A COLLECTION
OF
PROGRAMMING
PROBLEMS
AND
TECHNIQUES

D1570035

H. A. MAURER
and
M. R. WILLIAMS

University of Calgary
Calgary, Alberta,
Canada

A COLLECTION OF PROGRAMMING PROBLEMS AND TECHNIQUES

PRENTICE-HALL, INC., Englewood Cliffs, New Jersey

Library of Congress Cataloging in Publication Data

MAURER, HERMANN A. 1941–
  A collection of programming problems and techniques.

  1. Electronic digital computers—Programming
—Problems, exercises, etc.   I. Williams, M. R.,
1942–   joint author.   II. Title.
QA76.6.M38   001.6'42'076   71–39844
ISBN 0–13–139592–0

© 1972 by *Prentice-Hall Inc.*
Englewood Cliffs, New Jersey

Printed in the United States of America

10 9 8 7

Prentice-Hall International, Inc., London
Prentice-Hall of Australia Pty. Ltd., Sydney
Prentice-Hall of Canada, Ltd., Toronto
Prentice-Hall of India Private Limited, New Delhi
Prentice-Hall of Japan, Inc., Tokyo

CONTENTS

PREFACE

During the last decade there has appeared a large number of text-books on programming, programming languages and programming techniques. The vast majority of these books have a few programs to illustrate specific points and a few problems as exercise for the reader.

We believe that programming cannot be learned from simply reading a description of how it should be done, but rather is learned by doing. We have searched in vain for a supplementary text with a comprehensive collection of programming problems our students could attempt to solve. Having found none we have prepared a wide variety of problems ourselves and have included a brief description of the major methods required to solve them. We have collected these efforts in the form of this book in the sure knowledge that others will have experienced the same frustration in being unable to find a supplementary text of this type, and in the hope that the wide range of problems will both provide ample material for exercises and will stimulate an interest in the emerging discipline of Computing Science.

Throughout the book we have deliberately refrained from using any particular machine or programming language because of the proliferation and rapid change of both computing machinery and programming languages. All problems and algorithms are described in English sentences. Even the answer section is independent of which programming language is used. It does not contain program segments but rather contains the output produced by the programs and thus allows the student to check whether his program has worked correctly. We believe that this is often more valuable to the student than being able to check if his method of solving the problem conforms to someone else's way of solving it.

We wish to thank our colleagues at The University of Calgary for many helpful suggestions, our students, who have, by solving the problems, contributed to the answer section of this book, Mrs. A. Van Dieden for her impeccable typing of the manuscript, and the National Research Council of Canada for financial support.

A COLLECTION
OF
PROGRAMMING
PROBLEMS
AND
TECHNIQUES

INTRODUCTION

In this book many problems are presented that can be solved using a computer. The methods required for solving them are fairly representative of what is indeed often encountered in programming applications. Together with the formulation of the problems, techniques for their solution are briefly explained whenever such techniques are not obvious or whenever this gives the opportunity to elaborate on a more general programming method.

The problems in Chapter 1 are very simple compared to the quite difficult ones in Chapter 15. All other chapters are, in difficulty, in between, with later chapters not more inherently difficult than earlier ones. Since the problems within a chapter are generally quite independent of each other it is perfectly feasible to use the problems and chapters presented in any desired order.

With the exception of some problems in Chapters 6, 11, 13, and 15 no knowledge of mathematics beyond the high school level is required. The book is quite self-contained: Whenever an unknown term is encountered the extensive index can be used to find out where that term is defined in the book.

The Appendix gives partial solutions to the majority of the problems. The solutions provide enough information to get an idea whether a program designed for the particular task does indeed print the correct answers or not. For each problem the approximate number of simple statements† necessary

---

†For example, one FORTRAN, Algol 60, or PL/1 statement containing approximately 15 characters could be classified as "simple statement."

1

for its solution is also listed. The results for each of the problems in the book are produced by a medium-size, medium-speed computer† in a matter of minutes, in most cases in less than one minute.

For the purpose of explaining algorithms and techniques a combination of English and ordinary mathematical notation is used throughout the book: An algorithm consists of a Step 1, a Step 2, a Step 3, etc. These Steps are normally performed one by one except as mentioned in action 4 below. Each Step is an English sentence describing some action in a self-explanatory manner. The most common actions are

1. Assign a value to some variable. *Example:* Let $x_3 = -122$. This indicates that the value -122 is to be assigned to the variable x_3.
2. Read an input value and assign it to some variable. *Example:* Read m. This indicates that the next input data item is to be assigned to the variable m.
3. Print the value of a given quantity. *Example:* Print i^2. This indicates that the square of the current value of the variable i is to be printed.
4. The next step to be performed is the one specified. *Example:* Go to Step 3. This indicates that the next step to be performed is Step 3.
5. If a certain condition holds, then perform the action specified; otherwise perform the next step immediately following. *Example:* If $x > 3$, then go to Step 14. This indicates that if the current value of the variable x exceeds 3, then the next step to be performed is Step 14; otherwise the next step to be performed is the one following the sentence "If $x > 3$, then go to Step 14."

For further explanation two sample algorithms are given below. Algorithm 1 prints the values of $1^2, 2^2, 3^2, \ldots, 200^2$. Algorithm 2 reads 60 numbers $x_1, x_2, \ldots, x_{60}$ and then computes and prints the two quantities

$$m = \frac{x_1 + x_2 + \cdots + x_{60}}{60}$$

and

$$\sqrt{\frac{(m - x_1)^2 + (m - x_2)^2 + \cdots + (m - x_{60})^2}{60}}$$

called the "mean" and the "standard deviation" of the numbers $x_1, x_2, \ldots, x_{60}$.

ALGORITHM 1

Step 1. Let $i = 1$.

Step 2. Print i^2. (This prints the square of the current value of i.)

Step 3. Let $i = i + 1$. (This increases the value of i by 1.)

---

†The computer used for testing most programs was an IBM/360 model 50; any computer handling approximately 300 simple statements per second is suitable.

Step 4. If $i \leq 200$, then go to Step 2.

Step 5. Stop.

ALGORITHM 2

Step 1. Let $i = 1$ and let $n = 0$. (The variable n is used to calculate $x_1 + x_2 + \cdots + x_{60}$.)

Step 2. Read x_i.

Step 3. Let $n = n + x_i$ and let $i = i + 1$.

Step 4. If $i \leq 60$, then go to Step 2.

Step 5. Let $m = n/60$. (Now m is the mean of $x_1, x_2, \ldots, x_{60}$.)

Step 6. Let $i = 1$ and let $s = 0$. [The variable s is used to calculate $(m - x_1)^2 + \cdots + (m - x_{60})^2$.]

Step 7. Let $s = s + (m - x_i)^2$ and let $i = i + 1$.

Step 8. If $i \leq 60$, then go to Step 7.

Step 9. Print m and $\sqrt{s/60}$.

Step 10. Stop.

A number of functions are used occasionally throughout the book and are listed below.

Function	Value	Examples	Remarks
floor(x)	The largest integer not exceeding x	floor(5.3) = 5 floor($\sqrt{2}$) = 1 floor(-1.3) = -2	
mod(x,y)	The remainder on dividing x by y	mod(15,4) = 3 mod(23,7) = 2	$x \geq 1$ and $y \geq 1$ are integers
abs(x)	The absolute value of x	abs(-8) = 8 abs(3) = 3	
lcf(x,y)	The largest common factor of x and y	lcf(24,18) = 6 lcf(120,210) = 30	x and y are integers
lcf(x,y,z)	The largest common factor of x, y, and z	lcf(24,18,30) = 6 lcf(1,2,3) = 1	x, y, and z are integers
sin(x)	The trigonometric sine of x	sin(0) = 0 sin($\pi/4$) = $\sqrt{2}/2$	x in radians
cos(x)	The trigonometric cosine of x	cos(0) = 1 cos($\pi/4$) = $\sqrt{2}/2$	x in radians
ln(x)	The natural logarithm of x	ln(1) = 0 ln(10) = 2.3025851	$x > 0$
log(x)	The logarithm of x, base unspecified		
max(x,y)	The larger of the two numbers x and y	max($-1,2$) = 2	max is also used for three or more values
min(x,y)	The smaller of the two numbers x and y	min($-1,2$) = -1	min is also used for three or more values

Before attempting to solve any of the problems presented there are a number of important points that should be considered:

1. It is sometimes not possible or feasible to solve a problem exactly as formulated with the programming system at hand. *Example 1:* Some problems dealing with character manipulation may involve characters not available in some programming systems. Replacing these characters systematically by others removes the difficulty. *Example 2:* The algorithm for producing random numbers makes use of 15-digit decimal integers. In some programming systems such integers require multiple precision subroutines. Rather than making use of such routines it will generally be preferable to use smaller integers in the generation of random numbers. *Example 3:* Depending on the speed of the programming system used it might be wise to reduce the time required for solving some of the problems by producing shorter tables, using less input data, doing fewer simulations of some process, etc.

2. Many problems are not specified to the very last detail, leaving it to the programmer to fill in the remaining specifications. *Example 1:* For most problems requiring input the exact form of the input is not specified. Typically, it is left up to the programmer to decide how many numbers will be punched per card, what card columns will be used, if successive numbers are separated by some special character, if there is any restriction concerning the size of the numbers, etc. *Example 2:* It is also generally left up to the programmer to decide on a neat layout for the output produced, including headings, explanations, page numbers if applicable, etc. *Example 3:* Extraordinary situations arising are often not covered in detail. It is up to the programmer to take care of such situations by printing suitable messages, checking whether the input is legal, etc.

3. It is often desirable to write a program for a problem somewhat more general than formulated. *Example 1:* Rather than writing a program performing a certain calculation for one set of numbers, one should arrange the program to work for an arbitrary number of such sets of numbers. *Example 2:* It is often possible to combine a number of problems into a single one: Instead of writing an individual program for each of Problems 2.2.1–2.2.4, one could write a single program that for input MILES,65,KILOMETERS,100,1.61 produces the table of Problem 2.2.1, that for POUNDS,200,KILOGRAMS,90, .4536 produces the table of Problem 2.2.2, etc. *Example 3:* A problem can often be made more interesting by providing additional results or by combining it with other problems; in Problem 4.2.7 all cities actually visited when traveling from city i to city j could additionally be printed; Problem 4.3.4 can be extended by performing the computa-

tion using decimal numbers as well; Problem 3.2.10 could be expanded by printing for each n all prime numbers p and q for which $n = p + q$; and similar improvements are possible for almost every problem. Just let your imagination roam.

4. Whenever any changes, additions, deletions, and improvements are made to any problem as mentioned in points 1–3 it is essential that such changes are well documented and are stated in comments or headings in the program or the program output.

1

INTRODUCTORY PROBLEMS

1.1 INTRODUCTION

It is the purpose of this chapter to present a smorgasbord of simple introductory problems that may be solved on a digital computer. The majority of people tend to think of a computer as a machine that will do arithmetic at fantastic speed. However, a computer, rather than simply being a "number-crunching" machine, is essentially an information-processing device. The introductory problems will attempt to cover the field from purely numerical problems to character manipulative problems to problems requiring both arithmetic and manipulative capabilities. As the student works ahead to the other chapters it will become obvious that these two facets tend to blend together, so that the problems cannot be solved by the application of any one technique.

1.2 NUMERICAL PROBLEMS

Problem 1.2.1 (Cooling Time)

A number of automatic recording machines produce computer-readable input. Assume that there exists a machine that records the time taken (in seconds) for a steel bar to cool from 1000 degrees to 800 degrees and that it also records the time taken to cool from 800 degrees to 600 degrees and 600 degrees to 100 degrees. The machine records these three times on a punched card. Write a program to read this card and calculate and print the sum of the three integers (i.e., the time taken, in seconds, for the bar to cool from 1000 degrees to 100 degrees).

In all programs the output should be as meaningful as possible. For example, if the card contained the three numbers 57, 78, and 158, then the output should look something like the following:

THE THREE TIMES ARE   57   78   158
THE TOTAL COOLING TIME IS   293 SECONDS

Problem 1.2.2 (*Printing a Time*)

In printing an item such as a time (as in Problem 1.2.1) it is often more realistic to print out the time taken in hours, minutes, and seconds. Write a program that will read a five-digit positive integer representing an amount of time in seconds; then convert this to hours, minutes, and seconds; and print out the result with appropriate text. For example, the number 03812 should give as output

03812 SECONDS = 1 HOUR 3 MINUTES 32 SECONDS

Problem 1.2.3 (*Distance Conversion*)

With the world getting smaller and smaller it is a good idea to be able to convert the system of measurement used in one country to the system of measurement you may be familiar with. A number of conversion factors are readily obtainable; for example,

Multiply a distance in kilometers
$$\begin{cases} \text{by 3281 to obtain the distance in feet} \\ \text{by 0.6214 to obtain the distance in miles} \\ \text{by 1093.6 to obtain the distance in yards} \\ \text{by 0.5396 to obtain the distance in nautical miles} \end{cases}$$

Use these conversion factors to produce a table of kilometers from 0 to 200 and the corresponding distances in feet, yards, nautical miles, and miles. Your output should be of the form

Kilometers	Feet	Yards	Nautical Miles	Miles
0	0	0	0	0
1	3281	1093.6	0.5396	0.6214
2	6562	2187.2	1.0792	1.2428
.				
.				
.				

Problem 1.2.4 (*Temperature Conversion*)

Write a program to prepare a table (as in Problem 1.2.3) for temperatures in degrees centigrade and degrees Fahrenheit for the centigrade temperatures

$-40, -39, -38, \ldots, 100$. Use the formula n degrees centigrade $= (9n/5) + 32$ degrees Fahrenheit.

Problem 1.2.5 *(Table of Squares)*

Write a program that will calculate $1^2, 2^2, 3^2, 4^2, 5^2, \ldots, 100^2$ and print out the calculated numbers one per line.

Problem 1.2.6 *(Maximum)*

A great deal of computer time is spent in searching through large volumes of data to find the biggest or smallest item present. Consider a set of numbers $a_1, a_2, \ldots, a_n$. An algorithm for finding the largest number b of all numbers $a_1, a_2, \ldots, a_n$ and for finding the position j of b in the set (i.e., that number j for which $b = a_j$) is given below:

Step 1. Let $b = a_1$, let $j = 1$, and let $i = 2$.

Step 2. If $i > n$, then stop.

Step 3. If $a_i > b$, then let $b = a_i$ and let $j = i$.

Step 4. Let $i = i + 1$ and go to Step 2.

Ten cards are given, each containing an integer. Write a program that finds and prints the largest of these integers and also prints the number of the card it was punched on.

Problem 1.2.7 *(Sales Competition)*

The ABC Wigit Co. awards its top salesman of the year a month's holiday in Bermuda (all expenses paid, of course). ABC records each sale on a punched card in the following manner:

Card column 1	salesman number (1, 2, 3, 4, 5, 6, 7, 8, or 9)
Card columns 11–12	month of the sale (January is 01, February is 02, etc.)
Card columns 15–18	year of the sale (1970, 1971, etc.)
Card columns 25–29	number of Wigits sold

Write a program to read the sales cards of the ABC Wigit Co. and print out the number of the winning salesman and the number of wigits that he sold. Each salesman may have many cards so you will have to keep a total of all his sales as you read in the cards. Remember to check that all the sales are for the current year—it would not do to have any salesman attempting to obtain his holiday on last year's sales.

Problem 1.2.8 *(Sales Report)*

The sales records described in Problem 1.2.7 are typical of the records kept by many large firms. A great deal of analysis may be done from these records to show sales trends. Write a program to read the cards outlined in Problem 1.2.7 and print out the total sales for each month of the current year.

Problem 1.2.9 (*Commission*)

Assume that each wigit is sold for $1.27, except for salesman 4, who can sell them for $1.31 each. Use the data from Problem 1.2.7 and write a program to determine the salary for each salesman. Assume that the ABC Wigit Co. guarantees each salesman a salary of $4000.00 per year and then a 9% commission on all their sales over $1000 [i.e., a salesman's salary is $4000.00 + 0.09 (total sales − $1000.00)]. If he sells less than $5000.00 of wigits per year, then he is fired and the program should print out a message to that effect.

Problem 1.2.10 (*Mortgage Table*)

Given the amount of a mortgage, the rate of interest being charged, the monthly payment, and the amount of tax due on the property (per year), produce a table of the principal, interest, tax, payment, and the principal left for each month of the mortgage's existence. For example, if the principal is $20,000.00, the interest is 6%, the tax per year is $700.00, and the payment is $300.00 per month, then the output should be

Month	Principal ($)	Interest ($)	Tax ($)	Payment ($)	New Principal ($)
1	20,000.00	100.00	58.33	300.00	19,858.33
2	19,858.33	99.29	58.33	300.00	19,715.95
.					
.					
.					

Note: The last payment on the mortgage may be less than $300.00.

Problem 1.2.11 (*Nude plays*)

The use of break-even charts is an important part of the managerial decision-making process. A theatre company plans to hold a series of modern (i.e., nude) plays. The manager figures that, at a price of $2.50, he would be able to sell 120 tickets per performance. Each reduction in price by 5 cents would, he figures, increase the number of tickets sold by 15. It would also increase his expenses by 2 cents per patron (expenses used to defray legal suits, etc.). His expenses are currently running at 80 cents per patron (for 120 patrons). Write a program to print out a table of his expected profits for each price of ticket from the current $2.50 to $1.00 and an extra line advising him which price of ticket will reap the most reward.

Problem 1.2.12 (*Pi, Version 1*)

Given any circle of radius r and area A, the ratio A/r^2 is a number independent of the size of the circle chosen and is usually called π, $\pi = 3.14\ldots$. The value of the number π is known to great accuracy today. This was not always the case. The first recorded mention is in the Bible (1 Kings 7: 32 and 2 Chron. 4: 2), which gave the value as 3. The writer of the Rhind Papyrus (1650 B.C.) layed down the following rule: "Cut off 1/9 of a diameter and construct a square upon the remainder; this has the same area as the circle." This is not quite true, and if you work back from this rule the value of π thus obtained is

$$\pi = (\tfrac{16}{9})^2 = 3.16\ldots$$

Archimedes knew that π was less than $3\tfrac{10}{70}$ but greater than $3\tfrac{10}{71}$.

Write a program to compute, correct to three places of decimals, the value of π by the formula

$$\pi = 4 - \tfrac{4}{3} + \tfrac{4}{5} - \tfrac{4}{7} + \tfrac{4}{9} - \tfrac{4}{11} + \cdots$$

Hint: Consider a number A that is equal to an infinite "alternating" series (a series in which consecutive terms have opposite signs):

$$A = a_1 + a_2 + a_3 + \cdots \quad \text{with } \mathrm{abs}(a_1) \geq \mathrm{abs}(a_2) \geq \mathrm{abs}(a_3) \geq \cdots$$

It is known from calculus that

$$\mathrm{abs}(A - (a_1 + a_2 + \cdots + a_m)) < \mathrm{abs}(a_{m+1})$$

or, putting it another way, the sum of the first m terms of an alternating series gives the value of the series with an error not exceeding the absolute value of the $(m + 1)$st term of that series. One can thus calculate the value of A to n decimal places using an algorithm, as given below:

Step 1. Let $A = 0$ and let $i = 1$.

Step 2. If $\mathrm{abs}(a_i) < 10^{-n}$, then stop.

Step 3. Let $A = A + a_i$.

Step 4. Let $i = i + 1$ and go to Step 2.

It is important to realize that the calculation in Step 3 is performed on a computer using decimal numbers (or some variation thereof) with a finite number of decimal places. This can lead to inaccuracies and can have disastrous cumulative effects. It is thus necessary to carry out the computations in Step 3 with more than n decimal places of accuracy. To be completely safe at least $n + t$ decimal places should be used in Step 3, where t is the number of digits in k, k being the number of times Step 3 is being used.

For example, consider the calculation of π to $n = 3$ decimal places using $\pi = 4 - \tfrac{4}{3} + \tfrac{4}{5} - \cdots$. In this case $a_i = (-1)^{i-1}(4/(2i - 1))$ $(i = 1, 2, \ldots)$. The smallest k with $\mathrm{abs}(a_k) < 10^{-3} = \tfrac{1}{1000}$ is clearly $k = 2001$. Thus Step 3 will be used $k = 2001$ times. Since $k = 2001$ has four digits, one obtains $t = 4$ and the calculations in Step 3 should be carried out with at least $n + t = 7$ decimal places of accuracy.

Problem 1.2.13 (*Pascal's Triangle*)

Given any positive integer $n \geq 0$, the expression $(1 + x)^n$ can be written in the form $(1 + x)^n = b_{n,0} + b_{n,1}x + b_{n,2}x^2 + \cdots + b_{n,n}x^n$ for suitable numbers $b_{n,m}$ ($0 \leq m \leq n$). This can be obtained by multiplying $(1 + x)$ n times with itself and adding up equal powers of x.

As an example, $(1 + x)^3 = 1 + 3x + 3x^2 + x^3$ and thus $b_{3,0} = 1$, $b_{3,1} = 3$, $b_{3,2} = 3$, and $b_{3,3} = 1$.

The numbers $b_{n,m}$ ($n \geq 0, 0 \leq m \leq n$) are called "binomial coefficients."†
Collecting the binomial coefficients into a table of the form

$$b_{0,0}$$
$$b_{1,0} \qquad b_{1,1}$$
$$b_{2,0} \qquad b_{2,1} \qquad b_{2,2}$$
$$b_{3,0} \qquad b_{3,1} \qquad b_{3,2} \qquad b_{3,3}$$

one obtains "Pascal's triangle." Pascal's triangle has a very long history. It was mentioned by an early Chinese mathematician Chu Shih-chieh in 1303, and was known to Omar Khayyam, who lived from 1043 to 1123. It obtained its name because it appeared in Blaise Pascal's *Traite du Triangle Arithmetique*, which was published in 1653. The first six lines of the "triangle" are

```
            1
          1   1
        1   2   1
      1   3   3   1
    1   4   6   4   1
  1   5   10  10  5   1
```

Each number in Pascal's triangle is the sum of the two numbers in the previous line that are above the desired number.

Write a program that will print out the first 15 lines of Pascal's triangle.

Problem 1.2.14

Same as Problem 1.2.13 but for $n, m \geq 1$ use the formula

$$b_{n,m} = \frac{n(n - 1)(n - 2) \cdots (n - m + 1)}{m(m - 1)(m - 2) \cdots (3)(2)(1)}$$

†In mathematics, the symbol $\binom{n}{m}$ (read "n over m") is used rather than $b_{n,m}$.

Problem 1.2.15 (*Oscillating Frequencies*)

The most accurate methods of registering time over the last few centuries have all involved some oscillating device such as a swinging pendulum or a mass oscillating on a spring. It is only in the last few years that atomic clocks have passed the basic oscillating devices as the most accurate timekeepers. However, an atomic clock is not the type of device that is easily worn on the wrist or set up in the front hall; thus clock manufacturers still rely on the basic principles when designing their equipment. In designing a timepiece the manufacturer must know the frequency of oscillation of his device. Consider a mass suspended from a spring; this will oscillate with a frequency given by

$$f = \frac{1}{2\pi}\sqrt{\frac{k}{m}}$$

where f is the frequency in cycles per second, k is the constant of the spring (pounds per inch), and m is the mass (pound-square seconds per inch).

Write a program that will print a table of f when m takes the values 0.2, 0.5, 0.8, . . , 3.2 and when k takes on the values 10, 20, 30, . . . , 100.

Problem 1.2.16 (*Gravity Ratios*)

The problems produced by man's attempt to reach the moon and planets are not limited to the problems generated in simply getting off the earth. If man is to return to earth, then his rocket must be designed with the conditions of his destination in mind. For example, the power to lift a mass off the surface of the moon is only 0.16 of the power required to lift the same mass off the surface of the earth, and to lift it off Jupiter would require 2.64 times the power necessary on earth.

Given the following table, write a program to produce a table of the expected weights of masses from 1 to 200 pounds on each of the planets:

Planet†	Gravity Ratio
Mercury	0.27
Venus	0.85
Earth	1.00
Moon	0.16
Mars	0.38
Jupiter	2.64
Saturn	1.17
Uranus	0.92
Neptune	1.12

†The gravity ratio for Pluto is unknown.

Problem 1.2.17 (*The Rabbits of Leonardo Pisano*)

The sequence $F_1 = 1, F_2 = 1, F_3 = 2, F_4 = 3, F_5 = 5, F_6 = 8, F_7 = 13, F_8 = 21, F_9 = 34, \ldots$ in which each number F_i is the sum of the previous two numbers F_{i-1} and F_{i-2} is known as the "Fibonacci" sequence. This famous sequence was originated in 1202 by Leonardo Pisano (Leonardo of Pisa), who is sometimes called Leonardo Fibonacci (Filius Bonacci, son of Bonaccio). His book *Liber Abbaci* ("book of the abacus") contains the following problem: "How many pairs of rabbits are produced from a single pair within *n* months' time?" Assuming that each pair produces a new pair of offspring every month, each pair becomes fertile at the age of 1 month, and rabbits never die, the answer is F_n, the *n*th number in the Fibonacci sequence.

Write a program to determine $F_1, F_2, \ldots, F_{40}$ using the facts $F_1 = 1$, $F_2 = 1$, $F_i = F_{i-1} + F_{i-2}$ for $i \geq 3$.

Problem 1.2.18 (*Fibonacci Numbers*)

Same as Problem 1.2.17 but use the formula

$$F_i = \frac{\sqrt{5}}{5}\left(\left(\frac{1 + \sqrt{5}}{2}\right)^i - \left(\frac{1 - \sqrt{5}}{2}\right)^i\right) \qquad \text{for } i \geq 1$$

Hint: Calculate an approximate value A_i of F_i using as much accuracy as possible. Then round A_i to the nearest integer using the formula

$$F_i = \text{floor}(A_i + 0.5)$$

The values $F_2, F_3, \ldots, F_{40}$ obtained in this manner will indeed be the Fibonacci numbers if all calculations are carried out with at least 12 decimal digits of precision.

1.3 CHARACTER MANIPULATION

The problems in this section are suitable for solution using any programming language with some facilities for character manipulations such as PL/1, COBOL, some versions of FORTRAN, most assembly languages, etc. If a language has no character manipulation abilities such as "pure" Algol 60, there are often techniques for getting around these restrictions—one such technique being the coding of all characters as two-digit numbers, as indicated in Problem 1.3.4. It is beyond the scope of this book to discuss these techniques in detail.

Problem 1.3.1 (*Cryptography*)

A problem of interest to cryptographers is the detailed analysis of a given language, in particular the analysis of the frequency of occurrence of letters in a language. In the past this has taken a great deal of effort. However, it is essentially a simple job, of a repetitive nature, which is very easily programmed on a computer. Assume that a paragraph of a book has been punched onto cards, 80 characters per card. An additional card containing 45 characters (A–Z, 0–9, blank and punctuation characters) has been placed on top of the data deck. Write a program to count and print the number of times each of the 45 characters appears in the paragraph.

Problem 1.3.2 (*Customer File*)

Large business concerns, such as oil companies, generally keep all the data cards for one customer together. A typical customer's card file might include a card with his name, followed by a card with his address, followed by several cards indicating his credit card purchases. Assume that a card file is available consisting of three types of cards: name cards, address cards, and end card. The layout of each of these cards is as follows:

Name cards:

Col. 1	the character *N* indicating that this is a name card
Cols. 2–6	a five-digit account number identifying the customer
Cols. 7–27	the name of the customer
Col. 30	a one-digit code, 1 for Mr., 2 for Mrs., 3 for Miss, and 4 for Dr.

Address cards:

Col. 1	the character *A* indicating that this is an address card
Cols. 2–6	a five-digit account number identifying the customer
Cols. 7–8	a two-letter code, *AU* for address unknown in which case the rest of the card is blank and *AK* for address known in which case:
Cols. 11–30	a street address
Cols. 31–50	a city
Cols. 51–70	a province

End card:

Col. 1	the character *E* indicating that this is the end of the card file

Write a program that will read cards, ignore them until it reads a name card, and then prints out the customer's name preceded by Mr., Mrs., Miss, or Dr. as appropriate. If the next card is not an address card whose account number agrees with the account number on the preceding name card, the program will print the message FILE OUT OF ORDER; otherwise it will print the address below the name of the customer or ADDRESS UNKNOWN, whichever is applicable. In both cases the program repeats the process described until an end card is encountered; then the program terminates.

Problem 1.3.3 (*Matching Letters*)

A later problem (Problem 4.3.10) deals with the construction of a crossword puzzle. An instructive preparation for this task is this problem. Write a program that will read in a series of two English words, and, for each pair, determine how many letters, in corresponding positions of each word, are the same. For example, if the two words were C̲O̲A̲T̲S̲ and C̲A̲T̲T̲L̲E̲, they would have two matching letters, as indicated.

Problem 1.3.4 (*Coding*)

A study of cryptography and its growth as a science can shed light on the nature of languages and on certain aspects of history. For example, the level of education of the Boers in the Boer War can be noted from the fact that the British officers often sent messages written in normal schoolboy Latin, secure in the fact that if they did fall into the wrong hands, they could not be understood. One of the simplest codes (used from the times of the Greeks) is representing the letters of the alphabet by numbers. Some cards contain a series of two-digit integers. Each integer represents one character of the alphabet as follows:

> 00   represents a blank space
> 01   represents an A
> 02   represents a B
> 03   represents a C
> .
> .
> .
> 26   represents a Z

Write a program that reads the cards and prints the characters corresponding to the integers. The program should check that all integers are between 0 and 26. If this is not the case, the program should print a message indicating that the data card is invalid.

Problem 1.3.5 (*A's and B's*)

The study of computing science can lead to many fascinating fields. One of these is "programming linguistics," in which the properties of various languages (defined by a rigorous set of rules) are studied in depth. One such set of rules, of a language whose words consist of the letters A and B, is the following.

Consider the character string consisting of the letter S.

Step 1. Replace the first S in the character string so far obtained by either (a) SAAS, (b) ABAB, (c) ASBB, (d) AABSSB, or (e) BBAB.

Step 2. Go to Step 1.

Starting from the single character S, various character strings can be obtained. For example,

> S gives [by 1(a)] SAAS
> This gives [by 1(b)] ABABAAS
> This gives [by 1(d)] ABABAAAABSSB
> This gives [by 1(e)] ABABAAAABBBABSB
> This gives [by 1(b)] ABABAAAABBBABABABB

Write a program that finds all character strings with fewer than 21 characters and containing only A's and B's, which can be obtained from S as described above.

1.4 MISCELLANEOUS PROBLEMS

Problem 1.4.1 (*Printing a Date*)

Reports of sales figures, inventories, etc., are always out of date almost from the moment they are produced. It is common practice in the business world to put the date of production on each report so that the person reading it may have some idea of the relevance of the figures to the present-day situation. A number of the larger computers have facilities for making the date available to the program currently running; however, this date is generally in a form that is unnecessarily cumbersome. Problem 1.4.1 is an instructive exercise should you ever have to come to grips with this situation.

A number of cards are available, each containing three integers, d, m, and n. Write a program that will print for each card the name of the weekday corresponding to it ($d = 1$ means Monday, $d = 2$ means Tuesday, etc.), followed by the name of the month corresponding to m ($m = 1$ means January, $m = 2$ means February, etc.), followed by the value of n. As an example, the program will produce for $d = 2$, $m = 3$, and $n = 18$ the output TUESDAY MARCH 18. The program should check whether d is between 1 and 7, m is between 1 and 12, and n is between 1 and 31. If one of these conditions is not satisfied, the program should print a message indicating that the data card is invalid.

Problem 1.4.2 (*Ten-Pin Bowling*)

Almost everyone has seen, via television, how computers can be used to keep track of the results of sports events. They have been used extensively during the Olympic Games so that each competitor knows exactly his current standing in relation to all the others. For the computer to be used in this way it must be supplied with a set of programs to compute the score of each competitor in each game.

Assume that a card contains 22 positive two-digit integers n_1, m_1, n_2, $m_2, n_3, m_3, \ldots, n_{11}, m_{11}$ representing the score in a game of ten-pin bowling. Each pair n_i, m_i represents the score obtained on the ith frame, n_i the score obtained on the first ball, and m_i the score on the second ball. For example, $n_3 = 6$, $m_3 = 3$ indicates that the bowler knocked down six pins with his first ball of the third frame and knocked down three extra pins with his second ball of the third frame; $n_5 = 10$, $m_5 = 0$ indicates a strike in the fifth frame; $n_8 = k$, $m_8 = j$ (with $k + j = 10$) indicates a spare in the eighth frame.

According to the rules of ten-pin bowling, (a) $n_i, m_i \geq 0$ for $i = 1, 2,$ $\ldots, 11$; (b) $n_i + m_i \leq 10$ for $i = 1, 2, \ldots, 10$; (c) $n_{11}, m_{11} \leq 10$; (d) if $n_{10} + m_{10} < 10$, then $n_{11} = m_{11} = 0$; (e) if $n_{10} < 10$, then $m_{11} = 0$.

The score of a game of ten-pin bowling is the sum of the scores obtained in the first ten frames. The score f_i in the ith frame $(i = 1, 2, \ldots, 10)$ is calculated as follows:

$$f_i = \begin{cases} n_i + m_i & \text{if } n_i + m_i < 10 \\ n_i + m_i + n_{i+1} & \text{if } n_i < 10 \text{ but } n_i + m_i = 10 \\ n_i + n_{i+1} + m_{i+1} & \text{if } n_i = 10 \text{ and } i = 10 \text{ or} \\ & \text{if } n_i = 10 \text{ and } n_{i+1} < 10 \\ n_i + n_{i+1} + n_{i+2} & \text{if } n_i = 10, \ i \neq 10, \text{ and } n_{i+1} = 10 \end{cases}$$

Write a program to determine the score in each of the first ten frames of a given game of ten-pin bowling and the total score in that game. The program should make sure that the numbers n_i, m_i $(i = 1, 2, \ldots, 11)$ satisfy conditions (a)–(e) and thus do indeed represent a possible outcome of a game of ten-pin bowling.

EXAMPLE

Suppose that $n_1 = 3$, $m_1 = 6$, $n_2 = 10$, $m_2 = 0$, $n_3 = 9$, $m_3 = 1$, $n_4 = 6, m_4 = 3, n_5 = 7, m_5 = 2, n_6 = 8, m_6 = 1, n_7 = 10, m_7 = 0, n_8 = 10,$ $m_8 = 0$, $n_9 = 7$, $m_9 = 1$, $n_{10} = 9$, $m_{10} = 1$, $n_{11} = 3$, $m_{11} = 0$. Then f_1 $= 3 + 6 = 9$, $f_2 = 10 + 9 + 1 = 20$, $f_3 = 9 + 1 + 6 = 16$, $f_4 = 6 + 3$ $= 9$, $f_5 = 7 + 2 = 9$, $f_6 = 8 + 1 = 9$, $f_7 = 10 + 10 + 7 = 27$, $f_8 = 10$ $+ 7 + 1 = 18, f_9 = 7 + 1 = 8, f_{10} = 9 + 1 + 3 = 13$ and the total score is $f_1 + f_2 + \cdots + f_{10} = 138$.

Problem 1.4.3 (*For Five-Pin Bowlers Only*)

Write a program analogous to the one in Problem 1.4.2 for five-pin bowling.

Problem 1.4.4 (*Factorials*)

Write a program to calculate and print the ten numbers $1!$, $2!$, $3!$, $4!, \ldots, 10!$, where $n! = n(n - 1)(n - 2) \cdots (3)(2)(1)$. Thus, for example, $6! = (6)(5)(4)(3)(2)(1) = 720$.

Problem 1.4.5

Write a program that will read three numbers (representing the lengths of the sides of a triangle) and print out one of the following four words:

NONE   if the three lengths do not represent the sides of a triangle (i.e., if the sum of the lengths of any two sides is not greater than the third side)

GENERAL	if the lengths specify a general triangle (i.e., one whose sides are all of different lengths)
ISOSCELES	if any two sides are of equal length
EQUILATERAL	if all three sides of the triangle are of equal length

Write a program so that it will print out the lengths of the three sides along with the type of triangle they represent. The program should process an arbitrary number of sets of three numbers and will terminate upon reading a set of three numbers all of which are zero.

Problem 1.4.6 (*Multiple Choice Test*)

It is now becoming more and more common for schools and universities to give multiple choice tests. If properly constructed, they can provide an accurate assessment of the student's level of knowledge, and they can relieve the great burden of marking examination papers. There are several commercially available machines that will read a multiple choice answer sheet and produce both the mark obtained and a punched card that gives a list of choices the student has made. Assume that a number of cards are available. Each card is punched so that the first 20 columns contain information that identifies the student and the next 60 columns contain a sequence of the letters T and F, giving the student's answer to a 60-question true–false examination. Suppose that the correct answer to the nth question is true if n is exactly divisible by 2 or 3 and that otherwise it is false. Write a program to grade the test, listing for each student his identification followed by the number of correct answers out of 60 he has given.

Problem 1.4.7 (*Quadratic Equation*)

Given a positive integer n followed by n triples of numbers $a_1, b_1, c_1, a_2, b_2, c_2, \ldots, a_n, b_n, c_n$, determine for each triple a_i, b_i, c_i the solutions of the equation $a_i x^2 + b_i x + c_i = 0$ as follows: If $b_i^2 - 4a_i c_i < 0$, then the equation has no solution and a message to that extent is to be printed; if $b_i^2 - 4a_i c_i = 0$, the only solution is $-b_i/2a_i$; if $b_i^2 - 4a_i c_i > 0$, then there are the two solutions, $(-b_i + \sqrt{b_i^2 - 4a_i c_i})/2a_i$ and $(-b_i - \sqrt{b_i^2 - 4a_i c_i})/2a_i$.

Problem 1.4.8 (*Right Triangle*)

The "Pythagorean theorem" (which, incidentally, was known to Indian mathematicians a long time before Pythagoras) states that "the square of the hypotenuse of a right-angled triangle is equal to the sum of the squares of the other two sides." Putting it another way, if a triangle has a right angle between sides a and b, then for the third side c the relation $c^2 = a^2 + b^2$ holds. Three numbers a, b, and c satisfying the relation $c^2 = a^2 + b^2$ are called a "Pythagorean triple."

Write a program to determine all Pythagorean triples a,b,c with $1 \leq a < b \leq 60$ using the fact that all Pythagorean triples are obtained by considering three numbers $2uv$, $u^2 - v^2$ and $u^2 + v^2$ for all integers u,v with $u > v \geq 1$.

Problem 1.4.9 (*Fermat's Lost Proof*)

Pierre Fermat (1601–1655) was a busy lawyer, 30 years old, when he came across a copy of the book *The Arithmetic of Diophantus* dealing with, among other things, the equation $A^2 + B^2 = c^2$. Fermat developed a hobby of working out the ancient problems of Diophantus, putting notes of any proofs he had discovered in the margins of the book. In connection with the above-mentioned equation, Diophantus had a problem: "Divide a given square into two squares." Fermat, generalizing this, wrote in the margin of the book, "On the other hand it is impossible to separate a cube into two cubes, or a biquadrate into two biquadrates, or generally any power except a square into two powers of the same exponent. I have discovered a truly marvelous proof of this, which, however, the margin is not large enough to contain" [this is the same as saying that integer values cannot be found for a,b,c (a, b, and c all different and all greater than or equal to zero) such that

$$a^n + b^n = c^n$$

when n is greater than 2]. Mathematicians have been trying ever since Fermat's death to either rediscover Fermat's proof or prove him wrong. They have not yet succeeded.

Write a program to check all values of a,b,c between 1 and 30 for all values of n between 3 and 5 by determining all triples $1 \leq a < b < c$ for which $\text{abs}(a^n + b^n - c^n) \leq 15$.

2

MERGING

2.1 INTRODUCTION

Consider m collections of items (e.g., numbers, names, book titles) ordered in a certain manner (e.g., in ascending order, in alphabetical order). The process of combining the m collections into a single one that is ordered in the same manner is called "merging."

As an example, consider the merging of the three sequences A, B, and C of ascending numbers

$$A: \quad 1, 15, 16, 23, 51$$
$$B: \quad 0, 91, 101, 122, 130$$
$$C: \quad 32, 33, 34, 63, 200$$

into one sequence D of ascending numbers

$$D: \quad 0, 1, 15, 16, 23, 32, 33, 34, 51, 63, 91, 101, 122, 130, 200$$

The method generally used for merging can best be seen from the following example.

EXAMPLE

Given three sequences A_1, A_2, A_3, A_4, A_5; B_1, B_2, B_3, B_4, B_5; and C_1, C_2, C_3, C_4, C_5 of ascending three-digit integers, the following algorithm will merge the three sequences into a single sequence $D_1, D_2, \ldots, D_{15}$ of three-digit integers in ascending order.

20

Step 1. Let $A_6 = 9999$, let $B_6 = 9999$, and let $C_6 = 9999$.

Step 2. Let $i = 1$, let $j = 1$, let $k = 1$, and let $m = 1$.

Step 3. If $A_i \leq B_j$ and $A_i < C_k$, then let $D_m = A_i$, let $m = m + 1$, let $i = i + 1$, and go to Step 3.

Step 4. If $B_j \leq A_i$ and $B_j < C_k$, then let $D_m = B_j$, let $m = m + 1$, let $j = j + 1$, and go to Step 3.

Step 5. If $C_k = 9999$, then stop.

Step 6. Let $D_m = C_k$, let $m = m + 1$, let $k = k + 1$, and go to Step 3.

The reader unfamiliar with merging processes is urged to examine in detail how this algorithm will indeed merge the three sequences A, B, and C into the sequence D. Note that Step 1, by assigning 9999 (a number larger than any other number to be encountered) to A_6, B_6, and C_6, provides a convenient terminal condition in Step 5.

Merging processes are useful for preparing tables (see Problems 2.2.1, 2.2.2, 2.2.3, 2.2.4, 2.2.7, 2.2.8, and 2.2.9), for sorting (see Chapter 7), and for updating of files (consider a company with a file of customers ordered by account numbers that is updated every month by merging it with a file of new customers).

2.2 PROBLEMS

Problem 2.2.1 (*Mile Table, Version 1*)

Prepare a table with two columns, the first representing miles and the second kilometers, using the relation 1 mile = 1.61 kilometers. The table should contain for 1, 2, 3, . . . , 100 kilometers the corresponding number of miles, and for 1, 2, 3, 4, 5, . . . , 65 miles the corresponding number of kilometers. Both the first and second columns must contain numbers in ascending order.

Notes and Explanations: The table should start as follows:

Miles	Kilometers
0.62	1.00
1.00	1.61
1.24	2.00
1.86	3.00
2.00	3.22
.	.
.	.
.	.

Problem 2.2.2 (*Weight Table*)

Prepare a table as in Problem 2.2.1 for pounds and kilograms for 1, 2, . . . , 200 pounds and 1, 2, . . . , 90 kilograms using the relation 1 pound = 0.4536 kilograms.

Problem 2.2.3 (*Foreign Exchange Table, Version 1*)

Pick any two currencies and prepare a table as in Problem 2.2.1.

Problem 2.2.4 (*Temperature Table, Version 1*)

Prepare a table as in Problem 2.2.1 for degrees centigrade and degrees Fahrenheit for −40, −39, . . . , 100 degrees centigrade and −40, −39, . . . , 212 degrees Fahrenheit using the relation

$$n \text{ degrees Fahrenheit} = \frac{(n - 32)}{1.8} \text{ degrees centigrade}$$

Problem 2.2.5 (*Merging Two Sequences*)

Given a positive integer $n \leq 100$ followed by n pairs of five-digit integers $a_1,b_1, a_2,b_2, \ldots, a_n,b_n$ and assuming that the numbers $a_1, a_2, \ldots, a_n$ and $b_1, b_2, \ldots, b_n$ are in ascending order, write a program to print all $2n$ numbers in ascending order.

Problem 2.2.6 (*Merging Five Sequences*)

Given a positive integer $n \leq 50$ followed by n groups of five surnames $a_i, b_i, c_i, d_i,$ and e_i ($i = 1, 2, \ldots, n$) and assuming that the names $a_1, a_2, \ldots, a_n; b_1, b_2, \ldots, b_n; c_1, c_2, \ldots, c_n; d_1, d_2, \ldots, d_n;$ and $e_1, e_2, \ldots, e_n$ are in alphabetical order, write a program to print all $5n$ names in alphabetical order.

Problem 2.2.7 (*Mile Table, Version 2*)

Prepare a single table with six columns, the first representing miles, the second kilometers, the third geographical miles, the fourth nautical miles, the fifth Italian miles, and the sixth Austrian miles using the relations

$$1 \text{ mile} = 1.61 \text{ kilometers}$$
$$1 \text{ geographical mile} = 7.42 \text{ kilometers}$$
$$1 \text{ nautical mile} = 1.85 \text{ kilometers}$$
$$1 \text{ Italian mile} = 1.82 \text{ kilometers}$$
$$1 \text{ Austrian mile} = 7.25 \text{ kilometers}$$

The table should contain all the information for 1, 2, . . . , 100 kilometers; 1, 2, . . . , 65 miles; 1, 2, . . . , 14 geographical miles; 1, 2, . . . , 60 nautical miles; 1, 2, . . . , 60 Italian miles; and 1, 2, . . . , 15 Austrian miles, similar to the table in Problem 2.2.1.

Problem 2.2.8 (*Foreign Exchange Table, Version 2*)

Pick any six different currencies and prepare a table analogous to the one in Problem 2.2.7.

Problem 2.2.9 (*Temperature Table, Version 2*)

Prepare a single table with four columns, the first representing degrees centigrade, the second degrees Fahrenheit, the third degrees Reaumir, and the fourth degrees Kelvin using the relations

$$n \text{ degrees Fahrenheit} = \frac{(n-32)}{1.8} \text{ degrees centigrade}$$

$$n \text{ degrees Reaumir} = \frac{5n}{4} \text{ degrees centigrade}$$

$$n \text{ degrees Kelvin} = n - 273 \text{ degrees centigrade}$$

The table should contain all the information for $0, 1, 2, \ldots, 373$ degrees Kelvin; $-273, -272, \ldots, 100$ degrees centigrade; $-200, -199, \ldots, 80$ degrees Reaumir; and $-400, -399, -398, \ldots, 212$ degrees Fahrenheit.

Problem 2.2.10

Given $n \leq 10,000$ numbers $a_1, a_2, a_3, \ldots, a_n$ and four integers i, j, k, and l with $i < j$ and $k < l$, assume that the numbers $a_i, a_{i+1}, \ldots, a_j$ and a_k, $a_{k+1}, \ldots, a_l$ are in ascending order. Write a program segment ("subroutine," "subprogram") that will merge the sequences $a_i, a_{i+1}, \ldots, a_j$ and a_k, a_{k+1}, $\ldots, a_l$ into a single sequence of ascending numbers $c_1, c_2, c_3, \ldots, c_m$, where $m = j - i + l - k + 2$.

Problem 2.2.11 (*Alphabetical List*)

The students in a class of $n \leq 300$ students have obtained marks A, B, C, D, and F. On punched cards the number n followed by an alphabetical list of all students with mark A, followed by an alphabetical list of all students with mark B, $\ldots$, followed by an alphabetical list of all students with mark F is available. Write a program to print an alphabetical list of all students in the class together with their corresponding marks.

Problem 2.2.12 (*General Conversion*)

Write a program that combines all the problems involving the printing of conversion tables presented in this section.

Input information is available as follows:

(a) A sequence S of up to 80 characters representing a heading that is to appear on the first page of the table.

(b) A sequence R of up to 80 characters representing a running heading that is to appear on each page of the table except the first one and that is followed by a two-digit page number.

(c) A number n ($30 \leq n \leq 60$) indicating the number of lines to be printed per page of the table.

(d) A number m ($2 \leq m \leq 8$) indicating the number of different measurements to be considered; m therefore indicates the number of columns to be printed per page.

(e) m sequences $A_1, A_2, \ldots, A_m$ of up to 14 characters representing the names of the m measurements; these m names are to appear on top of the m columns on each page.

(f) m quintuples of numbers $(c_1, d_1, s_1, e_1, w_1)$, $(c_2, d_2, s_2, e_2, w_2), \ldots,$ $(c_m, d_m, s_m, e_m, w_m)$. Each quintuple $(c_i, d_i, s_i, e_i, w_i)$ indicates that k units of the measurement A_i are equal to $k \cdot c_i + d_i$ units of the measurement A_1 and that the quantities to be considered for measurement A_i are to range from s_i to e_i units in steps of w_i units.

The program is to produce a conversion table for the m measurements consisting of m columns of n lines per page, each page with headings and page numbers, the numbers in each column in ascending order analogous to what is described in Problem 2.2.1.

EXAMPLE

Given the input

1. $S = $ CONVERSION TABLE OF MILES AND KILOMETERS
2. $R = $ CONVERSION TABLE (CONTINUED)
3. $n = 40$
4. $m = 2$
5. $A_1 = $ KILOMETERS, $A_2 = $ MILES
6. $(c_1, d_1, s_1, e_1, w_1) = (1,0,1,100,1)$
   $(c_2, d_2, s_2, e_2, w_2) = (1.61,0,1,65,1)$

the program should produce a table as in Problem 2.2.1. Given the input

1. $S = $ CONVERSION OF TEMPERATURES
2. $R = $ TEMPERATURES (CONTINUED)
3. $n = 45$
4. $m = 4$
5. $A_1 = $ CENTIGRADE, $A_2 = $ FAHRENHEIT, $A_3 = $ REAUMIR, $A_4 = $ KELVIN
6. $(c_1, d_1, s_1, e_1, w_1) = (1,0,-273,100,1)$
   $(c_2, d_2, s_2, e_2, w_2) = (.55556,-17.77778,-400,212,1)$
   $(c_3, d_3, s_3, e_3, w_3) = (1.25,0,-200,80,1)$
   $(c_4, d_4, s_4, e_4, w_4) = (1,-273,0,373,1)$

the program should produce a table as required in Problem 2.2.9.

3

NUMBER
THEORY

3.1 INTRODUCTION

In the early days mathematicians were mainly concerned with the elucidation of properties of numbers. The ancient mystics were fascinated by numbers and attempted to explain why an omnipotent God should have created all things in 6 days, rather than 5 or 7 days, by examining the properties of the number 6; or why there were only 8 people in Noah's ark; or why the moon takes 28 days to circle the earth; or why there were only 5 (in ancient times) planets. These attempts at explaining natural (and supernatural) phenomena by the properties of the numbers involved soon lead to the study of numbers for their own sake. Of all the unsolved problems in modern mathematics, a large proportion of them are to be found in the field known as the "theory of numbers." The following problems are intended to introduce the student to this fascinating realm and to provide a framework for some nontrivial problems. A number of the problems presented here were unsolved as recently as 1950. In some cases (such as amicable numbers and arithmetic progressions of primes) problems had to await the advent of computers before any but the simplest examples were known to exist. The student is advised to think carefully before attempting any of the problems. The "brute force" method of attack will solve almost any problem; however, it will often take a very long time even on a powerful computer. A few moments of thought can often reduce the amount of computation by orders of magnitude.

25

3.2 PROBLEMS

Problem 3.2.1 (*Perfect Numbers*)

Six is the first "perfect" number. The Greeks called it "perfect" because it is the sum of all its divisors except itself (the only numbers that divide evenly into 6 are 1, 2, 3, and 6, and $6 = 1 + 2 + 3$). The ancient mystics explained that God chose to create the world in 6 days instead of 1 because 6 is the more perfect number. In the time since the Greeks the perfect numbers have taken on an aspect more ethical than practical. In the first century A.D. the numbers were separated into "abundant" (such as 12, whose divisors have a sum greater than 12), "deficient" (such as 9, whose divisors have a sum less than 9), and "perfect." The church mystics then layed down the moral and ethical properties of each type of number. In the twelfth century the study of perfect numbers was recommended for "healing of souls."

Write a program to list all the numbers 2 to 200 and classify each as abundant, deficient, or perfect and keep track of the number of numbers in each class. As a matter of interest, all known perfect numbers are even; it is unknown whether odd perfect numbers exist.

Problem 3.2.2 (*Partitions, Version 1*)

The theory of partitions is concerned with the number of ways in which a number can be represented as the sum of its parts. For example, the number 4 can be represented as

$$4$$
$$3 + 1$$
$$2 + 1 + 1$$
$$2 + 2$$
$$1 + 1 + 1 + 1$$

and the number 5 can be represented as

$$5$$
$$4 + 1$$
$$3 + 2$$
$$3 + 1 + 1$$
$$2 + 2 + 1$$
$$2 + 1 + 1 + 1$$
$$1 + 1 + 1 + 1 + 1$$

Denoting the number of partitions of a positive integer n by $P(n)$, one thus has $P(4) = 5$ and $P(5) = 7$.

Write a program to determine $P(n)$ for $n = 1, 2, \ldots, 12$.

Problem 3.2.3 (*Cubical Numbers*)

Nicomachus, in the first century A.D., wrote the book *Introductio Arithmetica* in which the question "How can the cubes be represented in terms of the natural numbers?" was answered by the statement that "Cubical numbers are always equal to the sum of successive odd numbers and can be represented this way." For example, $1^3 = 1 = 1$, $2^3 = 8 = 3 + 5$, $3^3 = 27 = 7 + 9 + 11$, $4^3 = 64 = 13 + 15 + 17 + 19$.

Write a program to find the successive odd numbers whose sum equals n^3 for n having the values from 1 to 20.

Problem 3.2.4 (*Sums of Digits*)

In all the integers > 1 there are only four that can be represented by the sum of the cubes of their digits. One of these numbers is $153 = 1^3 + 5^3 + 3^3$. Write a program to determine the other three.

Hint: All four numbers lie in the range 150 to 410.

Problem 3.2.5 (*Prime Numbers*)

A positive integer $n > 1$ is called "prime" if it is divisible by no positive integers other than 1 and n. Thus 2 is prime, 3 is prime, 4 is not prime because it is divisible by 2, 5 is prime, 6 is not prime because it is divisible by both 2 and 3, etc.

To find out if a number n is prime, it is necessary only to divide n by all the integers from 2 to $\sqrt{n}$. If any of these integers divide evenly into n, then n is "composite," i.e., not prime. Write a program that will read a series of numbers and print out the numbers along with an indication of whether they are prime or composite.

Problem 3.2.6 (*Prime Sieve*)

The following algorithm, essentially due to the Greek mathematician Erathosthenes, will print all prime numbers from 2 to n for any given positive integer n.

Step 1. Let $x_1 = 0$, let $x_2 = 0$, let $x_3 = 0, \ldots$, let $x_n = 0$.

Step 2. Let $k = 2$.

Step 3. If $x_k \neq 0$, then go to Step 7.

Step 4. Print k.

Step 5. Let $m = \text{floor}(n/k)$.

Step 6. Let $x_k = 1$, let $x_{2k} = 1$, let $x_{3k} = 1, \ldots$, let $x_{mk} = 1$.

Step 7. Let $k = k + 1$.

Step 8. If $k \leq \sqrt{n}$, then go to Step 3.

Step 9. If $x_k = 0$, then print k.

Step 10. Let $k = k + 1$.

Step 11. If $k \leq n$, then go to Step 9.

Step 12. Stop.

The reader not familiar with the "sieve of Erathosthenes" is urged to carry out the algorithm for $n = 40$ manually step by step.

Write a program that determines all prime numbers from 2 to 2000.

Problem 3.2.7 (*Prime Distribution*)

Prime numbers have been the subject of intensive study since the time of the early Greek mathematicians. Many people have attempted, without success, to find a formula that will generate all and nothing but prime numbers. The gaps between prime numbers vary widely. It is possible to prove that given any natural number n one can find a sequence of n consecutive natural numbers none of which is prime. For example, a consecutive sequence of five natural numbers, none of which is prime, is the sequence 24, 25, 26, 27, 28. In 1791 Gauss noticed (by a simple inspection of a table of prime numbers) that the average length of the gap between the first n primes was approximately given by

$$\frac{1}{1} + \frac{1}{2} + \frac{1}{3} + \frac{1}{4} + \frac{1}{5} + \cdots + \frac{1}{n}$$

If this is truly the case for all the primes, then the nth prime number P_n must be approximately equal to Q_n, where

$$Q_n = n\left(\frac{1}{1} + \frac{1}{2} + \frac{1}{3} + \frac{1}{4} + \cdots + \frac{1}{n}\right)$$

Write a program that will produce a table of n, P_n, and Q_n and then examine this table to see if Gauss' conjecture is correct (that Q_n is approximately equal to P_n) for all prime numbers less than 2000 (see Problem 3.2.6 for a "prime number generator"). The output should be a table such as

n	P_n	Q_n
1	2	1
2	3	3
3	5	5.5
4	7	8.3
5	11	11.4
.	.	.
.	.	.
.	.	.

Problem 3.2.8 (*Prime Twins*)

If a study is made of a list of prime numbers for any length of time, certain features soon become obvious. One of these is the occurrence of "prime twins." Prime twins are prime numbers that differ by 2. For example, 3 and 5 are prime twins, and so are 5 and 7, 11 and 13, 17 and 19, etc. It has often been speculated that there are only a finite number of prime twins; however, this has never been proved one way or the other.

Write a program to generate all the prime twins less than the number 2000.

Problem 3.2.9 (*Prime Twin Distribution*)

In 1923 Hardy and Littlewood conjectured that the number of prime twins (see Problem 3.2.8) less than the number n is roughly

$$\frac{1.32n}{(\frac{1}{1} + \frac{1}{2} + \frac{1}{3} + \frac{1}{4} + \frac{1}{5} + \cdots + 1/n)^2}$$

This remains unproved.

Write a program to check this conjecture for $n = 100, 500, 1000, 1500, 2000$.

Problem 3.2.10 (*Goldbach's Conjecture*)

Another conjecture, first made by Goldbach, whose proof has defied all attempts is that "every even number larger than two can be written as the sum of two prime numbers." For example, $4 = 2 + 2$, $6 = 3 + 3$, $8 = 3 + 5$, $10 = 3 + 7$, $100 = 89 + 11$, etc.

Write a program that determines for every even integer n with $2 \leq n \leq 200$ two prime numbers p and q such that $n = p + q$.

Problem 3.2.11 (*Complex Primes*)

"Complex numbers" are expressed as $a + ib$, where $i = \sqrt{-1}$ and a and b are ordinary numbers. When a and b are integers, $a + ib$ is called a "complex integer." Every ordinary integer a is clearly a complex integer since $a = a + i0$. A complex integer n is called a "complex prime number" if for any two complex integers c and d with $n = cd$ either $c = 1$, $c = -1$, $c = n$, or $c = -n$. It should be noted that some prime numbers are also complex prime numbers and that others are not. For example, 13 is a prime number since it is not divisible by any positive integers other than 1 and 13, but 13 is not a complex prime number since $(3 + 2i)(3 - 2i) = 9 - 4i^2 = 9 + 4 = 13$.

Write a program that determines for each prime number between 2 and 2000 whether it is a complex prime number or not.

Hint: An ordinary prime number p is not a complex prime if there exist two complex integers $m = a + ib$, $n = c + id$ such that $p = mn = (a + ib)(c + id) = ac - bd + i(ad + bc)$. From this it is easy to see that a prime number p is not a complex prime if there exist two integers $a > 0$ and $b > 0$ such that $p = (a + ib)(a - ib) = a^2 - i^2 b^2 = a^2 + b^2$, i.e., if p is the sum of the squares of two integers.

Problem 3.2.12 *(Prime Formula, Version 1)*

As mentioned in Problem 3.2.7 there have been many attempts to construct a formula for generating prime numbers. It is unknown who first discovered the formula $x_n = n^2 + n + 41$. However, he must have thought that he had discovered the elusive prime number formula. If it is evaluated for the first few integer values of n, the following table is obtained:

n	x_n
1	43
2	47
3	53
4	61
.	.
.	.
.	.

All the x_n's are prime numbers. Joy existed until further computation was done. It turns out that for some values of n the formula does not generate a prime number.

Write a program that uses the prime number generator of Problem 3.2.6 to determine for each value $n = 1, 2, \ldots, 43$ whether x_n is a prime number or not.

Problem 3.2.13 *(Prime Formula, Version 2)*

Another formula that will generate prime numbers is $y_n = n^2 - 79n + 1601$. This will actually generate more primes than the formula given in Problem 3.2.12. Write a program to determine for each value $n = 1, 2, \ldots,$ 90 whether y_n is a prime number or not.

Problem 3.2.14 *(Permutable Primes)*

Some prime numbers have been found that remain prime for all permutations of their digits. For example, the number 13 (a prime) will give 31 (also a prime) by permuting its digits, and the number 113 will yield the numbers 131 and 311 (all of which are prime) by permuting its digits.

Write a program that will determine if there are any other "permutable primes" less than 2000.

Hint: Ignore prime numbers, such as 1879, that, when permuted, may give numbers greater than 2000.

Problem 3.2.15

It has been conjectured that there exists a large number of prime numbers of the form $n^n + 1$. For example, $1^1 + 1 = 2$ (a prime) and $2^2 + 1 = 5$ (a prime).

Write a program to determine for each value $n = 1, 2, \ldots, 7$ whether $n^n + 1$ is a prime number or not.

Problem 3.2.16

Some prime numbers may be expressed in the form $n! + 1$. In fact it has been conjectured that there exist infinitely many prime numbers of this form. Write a program to find which primes (less than 2000) may be expressed as $n! + 1$ (see Problem 1.4.4 for the computation of $n!$).

Problem 3.2.17 (*Progression of Primes, Version 1*)

Several arithmetic progressions can be found in a list of prime numbers. For example, an arithmetic progression of three primes would be 3, 5, 7 (constant difference of 2) and one of four primes would be 251, 257, 263, 269 (constant difference of 6).

Write a program that will examine all the primes less than 2000 and print out all arithmetic progressions of three or four consecutive primes.

Note: It has been conjectured that there exist arbitrarily long arithmetic progressions formed of successive prime numbers; however, no progression of seven or more successive primes has ever been found.

Problem 3.2.18 (*Progression of Primes, Version 2*)

It is possible to find arithmetic progressions of nonconsecutive prime numbers. For example, an arithmetic progression of three nonconsecutive primes is 11, 17, 23 (constant difference of 6).

Write a program that will examine all the prime numbers less than 1000 and print out any arithmetic progression of three or four primes.

Problem 3.2.19 (*Switching Digits*)

Given an integer n it is often possible to form a prime number by changing one of its digits. For example, the number 18 can be formed into a prime by changing the digit 8 to 9, giving the number 19 (a prime), and the number 423 can be made into a prime by changing the digit 2 to 3, giving the number 433 (a prime).

Write a program that will determine the smallest number that cannot be made into a prime by changing any one of its digits.

Problem 3.2.20 (*Mersenne Primes*)

In the first half of the seventeenth century Father Martin Mersenne conjectured that the numbers of the form $2^p - 1$ are prime whenever the number p is a prime. These quickly became known as the "Mersenne primes" and they are denoted by M_p. The number $M_{127} = 2^{127} - 1$ held the record for the largest known prime number for many years and even in 1950 an attempt to find a larger prime failed. Unfortunately Father Mersenne's conjecture has not held up and, in fact, there are several examples of M_p (where p is a prime number less than 10) that are not primes.

Write a program to determine which values of p less than 12 (p always a prime number) result in M_p being prime.

It is interesting to note that, at the time of writing, the largest known prime is a Mersenne prime; in fact, it is $M_{11213} = 2^{11213} - 1$, a number with 3376 decimal digits.

Problem 3.2.21 (*Friendly Numbers*)

A pair of numbers m and n are called "friendly" (or they are referred to as an "amicable pair") if the sum of all the divisors of m (excluding m) is equal to the number n and the sum of all the divisors of the number n (excluding n) is equal to m ($m \neq n$). For example, the numbers 220 and 284 are an amicable pair because the only numbers that divide evenly into 220 are 1, 2, 4, 5, 10, 11, 20, 22, 44, 55, and 110 and $1 + 2 + 4 + 5 + 10 + 11 + 20 + 22 + 44 + 55 + 110 = 284$ (220's friendly number) and the only numbers that divide evenly into 284 are 1, 2, 4, 71, and 142 and $1 + 2 + 4 + 71 + 142 = 220$ (284's friendly number).

Write a program to find at least one other pair of amicable numbers.

Hint: There are many pairs of amicable numbers known; however, only one pair (220,284) is less than 1000. The next pair is in the range 1000-1500.

No example of three numbers x, y, and z is known such that the sum of the divisors of x is the number y, the sum of the divisors of y is the number z, and the sum of the divisors of z is the number x (x, y, and z all different).

Problem 3.2.22 (*Factors*)

All divisors ("factors")of a positive integer n can be found by noting each divisor a of n with $1 \leq a \leq \sqrt{n}$ and for each such divisor a the additional divisor $b = n/a$. Write a program using this method to find all divisors of ten six-digit positive integers given on punched cards.

Problem 3.2.23 (*Consecutive Compound Numbers*)

Write a program to determine a sequence of $n = 6$, 7, and 8 consecutive integers none of which is a prime number.

Problem 3.2.24 (*Largest Common Factor, Version 1*)

The "largest common factor" of two positive integers a and b is the largest integer that is both a divisor of a and b. It is denoted by $\mathrm{lcf}(a,b)$ throughout this book. The algorithm below, known as the "Euclidean algorithm," will calculate, given two positive integers a and b, a number c such that $c = \mathrm{lcf}(a,b)$.

Step 1. If $b = 0$, then let $c = a$ and stop.

Step 2. Let $d = \mathrm{mod}(a,b)$.

Step 3. Let $a = b$.

Step 4. Let $b = d$ and go to Step 1.

Given a positive integer n and n pairs of positive integers a_i,b_i ($i = 1, 2, \ldots, n$) write a program that determines for each pair a_i,b_i the largest common factor $\mathrm{lcf}(a_i,b_i)$ of a_i and b_i.

Problem 3.2.25 (*Largest Common Factor, Version 2*)

The largest common factor of three positive integers a, b, and c is the largest integer that divides a, b, and c. It is denoted by $\mathrm{lcf}(a,b,c)$ throughout this book and can be obtained as $\mathrm{lcf}(a,b,c) = \mathrm{lcf}(a,\mathrm{lcf}(b,c))$.

Given a positive integer n and n triples of positive integers a_i,b_i,c_i ($i = 1, 2, \ldots, n$), write a program that determines for each triple a_i,b_i,c_i the largest common factor $\mathrm{lcf}(a_i,b_i,c_i)$ of a_i, b_i, and c_i.

Problem 3.2.26 (*Smallest Common Multiple*)

The "smallest common multiple" of two positive integers a and b is the smallest positive integer that is divisible by both a and b. It is denoted by $\mathrm{scm}(a,b)$ and can be computed using the relation $\mathrm{scm}(a,b) = ab/\mathrm{lcf}(a,b)$.

Given a positive integer n and n pairs of positive integers a_i, b_i ($i = 1, 2, \ldots, n$), write a program that determines for each pair a_i,b_i the smallest common multiple $\mathrm{scm}(a_i,b_i)$ of a_i and b_i.

Problem 3.2.27

Given a positive integer n and n triples of positive integers a_i,b_i,c_i ($i = 1, 2, \ldots, n$) with $1 \leq a_i,b_i,c_i \leq 10000000$, write a program to determine for each such triple a_i,b_i,c_i the number $d_i = \mathrm{mod}(a_i^{b_i},c_i)$.

Hint: To calculate $d = \mathrm{mod}(a^b,c)$ for three large integers a,b, and c it is clearly not feasible first to compute a^b and then find the remainder upon dividing by c, since a^b can be an extremely large number. One can calculate $\mathrm{mod}(a^b,c)$, however, using the fact that

$$\mathrm{mod}(a^b,c) = \mathrm{mod}(1 \cdot \mathrm{mod}([\mathrm{mod}(a,c)]^b,c),c)$$

and that for arbitrary positive integers a, b, c, and r and the integer $h = \mathrm{mod}(a^2,c)$ the following relation holds:

$$\text{mod}(r\cdot\text{mod}(a^b,c),c) = \begin{cases} \text{mod}(r\cdot\text{mod}(h^{b/2},c),c), & \text{if } b \text{ is even} \\ \text{mod}(\text{mod}(r\cdot a,c)\cdot\text{mod}(h^{(b-1)/2},c),c),c), & \text{if } b \text{ is odd} \end{cases}$$

Thus, e.g.,

$$\begin{aligned} \text{mod}(738512^{118},7) &= \text{mod}(1\cdot\text{mod}(5^{118},7),7) = \text{mod}(1\cdot\text{mod}(4^{59},7),7) \\ &= \text{mod}(4\cdot\text{mod}(2^{29},7),7) = \text{mod}(1\cdot\text{mod}(4^{14},7),7) \\ &= \text{mod}(1\cdot\text{mod}(2^7,7),7) = \text{mod}(2\cdot\text{mod}(4^3,7),7) \\ &= \text{mod}(1\cdot\text{mod}(2,7),7) = \text{mod}(1\cdot 2,7) = 2 \end{aligned}$$

Problem 3.2.28 (*Pseudoprimes*)

A consequence of a famous theorem by Fermat is the fact that $\text{mod}(2^{p-1},p) = 1$ for every odd prime number p. An odd positive integer n satisfying $\text{mod}(2^{n-1},n) = 1$ is called a "pseudoprime." The number of pseudoprimes that are not primes is very small. Since it takes only on the order of $\log(n)$ steps to test whether $\text{mod}(2^{n-1},n) = 1$, one can determine that n is not a prime number for most numbers n in $\log(n)$ steps.

Write a program to determine a table of pseudoprimes and primes between 1500 and 2000. How many pseudoprimes do occur that are not prime numbers?

Problem 3.2.29

Write a program to determine for $n = 5000, 5001, \ldots, 5199$ the right-most seven digits of 2^n and 3^n.

Hint: Look at Problem 3.2.27.

4

SOME INTERMEDIATE PROBLEMS

4.1 INTRODUCTION

It is very difficult to separate the material in this chapter from the material in Chapter 1. If "beauty is in the eye of the beholder," then complexity is in the mind of the attempter. The problems presented here have no more inherent difficulty than those presented before; they simply require a slightly longer program to produce their complete solution.

The chapter is divided, rather arbitrarily, into four sections. The first deals with problems of a predominantly numeric nature and introduces some of the concepts used by "scientific" programmers. Section 4.3 is devoted to problems of a nonnumeric or manipulative nature, providing a broad spectrum of problems from the file-oriented "employee" problem to the manipulation of the representation of information in the problems on binary numbers. Section 4.4 is included because magic squares and tables provide a rich source of problems on array manipulation. The chapter concludes with a section devoted to a number of interesting problems that do not fit in any neat category.

4.2 NUMERICAL PROBLEMS

Problem 4.2.1 (Orbits)

As a first approximation satellites may be presumed to move in circular orbits around their parent (primary) bodies. The velocity of a satellite at sea level for the earth (if this were possible) is $V_s = 25{,}830$ feet per second (17,600 miles per hour). The velocity necessary to keep a satellite in orbit, known as "circular" velocity V_c, at a distance of h feet above the primary body is $V_c = (V_s\sqrt{R})/\sqrt{R + h}$, where R is the radius of the primary body (R_{earth} = 20,903,520 feet). The "parabolic" ("escape") velocity V_p at any particular altitude is equal to the circular velocity times the square root of 2; i.e., $V_p = V_c\sqrt{2}$.

Write a program to compute the circular velocity and the time taken for one orbit of a satellite orbiting the earth at X miles (1 mile $= 5280$ feet), where X varies between 100 and 300 miles in steps of 1 mile. Also compute the additional velocity that must be imparted to a deep space probe when launched from a vehicle orbiting X miles above the surface of the earth.

Problem 4.2.2 (*nth Root*)

A standard technique used in the solution of many numerical problems is known as "iteration." Iterative methods are used to obtain a solution or to improve upon an estimate of the solution by means of a repeated cycle of operations. For example, the iterative algorithm below will calculate, given positive numbers a and e, a number b such that abs$(a - b^2) < e$. To put it differently, the number b calculated is the square root of a with accuracy e.

Step 1. Let $b = a/2$.

Step 2. Let $b = (b^2 + a)/2b$.

Step 3. If abs$(a - b^2) \geq e$, then go to Step 2.

Step 4. Stop.

The above algorithm is a special case of the algorithm below, which will calculate, given positive numbers a and e, a number b such that abs$(a - b^n) < e$, i.e., which will calculate the nth root of a with accuracy e.

Step 1. Let $b = a/n$.

Step 2. Let $b = (b^n(n - 1) + a)/nb^{n-1}$.

Step 3. If abs$(a - b^n) \geq e$, then go to Step 2.

Step 4. Stop.

The formula in Step 2 is used a number of times, each time producing a new value of b that is closer to $\sqrt[n]{a}$ than the previous value of b. For a generalization of the formula in Step 2, see "Newton's method" in Chapter 6.

Write a program using the above process to calculate for each value $n = 2, 3, 4, \ldots, 10$ and $a = 2, 3, \ldots, 20$ a number b such that abs$(a - b^n)$ < 0.0001.

Note: If abs$(a - b^n) < e$, $b > 0$, and e is a small number in comparison to b, it is readily seen that abs$(\sqrt[n]{a} - b) < e/nb^{n-1}$. Since $b > 1$, $n > 1$, and $e = 0.0001$ in the problem, the numbers b calculated are indeed approximations of $\sqrt[n]{a}$ accurate up to at least four decimal places.

Problem 4.2.3 (*Pi, Version 2*)

Write a program to calculate the number π (see Problem 1.2.12) to four decimal places of accuracy using the fact that

$$\mathrm{abs}\left(\pi^2 - 6\left(1 + \frac{1}{2^2} + \frac{1}{3^2} + \cdots + \frac{1}{n^2} + \frac{1}{n}\right)\right) < \frac{6}{n(n+1)}$$

Hint: By choosing $n = 150$, first calculate a value a such that $\mathrm{abs}(\pi^2 - a) < 0.0003$. Then use the method described in Problem 4.2.2 to calculate a number b such that $\mathrm{abs}(a - b^2) < 0.0003$. It follows that $\mathrm{abs}(\pi^2 - b^2) < 0.0006$, and thus according to the note in Problem 4.2.2, $\mathrm{abs}(\pi - b) < 0.0006/2b < 0.0001$, as desired.

Problem 4.2.4 (*Vectors*)

A pair of numbers (a_1, a_2) is often called a "two-dimensional vector." The "representation of a vector (a_1, a_2)" is the line segment drawn from the origin of a coordinate system to the point with coordinates (a_1, a_2). For example, Fig. 4-1 shows the representation of the two vectors $(3,2)$ and $(2,-3)$.

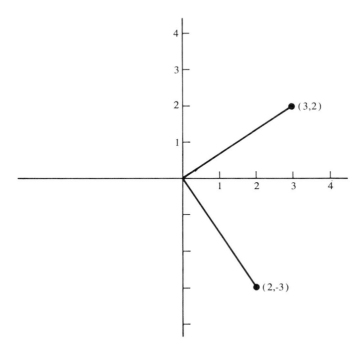

Figure 4-1

Two vectors are called "perpendicular" if their representations are perpendicular, i.e., if the two representations determine a right angle.

It is known from analytic geometry that two vectors (a_1, a_2) and (b_1, b_2) are perpendicular if and only if $a_1 b_1 + a_2 b_2 = 0$.

Write a program that will read ten pairs of numbers, each pair representing a vector, and that will determine which vectors are perpendicular to which.

Problem 4.2.5 (*Matrix Product*)

An "n by n matrix" or "n by n array" M is an arrangement of n "rows" of n numbers each. The first number in the first row of M is denoted by M_{11}; the second number in the first row of M is denoted by M_{12}; more generally, the jth number in the ith row of M is called M_{ij}.

As an example, if M is the 3 by 3 matrix

$$\begin{bmatrix} 6 & -5 & 16 \\ 0 & 8.2 & 9 \\ 2 & 5 & 8 \end{bmatrix}$$

then $M_{11} = 6$, $M_{12} = -5$, $M_{13} = 16$, $M_{21} = 0$, $M_{22} = 8.2$, $M_{23} = 9$, $M_{31} = 2$, $M_{32} = 5$, and $M_{33} = 8$.

If M and N are n by n matrices, one can define an n by n matrix P, called the "product" of M and N, in symbols $P = MN$, by defining $P_{ij} = M_{i1}N_{1j} + M_{i2}N_{2j} + \cdots + M_{in}N_{nj}$ for $1 \leq i,j \leq n$.

Given 32 integers $M_{11}, M_{12}, M_{13}, M_{14}, M_{21}, \ldots, M_{44}, N_{11}, N_{12}, \ldots, N_{44}$ representing two 4 by 4 matrices M and N, write a program to determine both the matrix $P = MN$ and $Q = NM$.

Problem 4.2.6 (*Road–Air Routes*)

Matrices often provide a convenient way for representing information. For example, consider n cities $1, 2, \ldots, n$ and their connections by various roads and air routes.

The road connections can be stored as an n by n matrix R as follows:

$$R_{ij} = \begin{cases} 0, & \text{if there is no direct road from city } i \text{ to city } j \\ 1, & \text{if there is a direct road from city } i \text{ to city } j \end{cases}$$

Similarly, a matrix A can be used to store the air routes.

For example, the matrix R for the four cities 1, 2, 3, and 4 with the connections as shown in Fig. 4-2 would be

$$R = \begin{bmatrix} 0 & 0 & 1 & 1 \\ 0 & 0 & 1 & 0 \\ 1 & 1 & 0 & 1 \\ 1 & 0 & 1 & 0 \end{bmatrix}$$

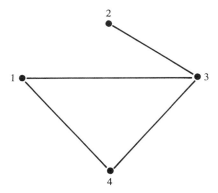

Figure 4-2

Given two matrices R and A representing road and air connections as explained and calculating $T = RA$, one can easily see that the value of T_{ij} (of the jth number in the ith row of T) gives the number of different ways of going from city i to city j, going the first part of the way by road and the second leg of the journey by air.

Write a program to read information giving the connections by road and by air for ten cities, and print out the number of possible ways of going from each city to each other city when the first leg of the journey is done by road and the second is done by air.

Problem 4.2.7 (*Holiday Travel*)

Write a program to read information giving the direct road connections between 15 cities as in Problem 4.2.6. Then the program is to compute for each pair of integers i,j with $1 \leq i,j \leq 15$ and $i \neq j$ the least number of cities to be visited when traveling from city i to city j.

Hint: Store the road connections in a 15 by 15 matrix R as described in Problem 4.2.6. Next compute 15 by 15 matrices $T^{(2)}, T^{(3)}, \ldots, T^{(15)}$ as follows: $T^{(2)} = R$, $T^{(n)} = T^{(n-1)}R$ for $n > 2$. Determine the smallest integer t for which $T_{i,j}^{(t)} \neq 0$ (i.e., for which the jth number in the ith row of the matrix $T^{(t)}$ is not equal to zero). The number t obtained is the least number of cities to be visited when going from city i to city j. If $T_{i,j}^{(t)} = 0$ for $t = 2, 3, \ldots, 15$, then there is no road from city i to city j.

Problem 4.2.8 (*Shortest Route*)

Information concerning the road connections between 15 cities 1, 2, 3, $\ldots$, 15 is given as follows: For each pair of cities i,j ($1 \leq i \leq j \leq 15$) an integer $R_{i,j}$ is provided; if $R_{i,j} = 0$, then there is no direct road from city

i to city j; if $R_{i,j} = t \neq 0$, then there is a direct road from city i to city j, t miles long.

Write a program that determines for each pair of cities the minimum road mileage between the two cities.

Problem 4.2.9 *(Multiplication of Polynomials)*

A basic course in algebra is included in most high school programs. One fundamental skill generally taught in such a course is the multiplication of two polynomials.

Assume that a card contains 22 numbers $a_0, a_1, \ldots, a_{10}$ and $b_0, b_1, \ldots, b_{10}$ representing the two polynomials $A(x) = a_0 + a_1 x + a_2 x^2 + a_3 x^3 + \cdots + a_{10} x^{10}$, $B(x) = b_0 + b_1 x + b_2 x^2 + \cdots + b_{10} x^{10}$. Write a program to print the number $c_0, c_1, c_2, \ldots, c_{20}$ representing the polynomial $C(x) = A(x)B(x) = c_0 + c_1 x + c_2 x^2 + \cdots + c_{20} x^{20}$. The numbers c_i ($0 \leq i \leq 20$) can be calculated by the formula $c_i = a_i b_0 + a_{i-1} b_1 + a_{i-2} b_2 + \cdots + a_0 b_i$, where $a_k = 0$ for $k > 10$ and $b_k = 0$ for $k > 10$.

Problem 4.2.10 *(Division of Polynomials)*

Given two polynomials $A(x) = a_0 + a_1 x + \cdots + a_{10} x^{10}$ and $B(x) = b_0 + b_1 x + \cdots + b_{10} x^{10}$, find two polynomials $C(x)$ and $R(x)$ such that $A(x)/B(x) = C(x) + (R(x)/B(x))$ and such that $\deg(R(x)) < \deg(B(x))$.

Note: The "degree" of a polynomial $R(x) = r_0 + r_1 x + \cdots + r_{10} x^{10}$ is denoted by $\deg(R(x))$ and is the largest number i such that $r_i \neq 0$. Determine $C(x)$ and $R(x)$ by dividing the polynomials $A(x)$ and $B(x)$ as is done in elementary algebra.

Problem 4.2.11 *(Largest Common Factor of Polynomials)*

The polynomial $R(x)$, calculated from two polynomials $A(x)$ and $B(x)$ as explained in Problem 4.2.10, is called the "remainder of dividing $A(x)$ by $B(x)$" and is usually denoted by rem($A(x),B(x)$). A largest common factor of two polynomials $A(x)$ and $B(x)$ is a polynomial $F(x)$ such that rem($A(x)$, $F(x)$) = 0, rem($B(x),F(x)$) = 0, and $\deg(F(x))$ is as large as possible.

To find a largest common factor $F(x)$ of two polynomials $A(x)$ and $B(x)$ one can use the Euclidean algorithm for polynomials as follows:

Step 1. If $B(x) = 0$, then let $F(x) = A(x)$ and stop.

Step 2. Let $F(x) = \text{rem}(A(x),B(x))$.

Step 3. Let $A(x) = B(x)$.

Step 4. Let $B(x) = F(x)$ and go to Step 1.

Given two polynomials $A(x)$ and $B(x)$ as in Problem 4.2.9, write a program to determine a largest common factor of $A(x)$ and $B(x)$.

4.3   MANIPULATION OF INFORMATION

A number in the usual decimal number system is a sequence constructed from the ten digits $0, 1, 2, \ldots, 9$. The value of a decimal number is so directly apparent that one hardly ever stops to consider how it is obtained. For example, the value of the decimal number 27 is given by $27 = 20 + 7 = 2 \cdot 10^1 + 7$, the value of 3849 is given by $3849 = 3 \cdot 10^3 + 8 \cdot 10^2 + 4 \cdot 10^1 + 9$, and, more generally, the value of the decimal number $a_n a_{n-1} \cdots a_2 a_1 a_0$ (where each a_i is one of the digits $0, 1, 2, \ldots, 9$) is given by $a_n \cdot 10^n + a_{n-1} \cdot 10^{n-1} + \cdots + a_2 \cdot 10^2 + a_1 \cdot 10^1 + a_0$.

The number 10 is called the "base" or "radix" of the decimal number system. The word *decimal* derives from the Latin word *decem* meaning "ten." Indeed it has been conjectured that we use a decimal system because we have ten fingers on our hands, and if our primitive ancestors had been blessed with only eight fingers, we would be using a number system that has 8 as its base.

Computers often use a base 2 or "binary" number system where each number is a sequence constructed from just two digits, 0 and 1. Such a "binary number" $b_n b_{n-1} \cdots b_2 b_1 b_0$ (where each b_i is one of the "bits" 0 or 1) has the value $b_n \cdot 2^n + b_{n-1} \cdot 2^{n-1} + \cdots + b_2 \cdot 2^2 + b_1 \cdot 2^1 + b_0$. For example, the binary number 11011 has the value $1 \cdot 2^4 + 1 \cdot 2^3 + 0 \cdot 2^2 + 1 \cdot 2^1 + 1$, i.e., has the same value as the decimal number 27.

Both Algorithm 1 and Algorithm 2 below will find, given a decimal integer $x > 0$, a binary number $b_n b_{n-1} b_{n-2} \cdots b_2 b_1 b_0$ whose value agrees with the value of x.

ALGORITHM 1

Step 1. Let $n = 0$.

Step 2. If $2^n \leq x$, then let $n = n + 1$ and go to Step 2.

Step 3. Let $n = n - 1$.

Step 4. If $2^n \leq x$, then let $x = x - 2^n$, let $b_n = 1$, and go to Step 6.

Step 5. Let $b_n = 0$.

Step 6. If $n = 0$, then stop.

Step 7. Go to Step 3.

ALGORITHM 2

Step 1. Let $n = 0$.

Step 2. Let $b_n = \text{mod}(x, 2)$.

Step 3. Let $x = $ floor$(x/2)$.

Step 4. If $x = 0$, then stop.

Step 5. Let $n = n + 1$ and go to Step 2.

Problem 4.3.1 (*Decimal to Binary Conversion*)

Use Algorithm 1 to write a program that will read ten ten-digit positive decimal integers and that will print for each integer a binary number with the same value.

Problem 4.3.2

Same as Problem 4.3.1 but use Algorithm 2.

Problem 4.3.3 (*Binary to Decimal Conversion*)

Consider ten cards each containing a sequence of 0's and 1's, each sequence of length 31, representing a binary number. Write a program to determine for each binary number its decimal value.

Problem 4.3.4 (*Addition of Binary Numbers*)

Two binary numbers can be added digit by digit, performing the calculation from the right to the left, almost like decimal numbers. The "addition rules" required are $0 + 0 = 0$, $0 + 1 = 1 + 0 = 1$, $1 + 1 = 0$ and a carry of 1 to the next column, and $1 + 1 + 1 = 1$ and a carry of 1 to the next column.

Write a program to read 40 0's and 1's representing two 20-bit binary numbers, add these numbers together, and print out the result in binary.

For example, if the two numbers are

$$00101010101101111001 \quad \text{and} \quad 00101110110110100110$$

then the result should be

$$01011001100100011111$$

Problem 4.3.5 (*Day of the Week, Version 1*)

Suppose that in a certain year January 1 happens to fall on a Wednesday. Write a program for determining which day of the week the nth day of the year is, and print the result along with suitable comments. (It can be assumed that the year at issue is not a leap year and thus has 365 days.)

Problem 4.3.6 (*Day of the Week, Version 2*)

Extend Problem 4.3.5 so that the program reads in the year and the weekday of January 1 (e.g., 1970, THURSDAY). The program should then behave in the same fashion as in the original problem except for the fact that it will take into account the possibility of the year being a leap year and also print out the date of the nth day of the year.

For example, if the data were

1970, THURSDAY, 116

then the program should print out

IN 1970 DAY NUMBER 116 IS SUNDAY APRIL 26

Problem 4.3.7 (*Desk Calculator*)

The common desk calculator is being replaced by the simple type-writer computer terminal in many engineering offices. This terminal is connected to a central computer that will do the arithmetic asked of it by the engineer. For example, if the engineer typed in the expression 150+60+20 −180, the central computer would type back the answer 50. Write a program to simulate this system by reading in a card that may contain up to 20 three-digit integers. These integers start in card column 1 and adjacent integers are separated by plus (+) or minus (−) signs. The program should calculate the value of the given expression. If the card contained

023+015+100−150+003

then the computer should print out

THE VALUE OF THE EXPRESSION IS −9

Problem 4.3.8 (*Diddling Numbers*)

Write a program that will read a three-digit number, subtract the "inverted" three-digit number, and print the result. The number 734 should give the result

734 − 437 = 297

Problem 4.3.9 (*Language Translation*)

Consider any two languages such as English and German. From a dictionary take about 100 important words in each language in their "main grammatical form." For example, you might choose LEARN–LERNEN, GO–GEHEN, LIVE–LEBEN, SCHOOL–SCHULE, WOOD–WALD, etc.

Write a program that takes a sentence in English (just consisting of some of the words chosen in their main grammatical form) and translates it word for word into the other language. Thus WE LEARN IN SCHOOL would give WIR LERNEN IN SCHULE.

You can improve on this somewhat by leaving words that have not been taken into the "dictionary" unchanged. Thus PETER LIVE IN CALGARY might give PETER LEBEN IN CALGARY even if the dictionary contains neither PETER nor CALGARY.

Translation programs for really good translations are very involved, so do not try too hard to add further improvements.

Problem 4.3.10 (*Crossword Puzzles*)

Most inventors of crossword puzzles will attempt to fit a series of words together into a crossword pattern and then construct the rules afterward.

Write a program that, when given an empty crossword puzzle pattern and a list of words, will attempt to fit them together to obtain a crossword puzzle.

For example, if the empty pattern is

	////		////	
		////		////
				////
			////	////

and the list of words included HOUSE, APPLE, TREE, NEXT, BI, RED, LEFT, MAX, ERG, NEW, TABLE, GRASS, PIER, UP, FG, SUN, LOT, HE, and FIVE, then a solution might be

T	////	U	////	H
A	P	P	L	E
B	I	////	O	////
L	E	F	T	////
E	R	G	////	////

Note: For simplicity consider only crossword puzzles with five columns and five rows. The empty crossword puzzle pattern is given on a punched card as a sequence of 25 0's and 1's, the 0's representing squares to be filled by letters, the 1's representing "black" squares, i.e., squares not to be filled by letters. In attempting to fit words into the puzzle, start with long words. The list should not contain more than 50 words.

4.4 MAGIC SQUARES AND LATIN SQUARES

A "magic square M of order n" is an n by n array M of numbers with the property that the numbers in each row, each "column," and both "diagonals" add up to the same "magic number" mag(M). It is easily seen that $\text{mag}(M) = (M_{11} + M_{12} + \cdots + M_{1n} + M_{21} + M_{22} + \cdots + M_{2n} + \cdots + M_{n1} + \cdots M_{nn})/n$; i.e., $\text{mag}(M)$ is the sum of all numbers in the magic square M divided by the order n of M. From the definition of magic square it follows that for every i,j $(1 \leq i,j \leq n)$ $\text{mag}(M) = M_{i1} + M_{i2} + \cdots + M_{in} = M_{1j} + M_{2j} + \cdots + M_{nj} = M_{11} + M_{22} + \cdots + M_{nn} = M_{1n} + M_{2,n-1} + \cdots + M_{n1}$. For example, a magic square A of order 3 constructed from the integers $1, 2, \ldots, 9$ is given below. The numbers in each row, column, and diagonal add up to $(1 + 2 + \cdots + 9)/3 = 15$.

$$A = \begin{array}{|c|c|c|} \hline 8 & 1 & 6 \\ \hline 3 & 5 & 7 \\ \hline 4 & 9 & 2 \\ \hline \end{array}$$

The addition of an integer to each element of a magic square does not change its magic properties. This is the basis of obtaining composite magic squares of order n^2 when given a magic square of order n. Given a magic square A of order n, constructed from the integers $1, 2, \ldots, n^2$, it is possible to produce a magic square of order n^2 as follows: Replace the number 1 by A itself, replace the number 2 by the square obtained by adding n^2 to each element of A, replace the number 3 by the square obtained by adding $2n^2$ to each element of A, and, more generally, replace each element i of A by the square obtained from A by adding $(i - 1)n^2$ to each element of A. In the case of generating a magic square of order 9 from the magic square A (given above) of order 3 the first two steps would result in

$$\begin{array}{ccc|ccc|ccc} 8 & 1 & 6 & & & & & & \\ 3 & 5 & 7 & & & & & & \\ 4 & 9 & 2 & & & & & & \\ \hline & & & & & & & & \\ & & & & & & & & \\ & & & & & & & & \\ \hline & & & & & & 17 & 10 & 15 \\ & & & & & & 12 & 14 & 16 \\ & & & & & & 13 & 18 & 11 \\ \end{array}$$

Problem 4.4.1 (*Big Magic Squares*)

Write a program that, when given the magic square A of order 3, will generate magic squares of order 9 and 81.

Problem 4.4.2 (*Odd Order Magic Squares*)

De la Loubère has found a method of generating magic squares of order n (where n is an odd number). Given two integers i,j with $1 \le i,j \le n$ the algorithm will determine $M_{i,j}$, the element of the magic square M in row i and column j.

Step 1. Let $b = j - i + ((n - 1)/2)$ and let $c = 2j - i$.

Step 2. If $b \ge n$, then let $b = b - n$ and go to Step 4.

Step 3. If $b < 0$, then let $b = b + n$.

Step 4. If $c > n$, then let $c = c - n$ and go to Step 6.

Step 5. If $c \le 0$, then let $c = c + n$.

Step 6. Let $M_{i,j} = bn + c$ and stop.

Write a program to produce magic squares of order 3, 5, 7, 9, 11, 13, 15, 17, and 19.

Problem 4.4.3

Combine the results of Problems 4.4.1 and 4.4.2 to produce a magic square of order 25.

Problem 4.4.4 (*Order 3 Magic Squares*)

Write a program that will read nine integers $a_1, a_2, \ldots, a_9$ and then will determine all magic squares of order 3 that can be formed using the given numbers.

Problem 4.4.5 (*Even Order Magic Squares*)

The generation of magic squares of even order is a more complicated procedure than that for magic squares of odd orders. In fact the method is too complex to be described easily.

Write a program that will attempt, by trial and error, to find a magic square of order 4 using the numbers 1, 2, 3, ..., 16.

Hint: Use the fact that there exists a magic square of order 4 such that the sum of any two adjacent numbers in any row and of the two numbers below is 34, i.e., the magic number of the square at issue. To put it another way, there exists a magic square M of order 4 constructed from the numbers 1, 2, ..., 16 such that for every pair i,j with $1 \le i \le 3$ and $1 \le j \le 3$, $M_{i,j} + M_{i,j+1} + M_{i+1,j} + M_{i+1,j+1} = 34$. It can further be assumed without loss of generality that either $M_{11} = 1$ or $M_{12} = 1$.

Problem 4.4.6 (*Border Squares*)

A "border square" is a magic square that remains magic when its border (top and bottom rows, right and left columns) are removed. One method of obtaining magic squares of even orders is to fit a border to a smaller magic square. One magic square of even order is

$$
B = \begin{array}{|c|c|c|c|}
\hline
1 & 12 & 7 & 14 \\
\hline
8 & 13 & 2 & 11 \\
\hline
10 & 3 & 16 & 5 \\
\hline
15 & 6 & 9 & 4 \\
\hline
\end{array}
$$

To fit a border to make this a magic square of order 6 it is necessary to add 20 numbers. First increase each element in the small square by 10, and then attempt to add the integers $1, 2, 3, \ldots, 10$ and $27, 28, 29, \ldots, 36$ around the border to make a magic square of order 6.

Write a program that will use the magic square B above to generate a magic square M of order 6 as described. Choose $M_{11} = 1$ and $M_{16} = 35$ and note that $M_{12} < M_{13} < M_{14} < M_{15}$, $M_{21} < M_{31} < M_{41} < M_{51}$, $M_{31}, M_{41}, M_{51} \geq 27$, and $M_{12}, M_{13} \leq 10$ can be assumed.

Problem 4.4.7 (*Latin Squares*)

A "Latin square L of order n" is an n by n array L of numbers containing the numbers $1, 2, 3, \ldots, n$ in such a manner that each row and column contains each number exactly once. If, in addition, both diagonals contain each number exactly once, L is called a "diagonal Latin square."

For example, the array A below is a Latin square of order 4 and B is a diagonal Latin square of order 4.

$$
A = \begin{array}{|c|c|c|c|}
\hline
1 & 2 & 3 & 4 \\
\hline
2 & 3 & 4 & 1 \\
\hline
3 & 4 & 1 & 2 \\
\hline
4 & 1 & 2 & 3 \\
\hline
\end{array}
\qquad
B = \begin{array}{|c|c|c|c|}
\hline
1 & 2 & 3 & 4 \\
\hline
3 & 4 & 1 & 2 \\
\hline
4 & 3 & 2 & 1 \\
\hline
2 & 1 & 4 & 3 \\
\hline
\end{array}
$$

Write a program that will produce a Latin square of order $4, 5, 6, \ldots, 10$.

Hint: One method for finding the entry $L_{i,j}$ in row i and column j of a Latin square L of order n is to use the formula $L_{i,j} = 1 + \mathrm{mod}(i+j, n)$.

Problem 4.4.8

Write a program to determine all diagonal Latin squares L of order 4 such that $L_{11} = 1$, $L_{14} = 2$, $L_{41} = 3$, and $L_{44} = 4$.

Problem 4.4.9

Write a program to determine all diagonal Latin squares L of order 5 such that $L_{11} = 1$, $L_{15} = 2$, $L_{51} = 4$, and $L_{55} = 5$.

Problem 4.4.10 (*Greco–Latin Squares*)

A "Greco–Latin square of order n" is an n by n array G of pairs of numbers

$$
G = \begin{array}{|c|c|c|c|}
\hline
a_{11},b_{11} & a_{12},b_{12} & \cdots & a_{1n},b_{1n} \\
\hline
a_{21},b_{21} & a_{22},b_{22} & \cdots & a_{2n},b_{2n} \\
\hline
\vdots & \vdots & & \vdots \\
\hline
a_{n1},b_{n1} & a_{n2},b_{n2} & \cdots & a_{nn},b_{nn} \\
\hline
\end{array}
$$

such that

$$
K = \begin{array}{|c|c|c|c|}
\hline
a_{11} & a_{12} & \cdots & a_{1n} \\
\hline
a_{21} & a_{22} & \cdots & a_{2n} \\
\hline
\vdots & \vdots & & \vdots \\
\hline
a_{n1} & a_{n2} & \cdots & a_{nn} \\
\hline
\end{array}
\quad\text{and}\quad
L = \begin{array}{|c|c|c|c|}
\hline
b_{11} & b_{12} & \cdots & b_{1n} \\
\hline
b_{21} & b_{22} & \cdots & b_{2n} \\
\hline
\vdots & \vdots & & \vdots \\
\hline
b_{n1} & b_{n2} & \cdots & b_{nn} \\
\hline
\end{array}
$$

are Latin squares of order n and such that every pair i,j with $1 \leq i,j \leq n$ occurs exactly once in G.

A Greco–Latin square is thus obtained by "superimposing" two suitable Latin squares. When Greco–Latin squares were first investigated Latin and Greek letters rather than numbers were used in the construction and hence their name. Greco–Latin squares were first introduced by Euler in 1782, and Euler indeed developed a method for constructing Greco–Latin squares of any order n, n odd. In 1900 Tarry established that no Greco–Latin square of order 6 can be constructed and in 1960 Parker proved that a Greco–Latin square of order n exists for every $n \neq 6$. Greco–Latin squares are useful for the design of experiments and are used in agronomic, biological, psychological, and sociological research.

A Greco–Latin square of order 4 is given below. Write a program to determine all Greco–Latin squares of order 4 that are obtained by super-imposing two diagonal Latin squares and that have the pair (1,4) in row 1, column 1; the pair (4,3) in row 1, column 4; and the pair (3,1) in row 4, column 4.

1,1	2,2	3,3	4,4
4,3	3,4	2,1	1,2
2,4	1,3	4,2	3,1
3,2	4,1	1,4	2,3

Problem 4.4.11 (*Magic Greco–Latin Squares*)

If both Latin squares K and L that go to make up a Greco–Latin square G are diagonal, then they can be used to form a magic square of the same order n using the formula $M_{ij} = K_{ij} + nL_{ij}$.

Write a program to determine a Greco–Latin square of order 4 as explained in Problem 4.4.10 and then use the method described to obtain a magic square of order 4.

4.5 MISCELLANEOUS PROBLEMS

Problem 4.5.1 (*Alloys*)

Some cards are given, each containing from two to four of the words ALUMINUM, IRON, COPPER, NICKEL, and ZINC, each word followed by a blank, a two-digit integer, and another blank.

Each such card represents a certain alloy. For example, ALUMINUM 30 IRON 50 NICKEL 20 represents an alloy consisting of 30% aluminum, 50% iron, and 20% nickel.

Taking the specific weights of aluminum, iron, copper, nickel, and zinc to be 2.63, 7.8, 8.72, 9.03, and 7.89, respectively, write a program to calculate the specific weights of the given alloys.

Problem 4.5.2 (*Molecular Weights*)

The atomic weights of some elements are as follows:

Al	26.98	Sb	121.75	S	32.06	Ba	137.34
Br	79.91	Ca	40.08	C	12.01	Cl	35.45
Cu	63.54	H	1.008	I	126.9	Fe	55.84
Pb	207.21	Mg	24.31	N	14.01	O	16.00

Write a program that, given some cards containing chemical formulae, will find the molecular weight for each formula. Each formula given is of the form:

element (number of atoms) element (number of atoms) element (number of atoms) . . . If (number of atoms) is omitted, then 1 is assumed. For example, water, H_2O, would have the formula H(2)O (with molecular weight $2(1.008) + 16 = 18.016$) and acetic acid CH_3COOH would have the formula CH(3)COOH or even C(2)H(4)O(2).

Note: The above method for representing chemical formulae cannot be used without changes for a more complete table of elements. For example, when incorporating the element Si (silicon) the meaning of the formula SI is not clear anymore. It could mean just one atom of silicon or it could mean a compound of one atom of sulphur (S) and one atom of iodine (I).

Problem 4.5.3 (*Old British Currency*)

Write a program that will read the three numbers P, S, and D (representing pounds, shillings, and pence) and convert this to the equivalent value in U.S. dollars. Assume that 1 pound = 20 shillings, 1 shilling = 12 pence, and 1 pound = $2.40 (thus 1 cent = 1 pence).

Problem 4.5.4

Write a program to read two pairs, m_1, d_1 and m_2, d_2, of integers representing two dates in a particular year, m_i the month and d_i the day in that month. The program is to compute and print the number of days between the two dates. It should check that m_i and d_i do indeed define a valid date (i.e., $1 \leq m_i \leq 12$, $1 \leq d_i \leq 31$) and it should provide for the case that the first date is later in the year than the second. Thus, if $m_1 = 1$, $d_1 = 2$ (January 2) and $m_2 = 1$, $d_2 = 7$ (January 7), the program should print a message indicating that there are 4 days between January 2 and January 7.

Problem 4.5.5 (*Easter*)

Easter (the "Western Easter" and not the Easter of the Eastern Orthodox Churches) falls on the first Sunday following the first full moon that occurs on or after March 21. The following algorithm, due to Gauss, will calculate for a given year y ($y \geq 1583$) a number representing the date of Easter as follows: If $d \leq 31$, then Easter is on March d, and otherwise on April f, $f = d - 31$. The intermediate values C, G, g, c, and E occurring in the algorithm can be briefly described as follows: C is the century; G is the "golden number," the number of the year in the "Metonic cycle" and is used to determine the position of the calendar moon; g is the "Gregorian correction" and is the number of years such as 1700, 1800, 1900, etc., when a leap year was not held; c is the "Clavian correction" for the Metonic cycle and amounts to about 8 days every 2500 years; and E is the "epact," the age of the moon on January 1 and thus may be used to find when the full moon occurs.

Step 1. Let $C = \text{floor}(y/100) + 1$.

Step 2. Let $g = \text{floor}(3C/4) - 12$.

Step 3. Let $G = \text{mod}(y,19) + 1$.

Step 4. Let $c = \text{floor}((8C + 5)/25) - 5 - g$.

Step 5. Let $e = \text{floor}(5y/4) - g - 10$.

Step 6. Let $E = \text{mod}(11G + 20 + c,30)$.

Step 7. If $E \neq 25$, then go to Step 9.

Step 8. If $G > 11$, then let $E = E + 1$.

Step 9. If $E = 24$, then let $E = E + 1$.

Step 10. Let $d = 44 - E$.

Step 11. If $d < 21$, then let $d = d + 30$.

Step 12. Let $d = d + 7 - \text{mod}(d + e,7)$ and stop.

Write a program to determine the date of Easter for the years 1800, 1801, ... , 2000.

Problem 4.5.6 *(Another Day-of-the-Week Problem)*

Given a date as a triple of numbers y,m,d with y indicating the year, m the month ($m = 1$ for January, $m = 2$ for February, etc.), and d the day of the month, the corresponding day of the week f ($f = 0$ for Sunday, $f = 1$ for Monday, etc.) can be found as follows:

Step 1. If $m > 2$, then go to Step 3.

Step 2. Let $m = m + 10$, let $y = y - 1$, and go to Step 4.

Step 3. Let $m = m - 2$.

Step 4. Let $c = \text{floor}(y/100)$ and let $a = \text{mod}(y,100)$.

Step 5. Let $b = \text{floor}((13m - 1)/5) + \text{floor}(a/4) + \text{floor}(c/4)$.

Step 6. Let $f = \text{mod}(b + a + d - 2c,7)$ and stop.

Write a program that will read five dates and print the corresponding day of the week.

Problem 4.5.7 *(Permutations)*

A family of six, Father, Mother, Peter, John, Sue, and Jane, is trying a different seating arrangement at a table for six people every day. Write a program to determine all possible seating arrangements.

Hint: An arrangement of n distinct objects in a row is called a "permutation of order n." Given all permutations of order n, all permutations of order $n + 1$ can be found by inserting into each permutation of order n the $(n + 1)$th object in all possible places. The given problem is equivalent to finding all possible permutations of order 6.

EXAMPLE

All permutations of order 2 of the two objects a,b are clearly $p_1 = a,b$ and $p_2 = b,a$. All possible permutations of order 3 of the three objects a,b,c can be obtained by inserting the object c in all possible places in both p_1 and p_2: p_1 yields c,a,b; a,c,b; and a,b,c; and p_2 yields c,b,a; b,c,a; and b,a,c.

Problem 4.5.8

Write a program to find all possible seating arrangements of a family of four, Father, Mother, Peter, and Sue, at a table for six people.

5

CHESS AND OTHER
GAMES

5.1 CHESS

Problem 5.1.1 (*Printing Chessboards*)

A chessboard may be considered as an 8 by 8 array. The chessmen may be represented by numbers in the following way:

	White	Black
Pawn	1	11
Knight	2	12
Bishop	3	13
Rook	4	14
Queen	5	15
King	6	16

Given eight data cards (representing the eight rows on a board) each of which contains eight numbers (a zero indicating an empty square, a number indicating a piece), write a program that will read these data and print out a neat listing of a chessboard with the pieces indicated on the squares.

Problem 5.1.2 (*Three Moves*)

Number the squares of a chessboard from 1 to 64 as follows:

```
 1   2   3   4   5   6   7   8
 9  10  11  12  13  14  15  16
17  18  19  20  · · ·
```

53

Write a program that will read in two numbers, M and P, where M is a number between 1 and 6 and represents a chessman (see the table in Problem 5.1.1) and P is a number from 1 to 64 that indicates his current position. Assuming the chessboard is empty, except for this one piece, print out the number of each square it could possibly visit in not more than three moves.

Problem 5.1.3 (Check)

Write a program that will read in a situation of a game of chess and then determine if black is in check.

Problem 5.1.4 (Checkmate)

Write a program that will read in a situation of a game of chess and then determine whether black is in checkmate. Remember that there are three ways for black to escape a check: (a) The black king moves out of check, (b) a black piece moves between the white attacker and the black king, and (c) a black piece captures the white attacker. Also take into account that the black king may be attacked by more than one piece.

Problem 5.1.5 (Take the Queen)

Write a program that will read in a situation in a game of chess and then determine if a black rook (if present) could take the white queen (if present) in not more than four moves if neither white pieces nor any other black piece are allowed to move in between the successive black rook's moves.

Problem 5.1.6 (Eight Queens)

In chess it is possible to place eight queens on the board so that no one queen can be taken by any other. Write a program that will determine all such possible arrangements for eight queens. Schachzeitung, the chess journal of Berlin, published in 1854, knew of 40 different arrangements of the eight queens. The great mathematician Gauss believed that there were 76 possible solutions. There are, in fact, 92 possible ways of arranging the eight queens.

Hint: The most obvious way to try to solve this type of problem is to consider all possible combinations of placing eight queens in the eight columns of a chessboard, one queen per column (giving 8^8 possible combinations), and then checking for each such combination whether all eight rows and all possible 30 diagonals contain at most one queen. Since the latter check requires more than 100 steps, in the order of 10^9 steps have to be carried out, too many for even a fast computer. More efficient methods for solving a problem of this type generally involve a technique called "backtracking." To be able to explain this technique for the case of placing eight queens on a chessboard, both the rows and columns of the board are considered to be numbered from 1 to 8. Further, an arrangement of queens on an otherwise empty board is called "conflict-free" if no two queens attack each other.

An algorithm for finding all conflict-free arrangements of eight queens is given below. It first places a queen in row 1 of column 1, then another queen conflict-free in column 2, etc., until either the eight columns contain a conflict-free arrangement of eight queens or until a column $c \leq 8$ is found in which no queen can be placed conflict-free. In the latter case the algorithm backtracks ("backs up") to column $c - 1$, trying to find a new conflict-free position for the queen in column $c - 1$; this is either possible, in which case column c is tried again, or it is impossible, in which case a further step of backtracking is necessary.

Step 1. Let $c = 1$.

Step 2. If $c > 8$, then print the current positions of the eight queens, let $c = 8$, and go to Step 5.

Step 3. Place a queen in row 1 of column c.

Step 4. If the arrangement is conflict-free, then let $c = c + 1$ and go to Step 2.

Step 5. If there is a queen in row 8 of column c and $c = 1$, then stop.

Step 6. If there is a queen in row 8 of column c, then remove it, let $c = c - 1$, and go to Step 5.

Step 7. Move the queen in column c to the next row and go to Step 4.

To write an efficient program based on the above algorithm it is essential to be able to check whether an arrangement is conflict-free or not using as few steps as possible. This can be done by keeping a record that indicates for each row and diagonal whether it already contains a queen or not. Using such a setup it is possible to check whether an arrangement is conflict-free or not in less than half a dozen steps.

Problem 5.1.7 *(Five Queens)*

It is possible to place five queens on a chessboard so that every square is dominated by at least one of the queens; i.e., if any other piece were placed on the board, it would be in danger of being captured by at least one of the queens. Write a program that will determine the position of each of the five queens.

Problem 5.1.8 *(Twelve Knights)*

It is possible to place 12 knights on a chess board so that they dominate all the other squares. Write a program to determine the position of each of the 12 knights.

It is also possible to place eight bishops in a "dominating" position.

Problem 5.1.9 (*Knight's Tour*)

It is possible to place a knight on any square of a chessboard and then in 64 moves have him visit every other square once and only once. Write a program that will attempt to find such a "knight's tour."

Hint: There are several ways of approaching this problem. One possibility is to use a method involving backtracking as described in Problem 5.1.4. It turns out that backtracking is quite slow for this particular problem and very careful programming is necessary to produce an acceptable program. A more efficient method is based on the following rules: For any square x on the chessboard let $p_i(x)$ ($i = 1, 2, \ldots$) be the number of squares accessible from x in i moves (not counting squares already visited). Always move the knight to a square x for which $p_1(x)$ is as small as possible. If various choices for x are possible, choose an x for which $p_2(x)$ is also as small as possible.

A method such as the above is called "heuristic": It is not guaranteed to work in every possible situation; for example, it is not guaranteed to work for a 50 by 50 "chessboard." It has been found to always work for a standard 8 by 8 chessboard. The fact that only the values of $p_1(x)$ and $p_2(x)$ are used is referred to as "double look-ahead" and in other situations a larger look-ahead proves advantageous.

Problem 5.1.10 (*Knight's Journey*)

Write a program that will determine the longest journey a knight may make without crossing his path. Use the program to find the length of the longest journey on a board with three, four, and five rows and columns.

Hint: Restrict the program to the case where the knight starts his journey in a corner square.

Problem 5.1.11 (*Chess Moves*)

Use the experience you gained by doing Problem 5.1.2 to write a program that will read in a situation in a game of chess and then list out all the possible moves open to each black piece on the board.

Problem 5.1.12 (*Good Next Move*)

If you are an avid chess player, then you will know some of the elementary "rules" of what constitutes a "good" position. For example,

It is good to have the opponent's king in checkmate.

It is good to have many pieces of high power.

It is good to attack the squares in the vicinity of the opponent's king.

It is good to have the opponent's men under attack.

It is not good to have a piece attacked by an opponent's piece of lower power.

It is not good to have an unprotected man attacked by an opponent's man.

Etc.

Think up a number of such rules. In accordance with these rules try to assign a numerical value $V(P)$ to each position P such that $V(P_1) > V(P_2)$ indicates that position P_1 is "better" than position P_2.

Expand the program of Problem 5.1.11 to evaluate each possible move that black can make by comparing the values of $V(P)$ for all possible positions P attainable in one move. The program should print out the best possible move(s) for the given situation.

5.2 OTHER GAMES

Problem 5.2.1 (*Tic-tac-toe*)

The game of "tic-tac-toe" (o's and x's, "naughts" and "crosses") is played by two players on a board with nine squares, arranged in three rows and three columns. The two players use pieces of different colors. At the beginning of the play the board is empty. The players make moves in turn, each move consisting of placing one piece in a still empty square of the board. A player wins ("makes a winning move") if he succeeds in filling one complete row, column, or diagonal with three of his pieces. A game is a draw if all squares of the board are occupied and no further move can be made.

Write a program that will simulate the playing of ten games of a player A (who starts every other game) with a player B, where the "strategies" of the two players are as follows: A makes a move at random (see Chapter 8). B acts as follows: If he has a winning move, then he makes a winning move; otherwise, if A can be prevented from making a winning move on A's next turn, then B prevents the winning move; otherwise B makes a move at random. The program should print for each game each move of both players and should determine the total number of draws and the total number of times B has won.

Note: If interactive facilities are available, the program should simulate only the player B; the moves of player A should be made by a human opponent.

Problem 5.2.2 (*Look-ahead for Tic-tac-toe*)

Improve the performance of player B in Problem 5.2.1 by incorporating more look-ahead (see Problem 5.1.9) as follows: (a) If B has a winning move, then B makes that move; otherwise (b) if B can prevent A from making a winning move on A's next turn, then B prevents the winning move; otherwise (c) if B can make a move such that, no matter how A reacts B has a winning move thereafter, then B makes that move; otherwise (d) if B can make a move such that, no matter how A reacts B can react such that A has no winning move thereafter, then *B* makes that move; otherwise (e) *B* places a piece such that the total number of rows, columns, and diagonals remaining without a piece of *B* is as small as possible. *B* chooses at random between moves if more than one is possible in accordance to one of the rules (a)–(e).

Note: The rules (a)–(d) are typical look-ahead rules. Rule (e), however, is a heuristic rule (see Problem 5.1.9): It does not guarantee success but it agrees with "common sense" and indeed turns out to be advantageous in many situations.

Problem 5.2.3 (*Gomoku*)

The game of "Gomoku" is similar to tic-tac-toe. It is played on an 8 by 8 chessboard, however, and a player wins if he succeeds in placing five consecutive pieces in any one row, column, or diagonal.

Write a program as in Problems 5.1.1 and 5.2.2 for the game of Gomoku. Because of the size of the board, look-ahead can be used only on a very limited scale. Heuristic rules such as (e) in Problem 5.2.2 prove more successful. Thus incorporate in your program more such rules and a modest look-ahead.

Problem 5.2.4 (*Three-Dimensional Tic-tac-toe*)

Extend the program of Problem 5.2.1 to play a three-dimensional game in a 4 by 4 cube. A player wins if he succeeds in filling one complete row, column, or diagonal with four of his pieces.

Problem 5.2.5 (*Nim, version 1*)

A popular version of the game of "Nim" is played with 12 counters that are arranged in three rows before the start of the game as follows:

```
  o   o   o
  o   o   o   o
  o   o   o   o   o
```

The game consists of removing counters according to rules detailed below. A pattern consisting of n_1 counters in the first, n_2 counters in the second, and n_3 counters in the third row can be conveniently represented by the triple (n_1,n_2,n_3). In particular, the pattern at the start of the game is represented by the triple (3,4,5).

The game is played by two persons who move in turns. Each move consists of removing one or more counters from one of the three rows. A player wins if he removes all remaining counters, i.e., if he reaches the situation (0,0,0).

Consider two players X and Y. A situation (n_1, n_2, n_3) reached by player X is called "winning" if, no matter what move is made by Y there is a move for X such that, no matter what move is made by Y there is a move for X such that, . . . , such that, no matter what move is made by Y there is a move for X leading to the situation $(0,0,0)$. Once a player X has attained a winning position he can systematically win by reacting to each move of the opponent Y by a move leading again to a winning situation. This strategy allows player X to eventually reach the situation $(0,0,0)$ and win the game. The knowledge of which situations are winning is therefore of crucial importance.

It is known that one can determine for the game of Nim whether a situation (n_1, n_2, n_3) is winning† or not as follows:

Step 1. Let the binary equivalent of n_1 be $b_1 b_2 b_3$, of n_2 be $c_1 c_2 c_3$, and of n_3 be $d_1 d_2 d_3$.

Step 2. Let $r_1 = b_1 + c_1 + d_1$, let $r_2 = b_2 + c_2 + d_2$, and let $r_3 = b_3 + c_3 + d_3$.

Step 3. If r_1, r_2, and r_3 are all even, then (n_1, n_2, n_3) is a winning situation; otherwise it is not.

For example, $(3,4,5)$ is not a winning situation since 3 in binary is $b_1 b_2 b_3 = 011$, 4 in binary is $c_1 c_2 c_3 = 100$, and 5 in binary is $d_1 d_2 d_3 = 101$ and thus $r_2 = 1 + 0 + 0 = 1$ is not even. Note that $(1,4,5)$, however, is a winning situation since 1 in binary is $b_1 b_2 b_3 = 001$, 4 in binary is $c_1 c_2 c_3 = 100$, and 5 in binary is $d_1 d_2 d_3 = 101$ and thus $r_1 = 0 + 1 + 1 = 2, r_2 = 0 + 0 + 0 = 0$, and $r_3 = 1 + 0 + 1 = 2$ are all even.

Write a program to simulate ten games of Nim of a player A (starting every other time) against a player B, where the strategies of A and B are as follows: Player A chooses at random between all possible moves; player B tries to reach a winning situation; if this is impossible, player B removes one counter in the first row possible. Note that player B will always win when starting, since he can obtain the winning position $(1,4,5)$ on his first move.

The program should print for each game each move of both players and an indication of who has won.

Note: If interactive facilities are available, the program should simulate only the player B; the moves of player A should be made by a human opponent.

Problem 5.2.6 (*Hexapawn*)

The game of "Hexapawn" is, in essence, a very limited form of chess. It is played on a 3 by 3 chessboard, each player starting with three pawns

---

†The algorithm given can be generalized for any game of Nim with any number of counters used, rows used, and starting patterns used. For a further discussion of Nim and the concept of a winning situation, see Chapter 10.

positioned as shown below:

The pawns move as in chess, i.e., either one square forward to an empty square or one square diagonally forward to a square occupied by an opponent's piece, which is then removed from the board. A player wins if he succeeds in moving one of his pawns two rows forward to the opposite side of the board or if his opponent is unable to move any of his pawns on his turn.

Write a program that will simulate the playing of ten games of a player *A* (who starts every other game) with a player *B*, where the "strategies" of the two players are as described in Problem 5.2.1.

Problem 5.2.7 (*Artificial Intelligence*)

The game of Hexapawn may be used to provide a very simple example of "artificial intelligence." Write a program to simulate the playing of 200 games of a player *A* (who starts every other game) with a player *B*, where both players move at random, but where player *B* "learns" from his own mistakes as follows: The program retains for each possible move in each possible board situation in Hexapawn a "weight" of the move, all weights initially being equal. Whenever it is player *B*'s turn the weights of all possible moves are considered and the move with the highest weight is chosen, a random choice between moves of same highest weight being made if necessary. For each game being played the program keeps track of all the moves made by player *B* during the game. When the game is over and has been won by player *B*, 1 is added to the weight of the first move made by player *B* in that game, 2 is added to the weight of the second move, etc. The weights are similarly decreased if *B* has lost the game.

The program should determine and print the winner for each of the 200 games and should, in addition, print out all moves made in games 1, 16, 31, 46, . . . , 196.

Note: If interactive facilities are available, proceed as above but let player *A* in games 1, 16, 31, . . . , 196 be played by a human opponent. Player *B* thus always plays 14 games against a player *A* who makes moves at random, having a chance to "learn," and will therefore display increasing skill when playing against a human opponent in games 1, 16, . . . , 196.

Problem 5.2.8 (*Checkers*)

Write a program that will, given a situation in a game of checkers, print out the "best possible" next move for black. The best move may be determined by a set of "rules" (see Problem 5.1.12) such as

It is good to create a new king.

It is good to capture a piece of the opponent.

It is not good to leave a piece in a position in which it could be captured.

It is good to have as many men as possible as far forward as possible.

Think up a number of such rules and proceed as in Problem 5.1.12.

6

EQUATIONS IN ONE VARIABLE

6.1 METHODS FOR SOLVING AN EQUATION IN ONE VARIABLE

A "function in one variable x" can be interpreted as a rule for computing a certain value, the "value of the function," given a value for the variable x. Functions are usually denoted by symbols such as $f(x)$, $g(x)$, etc.

For example, consider $f(x) = 3x^2 - x + 2$. This function represents a rule for a certain computation whose outcome depends on the choice of the value for the variable x. Taking $x = 2$ the value computed is $3 \cdot 2^2 - 2 + 2$, i.e., 12. This fact, that "the value of the function $f(x)$ for $x = 2$ is equal to 12," is expressed in symbols by writing $f(2) = 12$. Similarly one has $f(0) = 2$, $f(-1) = 6$, $f(1) = 4$, $f(10) = 292$, $f(1.2) = 5.12$, etc. For every choice of x one can find a "corresponding" value of the function $f(x)$.

Throughout this chapter the central problem is this: Given a function $f(x)$ how can one find a value for x such that the value of the function $f(x)$ is zero or close to zero? Or, putting it another way, how can one find a "solution" or "approximate solution" of the "equation" $f(x) = 0$?

Consider the function $f(x) = 3^x - 81$. To find a solution of the equation $3^x - 81 = 0$, application of high school algebra yields $3^x = 81$; i.e., $3^x = 3^4$. Thus $x = 4$ is obtained as the solution. Indeed, $f(4) = 3^4 - 81 = 0$ as desired.

Or consider the function $f(x) = x^2 + x - 2$. Solutions of the quadratic equation $x^2 + x - 2 = 0$ can be obtained using the standard formula as given in Problem 1.4.7. Applying this formula one finds the two solutions $x = (-1 + \sqrt{1 + 8})/2 = 1$ and $x = (-1 - \sqrt{1 + 8})/2 = -2$. Indeed, $f(1) = 0$ and $f(-2) = 0$.

Often the situation is not so simple. Consider the function $g(x) = x^3 - x - 1$. None of the usual methods allow the exact calculation of a solution of $x^3 - x - 1 = 0$. Still it is possible to compute an approximate value of the solution. First observe that $g(1) = -1 < 0$ and $g(2) = 5 > 0$. Thus if the value of x changes gradually from 1 to 2, it seems reasonable to assume that the value of $g(x)$ changes gradually from -1 to 5, from negative to positive.† Thus for some value of x between 1 and 2, as one says: "somewhere in the interval (1,2)," the value of $g(x)$ seems to be zero. Granted, the estimate of the solution that x must be between 1 and 2 is rather rough. But it is easy to improve this estimate as much as desired in the following systematic manner: It has been shown that $g(1) < 0$ and $g(2) > 0$. Thus the solution must be between 1 and 2. Consider now the number in the middle between 1 and 2, the "midpoint of the interval (1,2)." That number is $(1 + 2)/2$, i.e., 1.5. A simple calculation shows that $g(1.5) = 0.875$, i.e., $g(1.5) > 0$, and thus the solution must be between 1 and 1.5. The midpoint of the interval (1,1.5) is $(1 + 1.5)/2 = 1.25$, $g(1.25)$ can be seen to be negative, and thus the solution must be between 1.25 and 1.5. The midpoint of this new interval (1.25,1.5) is 1.375, $g(1.375)$ is positive, and thus the solution must be between 1.25 and 1.375. The midpoint of (1.25,1.375) is 1.3125, $g(1.3125)$ is negative, and thus the solution must be between 1.3125 and 1.375. This process can be carried on indefinitely, narrowing down the interval as much as desired. When the process is finally stopped it is an advisable precaution to compute $g(x)$ for some number x in the interval of solution determined. After all, $g(x)$ should be close to zero for any number x in that interval. In the particular case at issue the last interval calculated was (1.3125,1.375). Picking, e.g., $x = 1.32$ in this interval one finds $g(1.32) = -0.020032$, which is indeed reasonably close to zero.

The process described above is called the "binary search" or "interval halving" method. It is reliable and foolproof as long as the value of the function involved changes gradually as the value of the variable x changes gradually—as long as the function is what mathematicians call "continuous."

To understand the significance of this property it is helpful to examine the concept of the "graph" of a function.

The graph of a function $f(x)$ is obtained by plotting the points $(x, f(x))$ in a rectangular coordinate system. The graph of the function $f(x) = x^3 - x - 1$ is shown in Fig. 6-1.

It is now clear that finding a solution of an equation $f(x) = 0$ is equivalent to finding a point of intersection of the graph of $f(x)$ with the x-axis. Such a point of intersection must exist between two points a and b on the

---

†This is not always the case, as is discussed below.

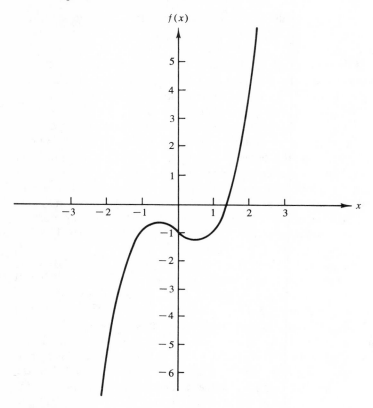

Figure 6-1

x-axis if $f(a) < 0$ and $f(b) > 0$ provided that the graph of $f(x)$ is "without jumps," i.e., is continuous. If, however, the graph of the function $f(x)$ has "jumps," as in Fig. 6-2, a point of intersection need not exist and the interval halving method may fail. One can summarize the results as follows:

Interval halving method for the approximate solution of an equation $f(x) = 0$, where $f(x)$ is a continuous function

Given values a and b with $f(a) < 0$, $f(b) > 0$, and $a < b$ (this is no restriction; consider $-f(x)$ if necessary) and a value $e > 0$, the algorithm below will have, when terminating, computed a value s such that abs $(f(s)) < e$.

Step 1. Let $s = (a + b)/2$.

Step 2. If abs$(f(s)) < e$, then stop.

Step 3. If $f(s) > 0$, then let $b = s$ and go to Step 1.

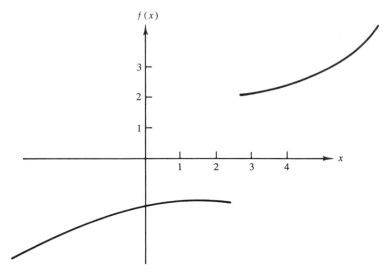

Figure 6-2

Step 4. If $f(s) < 0$, then let $a = s$ and go to Step 1.

If it is desired that the approximate solution is sufficiently close to the actual solution rather than that the value of the function at the approximate solution is sufficiently close to zero, it should be noted that Step 2 can be replaced by

Step 2. If $b - a < e$, then stop.

Whenever the interval halving method is applied it is imperative either to make sure that the function considered is continuous or to incorporate suitable checks in the algorithm used. Consider, e.g., the function $f(x) = 1/x$. One has $f(-1) = -1 < 0$ and $f(1) = 1 > 0$ but the equation $1/x = 0$ has no solution. As one can readily see from the graph of the function $f(x) = 1/x$ there is a jump, a "discontinuity," as the value of the variable x approaches zero.

Interval halving is a reliable method but often an unnecessary number of *iterations*, of halving the interval, are required to obtain a desired accuracy. Still, if the length of the initial interval is l, the length of the interval after 10 iterations is approximately $l/1000$, after 20 iterations $l/1,000,000$, etc. Thus the method is quite acceptable for a computer.

Among the many other methods known for finding an approximate solution of an equation in one variable is the "Newton–Raphson" method, explained below. As is the case for many other processes the Newton–Raphson method works better (i.e., fewer iterations are necessary) than the interval halving method if it works at all. In many situations, however, the Newton–Raphson method fails where interval halving can be used successfully.

Newton–Raphson method for the approximate solution of an equation $f(x) = 0$, where $f(x)$ is a function with derivative $f'(x)$†

Given a value $e > 0$ and a number s sufficiently close to the solution of $f(x) = 0$, the algorithm below will have, when terminating, computed a value s such that abs$(f(s)) < e$.

Step 1. If abs$(f(s)) < e$, then stop.

Step 2. Let $s = s - (f(s)/f'(s))$ and go to Step 1.

It should be noted that Step 2 and thus the Newton–Raphson method can be used only if $f'(s) \neq 0$. Further, the choice of the initial value s is often critical. In practice it is advisable to incorporate steps into the algorithm for checking whether the values obtained for s do indeed approach a solution of $f(x) = 0$. This can, e.g., be done by testing whether for successive values s and s', as calculated according to Step 2 above, abs$(f(s'))$ is indeed smaller than abs$(f(s))$.

Note that the calculation of the pth root of a number a can be interpreted as solving the equation $f(x) = x^p - a = 0$. For this type of function the formula in Step 2 above becomes

$$\text{Let} \quad s = s - \frac{s^p - a}{ps^{p-1}}, \qquad \text{i.e., let} \quad s = s\left(1 + \frac{a - s^p}{ps^p}\right)$$

in accordance to the formulae used in Problem 4.2.2.

For a more detailed discussion of the Newton–Raphson method and other iterative methods see, e.g., Dorn and Greenberg.‡

Both the interval halving and Newton–Raphson methods are iterative methods. In some special cases a solution of an equation of the form $f(x) = a_n x^n + a_{n-1} x^{n-1} + \cdots + a_2 x^2 + a_1 x + a_0 = 0$ ($n \geq 1$ is an integer; $a_0, a_1, \ldots, a_n$ are any numbers), of a so-called "polynomial equation," can be obtained directly.

If the numbers $a_0, a_1, a_2, \ldots, a_n$ are integers, all solutions of $f(x)$ of the form r/s, where r and s are integers, can be obtained using the fact, proven in algebra, that r must be a factor of a_0 and s a factor of a_n. Consider the equation $f(x) = x^3 + 2x - x^2 - 2$. The factors of $a_0 = 2$ are 1, -1, 2, and -2 and the factors of $a_3 = 1$ are 1 and -1. Thus, if $f(x) = 0$ has solutions of the form r/s, they must be among the numbers 1, -1, 2, and -2. Calculating $f(1) = 0$, $f(-1) = -6$, $f(2) = 6$, and $f(-2) = -18$ one finds that $x = 1$ is the only solution of $f(x) = 0$ of the form r/s.

---

†For an explanation of the term *derivative of a function*, see any introductory book on calculus.

‡W. S. Dorn and H. J. Greenberg, *Mathematics and Computing*, Wiley, New York, 1967.

If $n = 1$ in a polynomial equation $f(x) = a_n x^n + \cdots + a_1 x + a_0$, then $f(x) = 0$ is called a "linear equation" and the solution can be found immediately; if $n = 2$, then $f(x) = 0$ is called a "quadratic equation" and the formula of Problem 1.4.7 can be used; if $n = 3$, then $f(x) = 0$ is called a "cubic equation" and "Cardano's method," as given below, can be applied; for $n = 4$ a solution can be also obtained directly, but the method is of little practical value and is omitted here; for $n > 4$ it was shown by the Norwegian mathematician Abel in 1826 that no general formula can be found.

Cardano's method for finding a solution of a cubic equation

It clearly suffices to consider cubic equations of the form $x^3 + ax^2 + bx + c = 0$. By substituting the expression $x - a/3$ for x an equation of the form $x^3 + px + q = 0$ is obtained whose solutions differ by only $a/3$ from the solutions of the original equation. To find a solution s of an equation of the form $x^3 + px + q = 0$ using Cardano's method one proceeds as follows:

Step 1. Let $d = (4p^3 + 27q^2)/27$.

Step 2. Let $u = \sqrt[3]{\frac{1}{2}(-q + \sqrt{d})}$.

Step 3. Let $v = -(p/3u)$.

Step 4. Let $s = u + v$ and stop.

For example, this algorithm is applied to the equation $f(x) = x^3 - 3x^2 + 18x + 108 = 0$. Substituting the expression $x - (a/3) = x + 1$ for x yields $f(x + 1) = (x + 1)^3 - 3(x + 1)^2 + 18(x + 1) + 108 = x^3 + 15x + 124$. Now applying the algorithm to $g(x) = x^3 + 15x + 124$ one obtains $d = ((4)15^3 + (27)124^2)/27 = 15876$, $\sqrt{d} = \sqrt{15876} = 126$, $u = \sqrt[3]{\frac{1}{2}(-124 + 126)} = \sqrt[3]{1} = 1$, and $v = (-15)/3 = -5$. Thus a solution s of $g(x) = 0$ is $s = -4$. Since $g(x) = f(x + 1)$ one obtains $g(-4) = f(-4 + 1) = f(-3) = 0$ and -3 is thus a solution of $f(x) = 0$ as desired. Indeed, $f(-3) = (-3)^3 - 3(-3)^2 + 18(-3) + 108 = -27 - 27 - 54 + 108 = 0$.

It should be noted that for $d < 0$ Cardano's method leads to "complex" numbers. This situation occurs if the equation $x^3 + px + q = 0$ has three distinct real solutions, i.e., in the (in a sense) most important case. Despite the fact that the final result will be a real number, complex numbers do occur as intermediate results in this case. It has been established that this "detour" using complex numbers is unavoidable no matter what method is used. The case $d < 0$ is thus known as "*casus irreducibilis.*" Because of the awkward computations involved in Cardano's method, especially in the main case of three distinct real solutions, the method is little used in practice, and iterative methods are preferred.

In some cases a polynomial equation $f(x) = a_n x^n + \cdots + a_1 x + a_0$ can be reduced to a simpler polynomial equation $g(x) = b_m x^m + \cdots + b_1 x$

$+ b_0$ with $m < n$ using the fact, proven in algebra, that $g(x) = f(x)/\text{lcf}(f(x),$ $f'(x))$ has exactly the same solutions as $f(x)$. In the above formula $\text{lcf}(f(x), f'(x))$ is the largest common factor of the two polynomials $f(x)$ and $f'(x)$, as explained in Problem 4.2.11, and $f'(x)$, the "derivative" of $f(x)$, is given by $f'(x) = na_nx^{n-1} + (n-1)a_{n-1}x^{n-2} + \cdots + 2a_2x + a_1$.

6.2 PROBLEMS

Problem 6.2.1

Write a program to determine a number s such that $\text{abs}(s^s - 3s) < 0.00001$.

Problem 6.2.2

Write a program to determine an approximate solution s of the equation $2^x - 3x^2 = 0$ such that s agrees with the actual solution up to five decimal places.

Problem 6.2.3

Write a program to find an approximate solution s of the equation $x^4 - 10x^3 + 6x - 4 = 0$ such that $\text{abs}(s^4 - 10s^3 + 6s - 4) < e$, where $e > 0$ is a number read from a data card.

Problem 6.2.4

Write a program to determine an approximate solution s of the equation $f(x) = 1 + x \cos(x) - x^x = 0$. Note that $f(1) > 0$ but $f(2) < 0$.

Problem 6.2.5

Write a program to determine two different solutions s of the equation $\sqrt[x]{x} - 1.3 = 0$ such that $\text{abs}(\sqrt[s]{s} - 1.3) < 0.00001$ and such that s agrees with an actual solution up to four decimal places.

Problem 6.2.6

Write a program to determine an approximate solution s of the equation $3^{\cos(x)} - x = 0$.

Problem 6.2.7 *(Interval Halving for Polynomials, Version 1)*

A data card contains four numbers, a, b, c, and e, representing a cubic equation $f(x) = x^3 + ax^2 + bx + c = 0$ and a desired accuracy e. Using interval halving, write a program to determine an approximate solution s of the equation $f(x) = 0$ such that $\text{abs}(f(s)) < e$. Use as starting interval $(-h, h)$, where $h = 1 + \max(\text{abs}(a), \text{abs}(b), \text{abs}(c))$.

Note: This choice of starting interval is justified by the fact known from algebra that $f(-h) < 0$ and $f(h) > 0$.

Problem 6.2.8

Same as Problem 6.2.7 but after having found an approximate solution s of $f(x) = x^3 + ax^2 + bx + c = 0$ use the fact that one can write $(x^3 + ax^2 + bx + c) = (x - s)(x^2 + (a + s)x + (b + as + s^2))$ and that the possibly remaining two real solutions of $f(x) = 0$ can be found by calculating the solutions of the quadratic equation $x^2 + (a + s)x + (b + as + s^2) = 0$ according to Problem 1.4.7.

Problem 6.2.9 (*Newton–Raphson Method, Version 1*)

Write a program using the Newton–Raphson method to find an approximate solution s of the equation $x^5 - x^3 + x - 10 = 0$ in the interval $(1.5, 1.7)$ such that abs$(s^5 - s^3 + s - 10) < 0.00000001$.

Problem 6.2.10 (*Interval Halving for Polynomials, Version 2*)

A data card contains six numbers, a, b, c, d, e, and t, representing an equation $f(x) = x^5 + ax^4 + bx^3 + cx^2 + dx + e = 0$ and a desired accuracy t. Using interval halving write a program to determine an approximate solution s of the above equation $f(x) = 0$ such that abs$(f(s)) < t$. Use as starting interval $(-h, h)$, where $h = 1 + \max(\text{abs}(a), \text{abs}(b), \text{abs}(c), \text{abs}(d), \text{abs}(e))$.

Note: See Problem 6.2.7.

Problem 6.2.11 (*Interval Halving and Newton–Raphson Method*)

Same as Problem 6.2.10, but use a combination of the Newton–Raphson and interval halving methods as follows: Start with the interval $(-h, h)$ and the Newton–Raphson method, choosing as the starting value the right end point of the interval. If the Newton–Raphson process is not working successfully (is not "converging"), switch to interval halving for five iterations, and then back to Newton–Raphson, choosing as the initial value the right end point of the new interval, etc. For each set of input data, record also how often it was necessary to switch to the interval halving method.

Problem 6.2.12 (*Newton–Raphson Method, Version 2*)

Write a program using the Newton–Raphson method with the starting value $s = 2$ to find an approximate solution s of the equation $f(x) = x^7 - x - 110 = 0$ such that abs$(f(s)) < 0.00000001$. Do the same using interval halving starting with the interval $(1.5, 2)$. Print the solution s, the number of iterations required with the Newton–Raphson method, and the number of iterations required with interval halving.

Problem 6.2.13 (*Cardano's Method, Version 1*)

A data card contains two numbers, p and q, satisfying $4p^3 + 27q^2 > 0$, representing a cubic equation $x^3 + px + q = 0$. Write a program using Cardano's method to find a solution s of the given equation.

Problem 6.2.14 (*Cardano's Method, Version 2*)

A data card contains three numbers, a, b, and c, satisfying $4(b - (a/3))^3 + 27(c + (2a^3/27) - (ba/3))^2 > 0$, representing a cubic equation $x^3 + ax^2 + bx + c = 0$. Using Cardano's method write a program to find a solution of the given equation.

Problem 6.2.15 (*Rational Solutions, Version 1*)

Write a program to determine all solutions of the form r/s, where r and s are integers of the equation $1377x^6 - 17820x^5 - 8703x^4 + 99000x^3 + 6683x^2 - 10780x - 637 = 0$.

Problem 6.2.16 (*Rational Solutions, Version 2*)

Write a program to determine all solutions of the form r/s, where r and s are integers of the equation $x^3 + 2.3x^2 - 1.69x - 3.887 = 0$.

Problem 6.2.17 (*Rational Solutions, Version 3*)

A card contains four integers, a, b, c, and d, representing a cubic equation $ax^3 + bx^2 + cx + d = 0$. Write a program to find all solutions of the form r/s, where r and s are integers.

Problem 6.2.18 (*Rational Solutions, Version 4*)

A card contains five integers, a, b, c, d, and e, representing an equation $x^5 + ax^4 + bx^3 + cx^2 + dx + e = 0$. Write a program to find all solutions of the form r/s, where r and s are integers.

Problem 6.2.19 (*Reduction of Degree*)

Write a program to determine one solution of the equation $x^{12} - 9x^{10} - 4x^9 + 27x^8 + 36x^7 - 23x^6 - 108x^5 - 36x^4 + 108x^3 + 108x^2 - 108 = 0$.

Hint: This equation can be reduced to an equation $x^5 + a_4x^4 + \cdots + a_1x + a_0$ using the method explained at the end of Section 6.1.

Problem 6.2.20 (*General Root Finder*)

Write a program that combines some of the problems using interval halving and the Newton–Raphson method presented in this section.

As input the following information is available:

(a) An expression E involving one variable X, numbers, operators, standard functions, and brackets; to simplify the program E should be a valid expression in the programming language you are using; E represents a certain function $f(X)$.

(b) Two numbers a and b for which $f(a) \cdot f(b)$ is known to be negative.

(c) A number $e > 0$ representing the desired accuracy.

Write a program C that will produce as output a program P such that P will determine a number s between a and b with abs($f(s)$) $< e$ using a combination of interval halving and the Newton–Raphson method analogous to what is described in Problem 6.2.11.

EXAMPLE

Given the input

1. $E = X^X - 3X$
2. $a = 1, b = 3$
3. $e = 0.00001$

the program should produce a program for solving Problem 6.2.1.

Problem 6.2.21

Write a program C similar to the one described in Problem 6.2.20 that also takes care of problems such as Problem 6.2.7 where the program P generated by C requires input information itself.

7

SORTING

7.1 SORTING METHODS

The process of arranging a collection of items (e.g., numbers, names, book titles) into a certain order (e.g., ascending order, alphabetical order) is called "sorting."

Sorting is necessary for many data processing applications; a library might want to produce an alphabetical listing of all titles available, a store having charge accounts might find it useful to keep customer files arranged in ascending order by account number, etc. Sorting can also be used for certain mathematical applications such as the calculation of solutions of equations as in Problems 7.2.20–7.2.27.

It is basically not difficult to sort n items into a certain order. The number of items to be sorted is, however, sometimes very large so that time and space requirements of sorting methods are of critical importance. For example, Method 1 below for sorting n items can take up to n^2 steps. Thus to arrange $n = 400,000$ titles of a library in ascending order, 160,000,000,000 steps could be necessary and even a fast computer would require hundreds of hours for carrying out the process. Using Method 6 below, the same number of titles can be sorted in about 2,000,000 steps, a matter of minutes for a fast computer.

Thus in selecting a sorting method for a particular application three points have to be carefully considered: (1) programming effort, (2) time requirements, and (3) storage space requirements.

A number of well-known sorting methods are explained below. In each case it is assumed that $a_1, a_2, \ldots, a_n$ is a collection of n integers that is to be sorted into ascending order.

Method 1. Exchange sorting

Step 1. Let $c = 0$ and let $i = 1$.

Step 2. If $a_i > a_{i+1}$, then let $b = a_{i+1}$, let $a_{i+1} = a_i$, let $a_i = b$, and let $c = c + 1$.

Step 3. If $i < n - 1$, then let $i = i + 1$ and go to Step 2.

Step 4. If $c \neq 0$, then go to Step 1.

Step 5. Stop.

Note that Steps 2 and 3 check whether consecutive integers in the given sequence are in ascending order. If they are in ascending order, they are left unchanged and the next two integers are examined. If they are not in ascending order, they are exchanged (observe that this is done using the three statements let $b = a_{i+1}$, let $a_{i+1} = a_i$, and let $a_i = b$ since the two statements let $a_{i+1} = a_i$ and let $a_i = a_{i+1}$ would not have the desired effect of exchanging) and a count c (counting how often an exchange is performed) is increased by 1. Then the next two integers are examined. After the whole collection has been examined (and possibly modified) c is tested in Step 4. If an exchange has taken place ($c \neq 0$), the count c is reset to 0 and the process of examining and modifying the sequence of integers is repeated according to Steps 2 and 3. If, however, no exchange has taken place ($c = 0$), the sequence is now in ascending order and the sorting process is terminated.

Consider the effect of Method 1 when applied to the collection of five numbers $-3, 5, -8, 16, 2$. Applying Steps 2 and 3 repeatedly one obtains the sequence $-3, -8, 5, 2, 16$ and $c = 2$. By Step 4 the process is repeated giving $-8, -3, 2, 5, 16$ and $c = 2$. By Step 4 the process is repeated once more giving $-8, -3, 2, 5, 16$ and $c = 0$ and the process is terminated.

Method 2. Sorting by finding the smallest item

To print the numbers $a_1, a_2, \ldots, a_n$ in ascending order proceed as follows: First print the smallest of the n numbers $a_1, a_2, \ldots, a_n$, then print the smallest of the $n - 1$ remaining numbers, then print the smallest of the $n - 2$ remaining numbers, etc.

Method 3. Sorting by quadratic selection

To print the numbers $a_1, a_2, \ldots, a_n$ in ascending order proceed as follows:

Step 1. Divide the n numbers $a_1, a_2, \ldots, a_n$ into approximately $m = \sqrt{n}$ groups $G_1, G_2, \ldots, G_m$ of approximately $\sqrt{n}$ numbers each.

Step 2. Determine the smallest number in each group G_i and call it S_i.

Step 3. Find j such that S_j is the smallest of the numbers $S_1, S_2, \ldots, S_m$.

Step 4. Print S_j, remove S_j from G_j, and determine the smallest of the remaining numbers of G_j and call it S_j.

Step 5. If not all numbers have been printed yet, go to Step 3.

Step 6. Stop.

Consider the effect of Method 3 when applied to the sequence of the $n = 9$ numbers $19, 22, 15, 13, 6, -3, 18, 22, 11$. According to Step 1 one obtains $m = 3$; G_1: 19, 22, 15; G_2: 13, 6, -3; and G_3: 18, 22, 11. According to Step 2 one gets $S_1 = 15$, $S_2 = -3$, and $S_3 = 11$. By Step 3 $j = 2$. By Step 4 $S_2 = -3$ is printed and removed from G_2. S_2 changes to 6. By Step 3 $j = 2$. By Step 4 $S_2 = 6$ is printed and removed from G_2. S_2 changes to 13. By Step 3 $j = 3$. By Step 4 $S_3 = 11$ is printed and removed from G_3. S_3 changes to 18. By Step 3 $j = 2$. By Step 4 $S_2 = 13$ is printed and removed from G_2.

Note that now G_2 is exhausted. From now on $j \neq 2$ is used in Step 3. By Step 3 $j = 1$. By Step 4 $S_1 = 15$ is printed and removed from G_1. S_1 changes to 19. By Step 3 $j = 3$. By Step 4 $S_3 = 18$ is printed and removed from G_3. S_3 changes to 22. By Step 3 $j = 1$. By Step 4 $S_1 = 19$ is printed and removed from G_1. S_1 changes to 22. By Step 3 $j = 1$. By Step 4 $S_1 = 22$ is printed and removed from G_1.

Note that now G_1 is exhausted. From now on $j \neq 2$ and $j \neq 1$ are used in Step 3. By Step 3 $j = 3$. By Step 4 $S_3 = 22$ is printed and removed from G_3.

Since G_1, G_2, and G_3 are now exhausted the process terminates.

Method 4. Simulating a mechanical sorter

The following algorithm will sort a sequence of positive k-digit decimal integers (k arbitrary) into ascending order.

Step 1. Let $i = 1$.

Step 2. Generate a new sequence of numbers from the current sequence as follows: Take all numbers with 0 as ith digit from the right, followed by all numbers with 1 as ith digit from the right, . . . , followed by all numbers with 9 as ith digit from the right.

Step 3. If $i < k$, then let $i = i + 1$ and go to Step 2.

Step 4. Stop. The sequence last obtained is the sorted sequence.

Consider the effect of Method 4 when applied to the following sequence of 28 positive two-digit (i.e., $k = 2$) decimal integers: 98, 73, 16, 17, 10, 30, 63, 55, 15, 93, 08, 09, 27, 81, 82, 93, 39, 37, 16, 11, 57, 78, 25, 62, 18, 28, 92, 03. Applying Step 2 with $i = 1$ one obtains 10, 30, 81, 11, 82, 62, 92, 73,

63, 93, 93, 03, 55, 15, 25, 16, 16, 17, 27, 37, 57, 98, 08, 78, 18, 28, 09, 39. Applying Step 2 once more with $i = 2$ yields 03, 08, 09, 10, 11, 15, 16, 16, 17, 18, 25, 27, 28, 30, 37, 39, 55, 57, 62, 63, 73, 78, 81, 82, 92, 93, 93, 98, representing the given numbers in ascending order as desired.

Method 5. Sorting binary numbers

The following algorithm is a variation of Method 4 and will sort a sequence of positive k-bit binary numbers (for an explanation of binary numbers, see Problem 4.3.1) (k arbitrary) into ascending order.

Step 1. Let $i = 1$.

Step 2. Generate a new sequence of numbers from the current sequence as follows: Take all numbers with 0 as ith bit from the right followed by all numbers with 1 as ith bit from the right.

Step 3. If $i < k$, then let $i = i + 1$ and go to Step 2.

Step 4. Stop. The sequence last obtained is the sorted sequence.

Method 6. Sorting by two-way merging

For an explanation of "merging," see Chapter 2. Problem 2.2.10 will prove helpful in trying to implement the algorithm below.

Step 1. Rearrange the numbers in the given sequence $a_1, a_2, \ldots, a_n$ such that a_1, a_2 and a_3, a_4 and a_5, a_6, etc., are in ascending order. Now the given numbers are arranged in ascending sequences of length $2 = 2^1$. The following steps will produce longer and longer sequences of numbers arranged in ascending order.

Step 2. Merge a_1, a_2 and a_3, a_4 into an ascending sequence a_1, a_2, a_3, a_4; merge a_5, a_6 and a_7, a_8 into an ascending sequence a_5, a_6, a_7, a_8; etc. Now the given numbers are arranged in ascending sequences of length $4 = 2^2$.

Step 3. Merge a_1, a_2, a_3, a_4 and a_5, a_6, a_7, a_8 into an ascending sequence $a_1, a_2, a_3, a_4, a_5, a_6, a_7, a_8$; merge $a_9, a_{10}, a_{11}, a_{12}$ and $a_{13}, a_{14}, a_{15}, a_{16}$, etc. Now the given numbers are arranged in ascending sequences of length $8 = 2^3$.

Step i. Merge $a_1, a_2, \ldots, a_{2^{i-1}}$ and $a_{2^{i-1}+1}, a_{2^{i-1}+2}, \ldots, a_{2^i}$ into an ascending sequence $a_1, a_2, \ldots, a_{2^i}$, etc. Now the given numbers are arranged in ascending sequences of length 2^i.

Continue the process described until a single sequence of numbers in ascending order is obtained.

Consider the effect of Method 6 when applied to the following sequence of 16 integers: 98, 101, 313, 19, 21, 16, 44, 64, 32, 5, 11, 100, 62, 37, 71, 9. Applying Step 1 one obtains 98, 101;   19, 313;   16, 21;   44, 64;

5, 32;   11, 100;   37, 62;   9, 71. By Step 2 one gets 19, 98, 101, 313;
16, 21, 44, 64;   5, 11, 32, 100;   9, 37, 62, 71. Step 3 yields 16, 19, 21,
44, 64, 98, 101, 313;   5, 9, 11, 32, 37, 62, 71, 100. Step 4 finally gives
5, 9, 11, 16, 19, 21, 32, 37, 44, 62, 64, 71, 98, 100, 101, 313.

Method 7. Sorting by m-way merging

Similar to Method 6 but m sequences of numbers are merged at each step
to produce a longer sequence.

Method 8. Sorting by distribution

The method will be explained using an example: Suppose that 8000
three-digit positive integers (0 excluded) $a_1, a_2, \ldots, a_{8000}$ are given and have
to be printed in ascending order. Since the numbers are known to range
between 1 and 999 this can be done by just counting how often 1, how often
2, . . . , how often 999 occurs, as shown by the following algorithm.

Step 1. Let $c_1 = 0$, let $c_2 = 0, \ldots$, let $c_{999} = 0$.

Step 2. Let $i = 1$.

Step 3. Let $c_{a_i} = c_{a_i} + 1$.

Step 4. If $i < 8000$, then let $i = i + 1$ and go to Step 3.

Step 5. Let $i = 1$.

Step 6. Print the number i, c_i times.

Step 7. If $i < 8000$, then let $i = i + 1$ and go to Step 6.

Step 8. Stop.

Note that c_m counts how often m occurs for each $m = 1, 2, \ldots, 999$. The
critical step to be understood in this connection is Step 3. Suppose that
$i = 15$ and $a_{15} = 712$. Then the count of the number of times 712 has
occurred has to be increased by 1; i.e., $c_{712} = c_{712} + 1$. This is exactly
what is accomplished by Step 3 since c_{a_i} is c_{712} in the case considered. Steps
5–7 print the given numbers in ascending order. Suppose that $c_{680} = 19$,
indicating that the number 680 has occurred 19 times. Then for $i = 680$
Step 6 will indeed print the number 680 19 times.

The above method is applicable only if the numbers to be sorted are
in a small range, since for every number within the range a separate counter
has to be used. For numbers in a wider range suitable modifications can be
made. For one possible modification, see Problem 7.2.6. For further details
and other sorting methods, see, e.g., "Sort Symposium."†

This section is concluded by a table showing the approximate number
of steps required to sort n items using the sorting methods discussed.

---

†"Sort Symposium," *Communications of the Assoc. of Comp. Machinery*, Vol. 6, no. 5
(1963), pp. 199–280.

Method	Order of Magnitude of Maximum Number of Steps for Sorting n Positive Integers	Remarks
1	n^2	This method is very efficient if numbers are "globally" sorted with only "local disturbances"; otherwise it is not recommended
2	n^2	Easy to program but quite inefficient
3	$n\sqrt{n}$	
4	nm	m is the number of digits in largest number; this method is reasonably easy to program and is very fast but careful programming is necessary to avoid waste of (storage) space
5	nm	m is the number of bits in the largest number; this method can be highly recommended if the formula explained in Problem 7.2.14 can be efficiently implemented on the computing device available
6	$n \log (n)$	This very efficient method is not easy to program but it is the one most often used for sorting large collections of items; it can be quite easily used even if "external storage devices" (e.g., "tapes") have to be used because of the size of the collection
7	$n \log (n)$	
8	n	Fastest sorting method available, but not always applicable

7.2 PROBLEMS

Problem 7.2.1 (*Exchange Sort*)

Punched cards are available containing a number $k \leq 200$ followed by k eight-digit decimal integers $a_1, a_2, \ldots, a_k$. Write a program to sort the numbers $a_1, a_2, \ldots, a_k$ into ascending order using Method 1.

Problem 7.2.2 (*Digit Sort*)

Same as Problem 7.2.1 but use Method 4.

Problem 7.2.3 (*Two-Way Merging*)

Same as Problem 7.2.1 but use Method 6.

Problem 7.2.4 (*Quadratic Selection*)

Same as Problem 7.2.1 but use Method 3.

Problem 7.2.5 (*Distribution Sort*)

Punched cards are available containing numbers $a_1, a_2, \ldots, a_k, b$, where the a_i's are integers between -300 and $+300$ and where $b = 999$ (indicating the end of input data). Using Method 8, write a program to sort the numbers $a_1, a_2, \ldots, a_k$ into descending order.

Problem 7.2.6 (*Modified Distribution Sort*)

Punched cards are available containing a number $k \leq 300$ followed by k positive five-digit integers $a_1, a_2, \ldots, a_k$. Write a program to sort $a_1, a_2, \ldots, a_k$ into ascending order using a modification of Method 8.

Hint: Proceed as follows:

Step 1. Let $c_0 = 0$, let $c_1 = 0$, let $c_2 = 0, \ldots$, let $c_{999} = 0$. (*Note 1*: Throughout the algorithm the nonzero elements of $c_0, c_1, \ldots, c_{999}$ will be a sequence of numbers in ascending order.)

Step 2. Let $j = 1$.

Step 3. Let $i = \text{floor}(a_j/100)$. (*Note 2*: Observe that i will be between 0 and 999.)

Step 4. If $c_i = 0$, then let $c_i = a_j$.

Step 5. If $c_i \neq 0$, then insert a_j into the sequence of nonzero elements of $c_0, c_1, \ldots, c_{999}$ in its proper position in accordance with Note 1. (*Note 3*: Observe that this insertion can mean a considerable amount of rearranging of the nonzero elements of $c_0, c_1, \ldots, c_{999}$.)

Step 6. If $j < k$, then let $j = j + 1$ and go to Step 3.

Step 7. Stop. The nonzero elements of $c_0, c_1, \ldots, c_{999}$ are the numbers $a_1, a_2, \ldots, a_k$ in ascending order.

It is instructive to examine the above algorithm for the $k = 7$ numbers 56321, 92100, 56477, 56319, 56208, 55699, and 56318. For brevity only the nonzero elements of $c_0, c_1, \ldots, c_{999}$ will be listed.

1. For $a_1 = 56321$ one obtains $c_{563} = 56321$.
2. For $a_2 = 92100$ one obtains $c_{563} = 56321$ and $c_{921} = 92100$.
3. For $a_3 = 56477$ one obtains $c_{563} = 56321$, $c_{564} = 56477$, and $c_{921} = 92100$.
4. For $a_4 = 56319$ one obtains $c = \text{floor}(56319/100) = 563$, and since $c_{563} \neq 0$, $c_{563} > 56319$, and $c_{562} = 0$ one obtains $c_{562} = 56319$, $c_{563} = 56321$, $c_{564} = 56477$, and $c_{921} = 92100$.
5. For $a_5 = 56208$ one obtains, similar to 4, $c_{561} = 56208$, $c_{562} = 56319$, $c_{563} = 56321$, $c_{564} = 56477$, and $c_{921} = 92100$.
6. For $a_6 = 55699$ one obtains $c_{556} = 55699$, $c_{561} = 56208$, $c_{562} = 56319$, $c_{563} = 56321$, $c_{564} = 56477$, and $c_{921} = 92100$.
7. For $a_7 = 56318$ a major rearrangement becomes necessary yielding $c_{556} = 55699$, $c_{560} = 56208$, $c_{561} = 56318$, $c_{562} = 56319$, $c_{563} = 56321$, $c_{564} = 56477$, and $c_{921} = 92100$.

The described modification of Method 8 is generally very efficient and few rearrangements are necessary, unless the given numbers contain large groups of numbers very similar in magnitude. Note that in the example under consideration the ratio of the number of nonzero to the number of zero elements of $c_1, c_2, \ldots, c_{999}$ will never exceed $\frac{300}{1000} = \frac{3}{10}$. It should be clear that the number of rearrangements will increase as that ratio increases. As a rule of thumb that ratio should never exceed $\frac{1}{2}$. The method described above is often called "sorting by address calculation."

Problem 7.2.7 (*Examination of Distribution Sort*)

Write a program to generate ten groups of 200 random five-digit positive integers. (For a discussion of random numbers, see Section 8.1.) For each set of 200 random numbers examine the sorting method of Problem 7.2.6. In particular, determine the number of times a rearrangement becomes necessary.

Problem 7.2.8 (*Examination of Exchange Sort*)

Write a program to generate ten groups of 80 random integers between -100 and 900. (For a discussion of random numbers, see Section 8.1.) For each set of 80 numbers determine the total number of exchanges required to sort them into descending order using Method 1.

Problem 7.2.9 (*Alphabetic Sort*)

Punched cards are available containing a number $k \leq 100$ followed by the names and addresses of k persons. Using Method 2 write a program to print an alphabetical list of names together with the corresponding addresses.

Problem 7.2.10 (*Monthly Account Statements*)

Each entry ("record") of the file of a department store for customers with charge accounts contains

(a) An account number: a six-digit positive integer.
(b) Name and address of customer: a sequence of up to 50 characters.
(c) Present balance: a positive number for debits (i.e., if customer owes money to the store), a negative number for credits.

Assume that this file is available on punched cards, one card per customer. Assume further that the file is in no particular order ("unsorted"). For each purchase made by a customer a "charge card" is punched containing (a) the account number, (b) the word CHARGE, and (c) the amount of purchase, a positive number. For each payment made by a customer a "payment card" is punched containing (a) the account number, (b) the word PAYMENT, and (c) the amount paid, a positive number.

Using the charge cards, the payment cards, and the customer file as input, write a program that will (a) print a monthly statement for each customer and (b) print the updated customer file.

Note that for each customer no charge card or payment card can be present or that one or more charge cards or payment cards can be present. The monthly statement for each customer should show (a) the account number, (b) the name and address of the customer, (c) all payments, (d) all charges, (e) previous balance, and (f) new balance. Include in the charges a 1.5% interest and handling fee based on the balance in the customer file, if that balance is positive.

You may assume that the number of customers does not exceed 30 and that the number of charge cards and payment cards does not exceed 100 each.

Problem 7.2.11 (*Key-Word Index, Version 1*)

Punched cards are available containing $k \leq 50$ titles of books, each title consisting of at most eight words with at most 11 characters each. Write a program to prepare an alphabetical listing of all the words such that, for each word occurring in a title, one line is printed containing the word, followed by the complete title in which the word occurs. If a word occurs in more than one title, it should occur on a number of lines followed by those titles. If a word occurs more than once in the same title, treat the situation as if the word occurred only once.

Notes and Explanations: For $k = 2$ and the two book titles HISTORY OF THE ROMAN EMPIRE and THE THEORY OF NUMBERS the output should look like this:

```
EMPIRE      HISTORY OF THE ROMAN EMPIRE
HISTORY     HISTORY OF THE ROMAN EMPIRE
NUMBERS     THE THEORY OF NUMBERS
OF          HISTORY OF THE ROMAN EMPIRE
OF          THE THEORY OF NUMBERS
ROMAN       HISTORY OF THE ROMAN EMPIRE
THE         HISTORY OF THE ROMAN EMPIRE
THE         THE THEORY OF NUMBERS
THEORY      THE THEORY OF NUMBERS
```

Problem 7.2.12 (*Key-Word Index, Version 2*)

Same as Problem 7.2.11 but suppress printing of lines for words such as A, IN, THE, OF, WE, AND, NEXT, ALL, etc.

Problem 7.2.13 (*Bit Sort, Version 1*)

Punched cards are available containing a number $k \leq 200$ followed by k four-digit positive decimal integers. Write a program to convert the numbers to binary (for an explanation of binary numbers, see Problem 4.3.1), sort them into ascending order using Method 5, and print them in ascending order both in binary and decimal form.

Problem 7.2.14 (*Bit Sort, Version 2*)

Punched cards are available containing a number $k \leq 200$ followed by k four-digit positive decimal integers. Write a program to sort them into descending order using Method 5 without actually converting them to binary numbers. (For an explanation of binary numbers, see Problem 4.3.1.)

Hint: Given the binary representation b of a decimal integer n, the ith bit of b from the right can be computed directly from n as $\mod(\mathrm{floor}(n/2^{i-1}), 2)$. Thus the third bit from the right of the binary representation of the decimal number 18 is $\mod(\mathrm{floor}(18/2^2),2) = \mod(4,2) = 0$. Indeed, the binary representation of 18 is 10010.

Problem 7.2.15 (*Five-Way Merging*)

Six hundred twenty-five integers are available on punched cards. Using Method 7 with $m = 5$ (i.e., five-way merging) write a program to sort the numbers into ascending order.

Problem 7.2.16 (*Four-Way Alphabetical Merging*)

Punched cards are available containing a number $k \leq 1000$ followed by k names. Using Method 7 with $m = 4$ (i.e., four-way merging) write a program to sort the names into alphabetical order.

Problem 7.2.17

Punched cards are available containing an integer $k \leq 999$, followed by k eight-digit positive integers $a_1, a_2, \ldots, a_k$, followed by 20 integers $i_1, i_2, \ldots, i_{20}$, where $1 \leq i_n \leq k$ for $n = 1, 2, \ldots, 20$. Write a program to determine the i_1th smallest, the i_2th smallest, $\ldots$, the i_{20}th smallest of the k integers $a_1, a_2, \ldots, a_k$.

Problem 7.2.18 (*Intersection of Sets*)

Punched cards are available containing an integer $k \leq 200$ followed by two collections A and B of k integers. Write a program to determine all numbers that occur in both A and B.

Hint: Rather than comparing each of the k numbers in A with each of the k numbers in B (requiring some k^2 steps), take for each number n of A the number $2n$, take for each number m of B the number $2m + 1$, and sort the $2k$ numbers obtained in this manner into ascending order. Now determine all pairs of numbers of the form $(2p, 2p + 1)$ in the sequence obtained: For each such pair the number p occurs in both A and B. Note that by using Method 6 for sorting the order of magnitude of the number of steps involved in carrying out the process described will be $k \log(k)$, which is considerably smaller than k^2 for large k.

As an example, consider $k = 10$ and the following two collections A

and B of integers: A: 17, 9, 8, 3, 15, 20, 21, 7, 4, 14; B: 31, 21, 14, 19, 22, 33, 36, 2, 8, 9. By taking for each number n of A $2n$ and for each number m of B $2m + 1$ one gets 34, 18, 16, 6, 30, 40, 42, 14, 8, 28 and 63, 43, 29, 39, 45, 67, 73, 5, 17, 19. Sorting the 20 integers into ascending order yields 5, 6, 8, 14, 16, 17, 18, 19, 28, 29, 30, 34, 39, 40, 42, 43, 45, 63, 67, 73. Looking for all pairs of the form $(2p, 2p + 1)$ one finds (16,17), (18,19), (28,29), and (42,43). Thus the numbers occurring in both A and B are 8, 9, 14, and 21.

Problem 7.2.19 (*Club Memberships*)

The membership lists for the following four associations are available on punched cards: The Vegetarian Club of Canada, The Calgary Hunting Association, The Fly-to-the-Moon Club, and The Stay-on-Good-Old-Earth Association. Assume for simplicity that none of the above associations has more than 200 members. Using a method analogous to that used in Problem 7.2.18 write a program to determine

    (a) A list of all people belonging to all four associations.
    (b) A list of all people belonging to at least two of the four associations.
    (c) A list of "hypocrites" (a hypocrite is a person belonging to both the Vegetarian Club of Canada and the Calgary Hunting Association or to both the Fly-to-the-Moon Club and the Stay-on-Good-Old-Earth Association).

Problem 7.2.20 (*A Diophantine Equation*)

Write a program to determine the number of quadruples of integers (a,b,c,d) with $0 \leq a \leq b \leq 50$, $0 \leq c \leq 50$, and $0 \leq d \leq 50$ for which

$$a^3 + b^3 = c(c + 3) + d^2(d + 1) + 5$$

Hint: Take A to be the collection of all numbers of the form $a^3 + b^3$ and B to be the collection of all numbers of the form $c(c + 3) + d^2(d + 1) + 5$. Now proceed as in Problem 7.2.18.

Problem 7.2.21 (*Another Diophantine Equation*)

Same as Problem 7.2.20 but actually determine all quadruples of integers (a,b,c,d) satisfying $a^3 + b^3 = c(c + 3) + d^2(d + 1) + 5$.

Problem 7.2.22 (*Euler's Equation*)

The problem of finding integers (a,b,c,d) with $0 < a < b$, $c < d$, and $a < c$ satisfying the equation $a^4 + b^4 = c^4 + d^4$ was first solved by Euler by finding the solution $a = 59$, $b = 158$, $c = 133$, $d = 134$ and by indeed giving the formulae

$$a = u^7 + u^5v^2 - 2u^3v^4 + 3u^2v^4 + uv^6$$
$$b = u^6v - 3u^5v^2 - 2u^4v^3 + u^2v^5 + v^7$$
$$c = u^7 + u^5v^2 - 2u^3v^4 - 3u^2v^5 + uv^6$$
$$d = u^6v + 3u^5v^2 - 2u^4v^3 + u^2v^2 + v^7$$

which yield a solution for each pair of integers u and v. Using a method similar to the one in Problem 7.2.20 write a program to determine all quadruples of integers (a,b,c,d) satisfying $a < 59$, $b < 158$, $c < 133$, $d < 134$, $0 < a < b$, $c < d$, $a < c$, and $\text{abs}(a^4 + b^4 - c^4 - d^4) \leq 5$.

Problem 7.2.23 (*Still Another Diophantine Equation*)

Write a program to determine the number of sextuples of integers (a,b,c,d,e,f) with $0 < a \leq b \leq c \leq 15$ and $a < d \leq e \leq f \leq 15$ such that $a^2 + b^2 + c^2 = d^2 + e^2 + f^2$.

Problem 7.2.24 (*One More Diophantine Equation*)

Write a program to determine the number of sextuples of integers (a,b,c,d,e,f) with $0 < a \leq b \leq c \leq 15$ and $a < d \leq e \leq f \leq 15$ such that $a^3 + b^3 + c^3 = d^3 + e^3 + f^3$.

Problem 7.2.25 (*The Last Diophantine Equation*)

Write a program to determine the number of sextuples of integers (a,b,c,d,e,f) with $0 < a \leq b \leq c \leq 15$ and $0 < d \leq e \leq f$ such that $a^2 + b^2 + c^2 = d^3 + e^3 + f^3$.

Problem 7.2.26 (*Minimization*)

Using a method similar to the one suggested for Problem 7.2.20 write a program to determine that pair (x,y), where x and y are numbers of the set -1.00, -0.99, -0.98, . . . , 0.98, 0.99, 1.00, for which the value of $f(x,y) = x^3 - x - 3y^4 + y + 1$ is as small as possible.

Problem 7.2.27

Same as Problem 7.2.26 but determine all pairs (x,y) for which $-0.005 \leq f(x,y) \leq 0.005$.

8

RANDOM NUMBERS

8.1 INTRODUCTION

Take a six-sided die. Throw it 500 times, writing down the numbers occurring. You have written 500 "random integers uniformly distributed in the interval 1 to 6."

Take a globe. Give it a swirl and stop it by putting your finger on it. Write down the longitude of the position of your finger on the globe. Repeat the process 1000 times. You have written 1000 "random integers uniformly distributed in the interval 1 to 360."

Walk around on a parking lot, writing down the unit's digit showing on the speedometer of each car. You are writing "random integers uniformly distributed in the interval 1 to 10."

Take a coin. Flip it 200 times, writing down 0 for head and 1 for tail. You have written 200 "random integers uniformly distributed in the interval 0 to 1."

More generally, one can loosely define a "sequence of random numbers uniformly distributed in an interval m to n" as a sequence of numbers with no apparent pattern where each number between m and n occurs with about the same frequency. A more rigorous definition can be given by demanding that the sequence passes a number of statistical tests (see Chapter 12 and Problem 8.3.2) but the intuitive definition will be sufficient for the present purposes.

Random numbers are useful for many applications, as is best seen

84

from the problems below. Thus it is often necessary to obtain a sequence of random numbers. This is usually done not by using some mechanical device to produce random numbers but by using some algorithm to compute a sequence of numbers in a prescribed and completely deterministic manner that, however, does statistically qualify as a sequence of random numbers.

An algorithm for obtaining random numbers is given below. It is a special case of the so-called "linear congruential" method. It can be used for all problems in this section with satisfactory results. Before using any "random number generator" for more than exercise problems it is necessary to study the statistical properties of the generator in detail. For a detailed discussion of random number generators, see, e.g., Knuth.†

Method to generate uniformly distributed random integers in the interval m to n, where m and n are integers with $m < n$

Step 1. Let $d = 2^{31}$.

Step 2. Choose any integer Y such that $999999 > Y > 100000$.

Step 3. Let $i = 1$.

Step 4. Let $Y = \mathrm{mod}(15625\,Y + 22221, d)$.

Step 5. Let $X_i = m + \mathrm{floor}(((n - m + 1)\,Y)/d)$.

Step 6. Let $i = i + 1$.

Step 7. Go to Step 4.

For most choices of Y the numbers $X_1, X_2, \ldots$ form a sequence of random integers as desired. One possible recommended choice is $Y = 568731$.

To generate random numbers (not just integers) in an interval a to b with $a < b$ use the algorithm above, replacing the formula in Step 5 by: Let $X_i = a + (Y(b - a))/(d - 1)$.

Problem 8.1.1 (*Roulette*)

Write a program to generate and print 1000 random numbers between 1 and 32 and determine how often each number has occurred.

Problem 8.1.2

Write a program to generate and print 1000 random numbers between 0 and 0.999 with three digits to the right of the decimal point and determine how many numbers have occurred between 0 and 0.099, 0.1 and 0.199, . . . , 0.8 and 0.899, 0.9 and 0.999.

Hint: This can be done either by generating random numbers between 0 and 0.999 or by generating random integers between 0 and 999 and dividing by 1000.

†D. E. Knuth, *The Art of Computer Programming, Seminumerical Algorithms*, Vol. 2, Addison-Wesley, Reading, Mass., 1969.

Problem 8.1.3

Write a program to generate 1000 integers between 1 and 4 in a random fashion such that 1 occurs with a chance of 30%, 2 with a chance of 17%, 3 with a chance of 21%, and 4 with a chance of 32%. Determine how often 1, 2, 3, and 4 have actually occurred.

Hint: Generate 1000 random integers between 1 and 100. For each number x generated take 1 if $1 \leq x \leq 30$, 2 if $31 \leq x \leq 47$, 3 if $48 \leq x \leq 68$, and 4 if $69 \leq x \leq 100$. Then 1, 2, 3, and 4 will be generated randomly with a chance as prescribed.

8.2 GAMES

Problem 8.2.1 (*Throwing a Die, Version 1*)

Write a program that will do five separate simulations, each simulation consisting of 600 throws of a six-sided die. The program is to determine for each simulation

(a) The number of 1's, 2's, 3's, 4's, 5's, and 6's.
(b) The longest run of 1's, 2's, 3's, 4's, 5's, and 6's.
(c) The number of times a run 1, 2, 3, 4, 5, 6 has occurred.
(d) The number of times two 1's, 2's, 3's, 4's, 5's, and 6's have occurred consecutively.

Problem 8.2.2 (*Throwing a Die, Version 2*)

Write a program to simulate 2162 throws of a six-sided die. Print the result and determine for each triple (x,y,z) with x, y, and z between 1 and 6 how often a run x,y,z has occurred.

Note: Since there are 216 different triples (x,y,z) each run x,y,z should occur about ten times if the numbers generated are reasonably random. This idea is often used to test the randomness of a sequence of numbers.

Problem 8.2.3 (*Throwing Three Dice*)

Write a program to simulate 800 throws of three six-sided dice. Each throw will have between 3 points (three 1's) and 18 points (three 6's). The program should print all 800 throws and determine (a) the number of times a throw of 3, 4, 5, . . . , 18 points has occurred and (b) for each pair (x,y) with x and y between 3 and 18 how often successive throws x,y have occurred.

Problem 8.2.4 (*The "One is Zero" Game*)

The "one is zero" game for two or more persons is played with a six-sided die as follows: All players start with score zero and take turns; at each turn a player throws the die as often as he wants, say n times; if the points thrown are $p_1, p_2, p_3, \ldots, p_n$, the player adds $p_1 + p_2 + \cdots + p_n$ to his score provided that *all* p_i's are different from 1 and adds nothing to his score if at least one of the p_i's is equal to 1. A "game" consists of 20 turns for each player. The player with highest score wins.

(a) Suppose that a player adopts the strategy of finishing his turn after always exactly n throws. What is the best choice for n? Try to answer this question by writing a program that simulates ten games each for $n = 1, 2, 3, \ldots, 25$ and prints the average score obtained for each value of n.

(b) Suppose that a player adopts the strategy of finishing his turn after always having reached n points or more. What is the best choice for n? Try to answer this question by writing a program that simulates ten games each for $n = 4, 8, \ldots, 100$ and prints the average score obtained for $n = 4, 8, \ldots, 100$.

Problem 8.2.5 (*Dealing Bridge Hands*)

The card deck for a game of bridge consists of cards of the four suits clubs, diamonds, hearts, and spades. Each suit consists of the 13 cards ace, king, queen, jack, 10, 9, 8, 7, 6, 5, 4, 3, and 2. Four players, called North, East, South, and West, participate in a game of bridge, each obtaining 13 cards. Using random numbers write a program to simulate the dealing of 50 games of bridge. Counting ace as four points, king as three, Queen as two, Jack as one, and all other cards as zero, determine whether North and South or East and West have 31 points or more together (a "slam bid" is possible) or whether one of the players has more than 7 cards in any one suit. If one of the conditions is met, print the cards of the four players in a neat manner.

Problem 8.2.6 (*Cricket*)

The game of cricket can be played with two dice. The first has on five of its faces the numbers 1, 2, 3, 4, and 6 and on the remaining face the words "how's that"; the second has on its six faces the words "caught," "bowled," "leg-before-wicket," "stumped," "no ball," and "not out." The player throws the first die, and if one of the numbered faces falls uppermost, the corresponding number is counted toward the score of the player. He continues to throw the die until the face "how's that" falls uppermost. The second die is then thrown, and unless "no ball" or "not out" falls uppermost, the player's turn ("innings") is ended. If "no ball" or "not out" appears, he continues his innings as before by throwing the first die, adding one extra to the score in the case of "no ball."

Write a program to simulate 1000 innings and determine the average score obtained.

8.3 SIMULATION PROBLEMS

Problem 8.3.1 (*A Simple Harbor System*)

Consider a small harbor with unloading facilities for ships. Only one ship can be unloaded at a time. The time between the arrival of successive ships varies irregularly (i.e., in a random manner) from 10 to 130 minutes.

The unloading time per ship depends on the quantity and type of cargo carried by the ship and varies irregularly from 40 to 90 minutes.

Write a program, using random numbers, to do five separate simulations of the arrival and unloading of 500 ships. For each of the five simulations determine (a) the average and maximum time per ship in the harbor, (b) the average and maximum "waiting time" per ship (waiting time is the time between arrival and start of unloading), (c) the total amount of idle time of the unloading facilities, (d) the average and maximum number of ships in the waiting line, and (e) whether the harbor system is "unstable" (unstable means that the waiting time is more or less increasing throughout the simulation; a rather arbitrary but frequently used method for determining whether such a system is unstable is the following: Let A be the average waiting time for the first 100 ships; the system is unstable if the waiting time for each of the last 100 ships exceeds A).

Problem 8.3.2 (*A Simple Traffic Problem*)

Consider an intersection of two one-way streets controlled by a traffic light. Assume that a random number of cars (between 5 and 15) going in direction 1 arrive at the intersection every 10 seconds, and that between 6 and 24 cars arrive every 10 seconds going in direction 2. Suppose that 36 cars per 10 seconds can cross the intersection in direction 1 and that 20 cars per 10 seconds can cross the intersection in direction 2, if the traffic light is green. No turning is allowed. Write a program using random numbers to examine the following switching periods (in seconds) of the traffic light in direction 1:

Green	Red
10	90
20	80
.	.
.	.
.	.
90	10

For each choice of green–red simulate three times the situation for 5 minutes. For each simulation determine the switching period for which the total waiting time for both directions is as small as possible.

Problem 8.3.3 (*One Check-out Counter*)

A store has one check-out counter. The time between the arrival of successive customers at the counter varies in a random manner from 10 to 490 seconds. Check-out time varies randomly between 100 and 300 seconds. Write a program using random numbers to do ten separate simulations of the arrival and checking out of 200 customers. For each of the ten simulations determine (a) the average overall check-out time per customer (this is to include waiting time and check-out time), (b) the average and maximum number of customers in the waiting line, and (c) those ten customers with the largest overall check-out time. (Print the number of the customer and the overall check-out time for the customer in the form OVERALL CHECK-OUT TIME FOR CUSTOMER 15 WAS 352 SECONDS.)

Problem 8.3.4 (*Three Check-out Counters, Version 1*)

A store has three check-out counters. The time between the arrival of successive customers varies in a random manner between 0 and 160 seconds. Check-out time at each counter varies randomly between 100 and 360 seconds. Assume that a customer arriving at the check-out counters joins the shortest of the three available waiting lines. Once he has joined a waiting line he will not switch to another waiting line later on. Write a program that uses random numbers to do five separate simulations of the arrival and checking-out of 600 customers similar to Problem 8.3.3.

Problem 8.3.5 (*Three Check-out Counters, Version 2*)

Same as Problem 8.3.4 but assume that the last customer in a waiting line will switch waiting lines if a shorter waiting line becomes available.

Problem 8.3.6 (*Random Walk, Version 1*)

Consider the following road plan of a city:

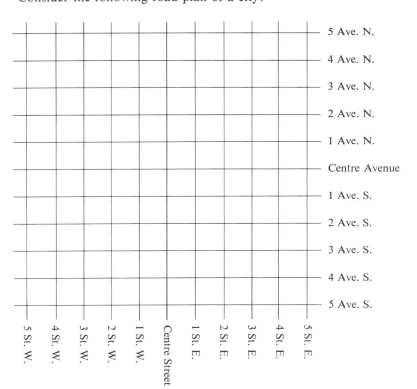

Assume that all streets and avenues leaving the city are closed, with the exception of 2 Avenue North in an easterly direction. Somebody is standing at Centre Street–Centre Avenue and will walk around as follows: At each intersection he will make a random choice as to whether to turn north, east, south, or west.

If the choice made is impossible (road closed), he will make another choice.

Write a program to do ten separate simulations of such a "random walk." Each simulation should continue until the person has done 500 steps or until the person leaves the city via 2 Avenue North in an easterly direction.

After how many steps, if at all, did the person leave the city in simulation 1, simulation 2, . . . , simulation 10? How often during each walk did the person come back to the junction Centre Street–Centre Avenue? How often was a closed road encountered?

Problem 8.3.7 (*Random Walk, Version 2*)

Consider the road plan of the city in Problem 8.3.6. Somebody is standing at Centre Street–Centre Avenue and will walk around as follows: At each intersection he will make a random choice as to whether to turn north, east, south, or west subject to the following restrictions: (a) The person will never leave the city and (b) the person will never visit an intersection he has visited before.

Write a program to do ten separate simulations of such a random walk. Each simulation should continue until the person has done 100 steps or until the person cannot make any further steps without violating (a) or (b). For each simulation, print the roadplan of the city with an indication of the walk. A typical output might look like

```
       5   4   3   2   1   C   1   2   3   4   5
   5
   4
   3                               S   W
   2                       E   S   T   N
   1                   E   N   E   E   N
   C                   N   E   E   E   S
   1                   N                   S
   2                   N       S   W   W
   3                   N   W   S
   4                       N   W
   5
```

In the above, E, S, W, and N indicate that the person has turned east, south, west, or north, respectively. T indicates the end of the random walk.

Problem 8.3.8 (*Random Walk, Version 3*)

Same as Problem 8.3.7 but replace restriction (b) by the following: If visiting an intersection visited before, the person will not leave that intersection in the same direction as before.

Problem 8.3.9 (*Random Walk, Version 4*)

Same as Problem 8.3.6 but at each step the chance of turning north is $A\%$, of turning east is $B\%$, of turning south is $C\%$, and of turning west is $D\%$. A, B, C, and D are positive integers, with sum 100, which are to be read from data cards.

Problem 8.3.10 (*Random walk, Version 5*)

Banff National Park, in southwestern Alberta, Canada, was established as that country's first national park in 1885 when an area of 10 square miles surrounding the newly discovered hot mineral springs at Banff was set apart for public use. The park, which includes some of the finest Alpine scenery in the Canadian Rockies, has been enlarged to more than 2500 square miles and is noted for its wildlife, including bighorn sheep, Rocky Mountain goats, elk, moose, deer, and black and grizzly bears.

One of the buildings of the famed Banff Springs Hotel has eight floors. Each of the floors has four rows of ten rooms. Assume that any two adjacent rooms are connected by a door and that stairs lead to the next higher and lower floor in each of the four corner rooms of each floor. Assume that two people are standing initially in two different rooms at least six floors apart. They are trying to find each other. Both persons walk around in a random fashion as follows: If a person is in one of the corner rooms, the chance of going upstairs or downstairs is 80% (40% for each direction, if both are possible, and 80% in the only possible direction otherwise) and the chance of going in any of the other two possible directions (without changing the floor) is 10% each. If the person is in any other room, the chance of going in a direction leading to the nearest corner is 64% (32% for each direction, if two are possible, and 64% in the only possible direction otherwise) and the chance of going away from the nearest corner is 36% (18% for each of the directions possible). Assume that the people will find each other if they ever come to adjacent rooms on the same floor. Assume that both people move at the same speed.

Write a program using random numbers to do five separate simulations (each of at least 800 steps) to determine whether the two people ever meet, and if they do, after how many steps. Determine also how often the people are on the same floor, how often each person changes to a different floor, and other relevant information.

Problem 8.3.11 (*Paint Throwing, Version 1*)

During a recent student disturbance some students came into the back of the lecture hall and threw bags of red paint at random over people. Assume that the lecture hall consists of 15 rows of 10 seats each. Assuming that one bag of paint falling on a certain seat leaves 2 cups of paint over the person in that seat and 1 cup of paint over each person in an adjacent seat, write a program, using random numbers, to calculate the number of cups of paint that would be received by the people in each seat if 22 bags of paint were thrown. Simulate the situation 40 times.

Problem 8.3.12 (*Paint Throwing, Version 2*)

Consider the paint-throwing incident as described in Problem 8.3.11 and determine for each of 100 simulations the number of bags necessary to ensure that every person has received at least 1 cup of paint.

Problem 8.3.13 (*Trout Fishing in Alberta*)

The lakes and streams of Alberta offer excellent trout fishing as shown by the Alberta trout fishing records: Brook Trout, 12 pounds and 14 ounces (1967); Cutthroat Trout, 9 pounds and 8 ounces (1966); Dolly Varden Trout, 14 pounds and 13 ounces (1969); Golden Trout, 4 pounds and 7 ounces (1965); Rainbow Trout, 15 pounds (1967); Lake Trout, 52 pounds and 8 ounces (1928). Despite the size and abundance of trout few people have ever had success without careful examination of their fishing method using random numbers.

Take a rectangular pool and consider it to be divided into 50 rows of 40 little squares each. The pool contains 260 squares used as hiding places for trout (select these 260 hiding places at random). Sixty of the hiding places selected at random are initially occupied by one trout each. Trout tend to swim around in a random manner, but they never swim more than 2 squares away from their hiding place, unless scared away. Assume that every 5 seconds each of the trout makes a decision whether to stay in the present square (40% chance) or swim 1 square north, west, south, or east (15% chance each). An exception to the above occurs only in one of two cases: (a) If a bait is dropped into the square currently occupied by a trout, the fish is terrified by the splash of the bait, dashes (at random) to any of the 260 hiding places, and refuses to take a bait for the next minute. (b) If a bait is already located in the square occupied by a trout, the fish takes the bait and can be considered caught.

How often should one throw the bait to obtain the largest catch? Write a program using random numbers to determine the catch when throwing the bait every 10 seconds, every 20 seconds, . . . , every 300 seconds. The program is to do five separate simulations, each simulation covering a period of 2500 seconds.

Problem 8.3.14 (*The Pipe Smoker*)

A pipe smoker has two booklets of matches in his pocket, each containing 40 matches initially. Whenever a match is required he picks one of the booklets at random, removing one match. Write a program using random numbers to simulate the situation 100 times and determine the average number of matches that can be removed until one booklet is completely empty.

Problem 8.3.15 (*Seat Reservation*)

A theatre has 20 rows of 10 seats each. On punched cards a number n followed by n "requests" is available. Each request is for a certain number of adjoining seats in a certain row.

Write a program that uses random numbers to process the requests one by one as follows: If the request can be satisfied, a reservation is made; if the request cannot be satisfied in the desired row but can be satisfied in a number of other rows, a random choice is made and a message indicating the choice is printed; if the request cannot be satisfied at all, a message to that extent is printed and the request is ignored. When all requests have been processed a list of still available seats is to be printed.

8.4 MATHEMATICAL APPLICATIONS

A large number of mathematical applications ("Monte Carlo" applications) of random numbers are variations of the following situation.

Consider two finite sets M and N, N containing M. Let the number of elements in M be m, let the number of elements in N be n, and suppose that an approximate value of m/n has to be determined. One can obtain an estimate of m/n by choosing y random elements of N, determining the number x of these y elements in M, and calculating x/y.

The method can also be applied to infinite sets. Consider two plane regions A and B, B containing A, of area a and b, respectively. By choosing y random elements (i.e., points) in B, determining the number x of these points in A, and calculating x/y, an approximate value of a/b is obtained.

Note that if b is known, a can be calculated. Thus the method can be used to determine the area of a plane region. It is well known that random numbers cannot be used for this type of application if high accuracy is desired. (The "convergence" is very slow: One can show that increasing the number of random numbers used 100 fold increases precision only roughly 10 fold, see, e.g., Hull.[†]) Thus random numbers should be used for applications of this type only if no other simple methods are available and if a rough estimate of the answer is sufficient.

[†]T. E. Hull, "Random Number Generators," *SIAM Review*, Vol. 4, no. 3 (1962), pp. 230–254.

For many applications of the above type it is necessary to obtain random points of a region in n-dimensional space. This is usually done by generating n random numbers $z_1, z_2, \ldots, z_n$, which are taken to represent a point P with coordinates $(z_1, z_2, \ldots, z_n)$. Thus to determine random points in a plane region (two-dimensional space) one generates two random numbers z_1 and z_2 and interprets them as point P with coordinates (z_1, z_2).

Problem 8.4.1 (*Number of Lattice Points in a Sphere*)

Given a three-dimensional coordinate system with origin O, write a program to determine the approximate number of lattice points in a sphere of radius $r = 2000$ centered in the origin.

Note: A point P with coordinates (x,y,z) is called a "lattice point" if x, y, and z are integers. A point P is in a sphere S_r of radius r centered in O if $x^2 + y^2 + z^2 \leq r^2$. Note that the cube C_r with diameter $2r$ centered in O contains exactly $(2r + 1)^3$ lattice points and contains the sphere S_r. Let m be the number of lattice points in S_r and n be the number of lattice points in C_r. Thus m/n can be calculated approximately by using random points chosen in C_r. Since $n = (2r + 1)^3$ is known, m can be determined approximately. For this problem choose 2000 random points.

Problem 8.4.2 (*Lattice Points*)

Write a program to determine the approximate number of lattice points in the region R whose points P, with coordinates (x,y,z), satisfy all the conditions

(a) $x^2 + 2y^2 + z^2 \leq 720{,}000.$
(b) $2x^2 - 5y^2 + 5z^2 \leq 800{,}000.$
(c) $z - x - y \geq 0.$

Problem 8.4.3 (*Square Root of 5*)

Write a program to determine the approximate value of $\sqrt{5}$ using 2000 random numbers.

Note: $\sqrt{5}$ is between 2 and 3. Choose 2000 random numbers between 2 and 3 and determine m, the number of these numbers less than $\sqrt{5}$ (a number x is less than $\sqrt{5}$ if x^2 is less than 5). The value $a = 2 + (m/2000)$ gives an approximate value of $\sqrt{5}$.

Problem 8.4.4

Write a program to determine the approximate value of $\sqrt[3]{7}$ and $\sqrt[7]{3}$ using 2000 random numbers.

Problem 8.4.5 (*Root and Cube Root*)

Read a positive number n from a data card. Using 2000 random numbers, write a program to calculate $\sqrt{n}$ and $\sqrt[3]{n}$.

Problem 8.4.6 (*Pi, Version 3*)

Write a program to determine an approximate value of π using random numbers.

Note: In a two-dimensional coordinate system the conditions (a) $x^2 + y^2 \leq 1$, (b) $x \geq 0$, and (c) $y \geq 0$ describe a quartercircle Q with radius 1. Consider 5000 random points $P = (x,y)$ in the square S: $0 \leq x \leq 1$, $0 \leq y \leq 1$. Determine n, the number of these points in Q. Using the fact that (roughly) $n/5000$ = area of Q/area of $S = \pi/4$, one can calculate $\pi = n/1250$.

Problem 8.4.7 (*Pi, Version 4*)

Write a program to determine π using random numbers as explained in Problem 8.4.6. First use 500, then 1000, then 1500, . . . , then 8000 random numbers and print the 16 different approximations of π.

Problem 8.4.8 (*Area of Union of Simple Areas*)

Using 5000 random numbers, write a program to determine the area of the region R defined as follows: A point $P = (x,y)$ is in R if and only if $x^2 + 2y^2 \leq 54$ or $3x^2 + y^2 \leq 36$ or $(x - 2)^2 + (y - 1)^2 \leq 50$.

Problem 8.4.9 (*Volume of Intersection of Simple Bodies*)

Write a program, using 9000 random numbers, to determine the area of the three-dimensional region R defined as follows: A point $P = (x,y,z)$ is in R if and only if $x^2 + y^2 + 2z^2 \leq 100$ and $3x^2 + y^2 + z^2 \leq 150$.

Problem 8.4.10

Write a program, using 850 random numbers, to determine the approximate number of prime numbers among the 100,000 numbers floor $(1.93x + 0.82)$, $x = 1, 2, 3, . . . , 100000$.

Note: An integer $n > 1$ is called a "prime number" if 1 and n are the only integers dividing n evenly. For a discussion of prime numbers, see Chapter 3.

Problem 8.4.11

Write a program, using 6000 random numbers, to determine the approximate number of complete squares among the 20,000,000 numbers floor $(2.1111x)$, $x = 1, 2, 3, . . . , 20000000$.

Note: A number y is called a "complete square" if $y = n^2$ for some integer n.

Problem 8.4.12 (*Integration*)

Write a program, using 5000 random numbers, to determine the area of the region R defined as follows: A point $P = (x,y)$ is in R if and only if (a) $0 \leq y \leq 2^{(x^2)}$ and (b) $0 \leq x \leq 1$.

Note: The calculation amounts to evaluating the integeral

$$\int_0^1 2^{(x^2)}\,dx$$

Problem 8.4.13 (*General Monte Carlo*)

Write a program that produces programs for solving problems such as Problems 8.4.1–8.4.9 if the following input information is supplied:

(a) A number n indicating the number of random points to be used.

(b) A number t ($1 \le t \le 3$) indicating that the variables $X_1, \ldots, X_t$ are used.

(c) t pairs of integers (a_i, b_i) for $i = 1, \ldots, t$ indicating that the variable X_i will take on random integer values between and including a_i and b_i ($i = 1, \ldots, t$).

(d) A condition C defining a certain region R inside the region Q given by the inequalities $a_i \le X_i \le b_i$ ($i = 1, \ldots, t$).

The program is to produce as output a program to calculate an approximate value of the region R by generating n random points in the region Q, by determining the number m of these points inside region R (i.e., satisfying condition C), and by using the fact that value of R/value of Q is approximately equal to m/n and that the value of Q is the product of the quantities $(b_i - a_i + 1)$ for $i = 1, \ldots, t$.

EXAMPLES

Given the input

1. $n = 8000$
2. $t = 3$
3. $a_1 = -2000$, $b_1 = 2000$, $a_2 = -2000$, $b_2 = 2000$, $a_3 = -2000$, $b_3 = 2000$
4. $C = X_1^2 + X_2^2 + X_3^2 \le 2000^2$

the program should produce a program for solving Problem 8.4.1.

Given the input

1. $n = 8000$
2. $t = 1$
3. $a_1 = 200$, $b_1 = 299$
4. $C = X_1^2 < 50000$

the program should produce a program for finding an approximate value of $\sqrt{50000} - 200 = 100(\sqrt{5} - 2)$, i.e., for solving, essentially, Problem 8.4.3.

Given the input

1. $n = 5000$
2. $t = 3$

3. $a_1 = -849$, $b_1 = 849$, $a_2 = -600$, $b_2 = 600$, $a_3 = -849$, $b_3 = 849$
4. $C = (X_1^2 + 2X_2^2 + X_3^2 \leq 720000)$ and $(2X_1^2 - 5X_2^2 + 5X_3^2 \leq 800000)$ and $(X_3 - X_1 - X_2) \geq 0)$

the program should produce a program for solving Problem 8.4.2 using 5000 random points.

9

INPUT AND OUTPUT PROBLEMS

9.1 INPUT PROBLEMS

Problem 9.1.1 (*Digits*)

Write a program that will read a card and determine whether the 80 characters are all digits (0 to 9, blank counting as a digit). Print out the card along with an indication of it being an all-digit card or not.

Problem 9.1.2 (*Morse Code*)

Punched cards are available containing a message in Morse code, where each Morse code letter is separated from the next by a comma. Write a program to read these cards and print out the message. A table of the Morse code is given below:

A	·-	F	··-·	K	-·-	P	·--·	U	··-
B	-···	G	--·	L	·-··	Q	--·-	V	···-
C	-·-·	H	····	M	--	R	·-·	W	·--
D	-··	I	··	N	-·	S	···	X	-··-
E	·	J	·---	O	---	T	-	Y	-·--
				Z	--··				

Problem 9.1.3 (*Squaring Numbers*)

A number of cards contain an arrangement of digits and asterisks, followed by blanks. Write a program that will print each card together with the square of the number that is obtained by ignoring the asterisks.

98

EXAMPLE

For a punched card containing 1***2*** the program should print 144, for a card containing ***0****4*** the program should print 16, etc.

Problem 9.1.4 (*Free Field Reading*)

A number may be written in quite a few different ways. It is often necessary to design program segments (often called "free field reading routines") that will read the next legitimate number from a card.

Suppose that a number may be written

(a) With or without a leading sign, e.g., 3, +3, −79, etc.
(b) With or without a decimal point, e.g., 3., 3.0, 3, 1.9462, etc.
(c) With or without an "exponent" (either positive or negative and with or without sign), in the form aEb meaning $a \cdot 10^b$, e.g., 3.941, 3941E−3, 0.03941E2, 0.03914E+2.

Write a program that will read punched cards character by character and determine the numbers that are punched on them. The program should assume that the numbers are separated by either one or more blank spaces or by one or more characters that cannot be part of a number (i.e., commas, semicolons, any letter except E, etc.).

EXAMPLE

For a punched card containing ABCD21PQR+3.1415;;946.7E−3AB −396E+2 the program should print the four numbers 21, 3.1415, 0.9467, and − 39600.

Problem 9.1.5 (*Spelling Chicken*)

A well-known distributor of fried chicken has attempted (in many cases successfully) to obtain a telephone number such as 2442536, which, when dialed on a telephone with letters as well as numbers, spells out the word CHICKEN. There are three letters associated with each number on the dial, ABC with the number 2, DEF with 3, etc. Write a program that will read a telephone number and print out all the possible seven-letter words it might form.

Problem 9.1.6 (*Coded Expressions*)

Write a program that will read a number of cards. The cards will contain a positive three-digit integer m followed by m positive two-digit integers $n_1, n_2, n_3, \ldots, n_m$. Each two-digit integer is either of the form $0i$ or $j0$, where i is 0, 1, 2, 3, $\ldots$, 9 and j is 1, 2, 3, or 4. The two digits $0i$ are to be considered as the number i and the digits 10 stand for +, 20 for *, 40 for), and 30 for (. The program should check to see if the sequence of two-digit integers, interpreted as above, forms a valid expression.

Note: It is not clear to start with what constitutes a valid expression. According to some definitions, $+++3$ and $+(+((((3)))))$ could be valid; according to other definitions, they might not be valid. Be sure that the program prints the exact rules used in determining whether an expression is valid or not before it examines the expressions on the punched cards. A typical set of rules you might decide to use is this:

(a) For every opening parenthesis (there must be a closing parenthesis) farther to the right.

(b) A closing parenthesis) must be followed by either $+$ or $*$ or another closing parenthesis) or must occur at the end of the expression.

(c) An opening parenthesis (must be preceded by either $+$ or $*$ or another opening parenthesis (or must occur at the beginning of the expression.

(d) An opening parenthesis (cannot be immediately followed by a closing parenthesis).

(e) $+$ and $*$ must be preceded by either a number or a closing parenthesis).

(f) $+$ and $*$ must be followed by either a number or an opening parenthesis (.

EXAMPLE

00730031002402006 is interpreted as $(3+2)*6$ and is thus a valid expression. 00730301002402006 is interpreted as $((+2)*6$ and is invalid.

Problem 9.1.7 (*Scrambling Code*)

A large number of elementary codes rely on the substitution of one symbol for another. For example, replace all A's by 1's, all B's by 2's, etc. This simple substitution code is easily broken if one has a table of the frequency of occurrence of letters in the language under consideration. A coding system that is not so easily broken is represented in this problem.

Some punched cards contain a number $n \le 200$, followed by a sequence $x_1, x_2, x_3, \cdots, x_n$ of letters $A, B, C, \ldots, Z$. For any letter x of the alphabet let $p(x)$ be the "position" of x in the alphabet; i.e., $p(A) = 1, p(B) = 2, \ldots,$ $p(Z) = 26$. Write a program to read the cards and determine a sequence $a_1, a_2, a_3 \ldots a_n$ of two-digit numbers as follows: $a_1 = p(x_1)$, $a_i = \mod(p(x_i) + a_{i-1}, 40)$ for $i \ge 2$.

Problem 9.1.8 (*Unscrambling the Code*)

This problem is the converse of Problem 9.1.7, i.e., converting the code back into the plain text. Some punched cards contain a number $n \le 200$, followed by a sequence $a_1, a_2, a_3, \ldots, a_n$ of positive integers not exceeding 39. Write a program to determine whether there exists a sequence $x_1, x_2, x_3, \ldots, x_n$ of letters such that $a_1 = p(x_1)$, $a_i = \mod(p(x_i) + a_{i-1}, 40)$ for $i \ge 2$.

The program should print the sequence $x_1, x_2, x_3, \ldots, x_n$ corresponding to $a_1, a_2, a_3, \ldots, a_n$ if such a sequence exists.

Problem 9.1.9 (*Palindromes*)

A character string W not containing the character $*$ is available in the form $*W*$ on punched cards. Write a program to determine whether W reads the same forward and backward. Ignore blanks in W.

EXAMPLE

The famous sentence attributed to Napoleon when exiled to Elba, ABLE WAS I ERE I SAW ELBA, and the rather odd German sentence EIN NEGER MIT GAZELLE ZAGT IM REGEN NIE telling about a man with an antelope who is not afraid when it rains both read the same forward and backward, but the sentence THIS READS THE SAME FORWARD AND BACKWARD does not.

Problem 9.1.10 (*Letter Pairs*)

Write a program to read an essay of about $n = 3000$ characters and determine how often the character A is followed by the character B, B by C, C by $D, \ldots, Y$ by Z. Ignore blanks and punctuation marks.

9.2 OUTPUT PROBLEMS

Problem 9.2.1 (*Plot*)

It is possible to use the computer printer as a plotting device. To plot the graph of a function $y = F(x)$ it is necessary only to "draw," by using asterisks or periods, a set of axes on a sheet of printer paper and then print an $*$ in the appropriate place on each line. For example,

is a plot of the straight line $y = x$.

Write a program that will read in 40 pairs (x,y) of numbers and plot the 40 points with coordinates (x,y) on a single piece of paper. For simplification you may assume that the x's are integers between 1 and 50 and that the y's are integers between 1 and 120.

Problem 9.2.2 *(Scaling, Version 1)*

At times it is necessary to scale numbers so that a plot will fit neatly onto a page. For instance, the function $F(x) = \sin(x)$ will only take on values from -1 to 1 that, to give a good plot, should be scaled to the values 1 to 100. Write a program to plot the function (a) $F(x) = \sin(x)$ and (b) $F(x) = \cos(x)$ for the values of x from $0°$ to $180°$ in steps of $5°$.

Problem 9.2.3 *(Scaling, Version 2)*

Sometimes the largest and smallest values of a function $F(x)$ are not known beforehand. In such a case the program must calculate $F(x)$ for all values of x that will be plotted and then scale these values appropriately. Write a program to plot the graph of $F(x) = (x + 1956)/(x^2 - 49)$ for $x = 0, 2, 4, 6, 8, \ldots, 80$.

Problem 9.2.4 *(Positioning Problem)*

Write a program to read two integers x and y (both in the range 0 to 9) and produce the output

```
        0   1   2   3   4   5   6   7   8   9

    0                                           0
    1                                           1
    2                                           2
    3                                           3
    4                                           4
    5                                           5
  x 6                   +                       6
    7                                           7
    8                                           8
    9                                           9

        0   1   2   3   4   5   6   7   8   9
                        y
```

with the letters x and y opposite their values and the $+$ at the point with coordinates (x,y), the example shown corresponding to $(x,y) = (6,3)$.

Problem 9.2.5 *(General Relativity)*

Write a program that will read a three-digit integer, add the number 11 to this integer, and print out the result (possibly a four-digit integer) with one asterisk between each digit.

EXAMPLE

For 812 the program should produce 8*2*3, for 992 the program should produce 1*0*0*3, etc.

Problem 9.2.6 (*Justification*)

Write a program that will read a number of English sentences punched on cards (ignore the card boundaries) and print these out in the middle 50 positions of a page in such a manner that the right and left margins of the text are in straight lines and each word is completely in one line. This can be done by inserting extra blanks between words to ensure that each output line occupies exactly 50 characters.

Problem 9.2.7 (*Giant Letters*)

Write a program that will read a word from cards and then print this word in giant letters in the middle of a page. For example, if the word read is JOB, then the program should produce

```
          JJ      OOOOOOOOOO      BBBBBBBBBBBB
          JJ      OOOOOOOOOOOO    BBBBBBBBBBBBBB
          JJ      OO        OO    BB          BB
          JJ      OO        OO    BB          BB
          JJ      OO        OO    BB          BB
          JJ      OO        OO    BBBBBBBBBBBB
          JJ      OO        OO    BBBBBBBBBBBB
    JJ    JJ      OO        OO    BB          BB
    JJ    JJ      OO        OO    BB          BB
    JJJJJJJJJJJ   OO        OO    BB          BB
    JJJJJJJJJJ    OOOOOOOOOOOO    BBBBBBBBBBBBBB
    JJJJJJJJJ     OOOOOOOOOO      BBBBBBBBBBBB
```

Make your giant A out of a series of A's, your giant B out of a series B's, etc.

Problem 9.2.8 (*Ripple Printing*)

Take a line of text and write a program that will produce a full page of "ripple printing." For example, if the text was THIS IS AN ANSWER TO PROBLEM 9.2.8, then a ripple print would look like

```
THIS IS AN ANSWER TO PROBLEM 9.2.8
THIS IS AN ANSWER TO PROBLEM 9.2.8
.8  THIS IS AN ANSWER TO PROBLEM 9.2
.2.8 THIS IS AN ANSWER TO PROBLEM 9
       .
       .
       .
```

Write your program so that you can read in the line of text and the amount it should be shifted in each line.

Problem 9.2.9 (*Output Editing*)

Write a program that reads ten positive integers of between two and ten digits and that prints each number without leading zeroes, with the character $ inserted immediately preceding the leftmost digit and with the character , (comma) separating groups of three digits, starting from the right end of the number.

EXAMPLE

036892 should be printed as $36,892.

Problem 9.2.10 (*Random Blocking*)

Write a program to read an essay of about $n = 3000$ characters and print the essay without blanks and punctuation marks, inserting a blank every two, three, four, five, or six characters, the choice being made at random (see Chapter 8).

Problem 9.2.11 (*Calendar, Version 1*)

A punched card contains a four-digit positive integer n followed by the name of a day of the week x; n and x indicate that January 1 of year n falls on weekday x. Using this information write a program to print a calendar for the year n. The calendar should consist of 12 small pages, 1 page per month. A typical page for a month should look like this:

			October 1973			
Sun	*Mon*	*Tue*	*Wed*	*Thur*	*Fri*	*Sat*
					1	2
3	4	5	6	7	8	9
10	11	12	13	14	15	16
17	18	19	20	21	22	23
24	25	26	27	28	29	30
31						

The program should take into account that February has 29 days if either mod(n,4) $= 0$ and mod(n,100) $\neq 0$ or mod(n,400) $= 0$.

Problem 9.2.12 (*Calendar, Version 2*)

Given a number n, the day of the week x of January 1 in year n can be calculated according to Problem 4.5.6. Write a program to read two integers n,m with $n \leq m$ and print a calendar for all years $n, n + 1, \ldots, m$ similar to Problem 9.2.11.

Problem 9.2.13 (*Clock*)

When using the 24-hour notation for time, 9:15 A.M. is written as 0915, 1:28 P.M. is written as 1328, etc. Write a program that will read a time, in 24-hour notation, and print out a picture of a clock face with indication of the position of the hands of the clock. Be sure to make one hand big and the other little.

9.3 INPUT-OUTPUT PROBLEMS

Problem 9.3.1 (*Printing Bridge Hands*)

The card deck for a game of bridge consists of cards of the four suits CLUBS, DIAMONDS, HEARTS, and SPADES. Each suit consists of 13 cards ACE, KING, QUEEN, JACK, 10, 9, 8, 7, 6, 5, 4, 3, and 2. Each player in a game of bridge has 13 cards. Write a program that will read four punched cards, each card containing 52 0's and 1's that correspond to the cards of the four players. The 1's correspond to the cards a player has got and the 0's to the cards he does not have. The first group of 13 numbers on each card corresponds to the suit CLUBS, the second group of 13 numbers to the suit DIAMONDS, etc. The first number in each group corresponds to ACE, the second to KING, etc. Thus the sequence

1010000010011000001100000011110000000100000010000000

corresponds to

          CLUBS: ACE, QUEEN, 6, 3, 2
          DIAMONDS: 9, 8
          HEARTS: ACE, KING, QUEEN, JACK, 3
          SPADES: 9

The program should print out the names of the cards for each player around a box that represents the bridge table. A typical output could look like this:

                    CLUBS: A, Q, 6, 3, 2

                    DIAMONDS: 9, 8

                    HEARTS: A, K, Q, J, 3

                    SPADES: 9

                    . . . .
CLUBS: 9, 5   .   .   CLUBS: K, 8, 4
                       .   .
DIAMONDS: J, 10, 3   .   .   DIAMONDS: A, 7, 5, 4, 2
                       .   .
HEARTS: 10, 8, 6, 5, 2 .   .   HEARTS: 9, 4
                       .   .
SPADES: K, 8, 6   .   .   SPADES: A, 10, 7
                    . . . .
                    CLUBS: J, 10, 7

                    DIAMONDS: K, Q, 6

                    HEARTS: 7

                    SPADES: Q, J, 5, 4, 3, 2

Problem 9.3.2 (*Printing a Chessboard*)

A chessboard can be considered as an 8 by 8 array. Suppose that the pieces of a game of chess are numbered as follows:

	White	*Black*
PAWN	1	11
KNIGHT	2	12
BISHOP	3	13
ROOK	4	14
QUEEN	5	15
KING	6	16

Write a program that, when given a situation of a game of chess (as data on punched cards), will print out a pictorial representation of the chessboard with the names of the pieces in the appropriate squares. The picture of the chessboard should somehow indicate the color (white or black) of each square. For example, part of the board might look like

```
.  .  .  .  .  .  .         .  .  .  .  .  .  .
.        .  xxxxxxxx  .     .  .  xxxxxxxx  .
.        .  x      x  .     .  x        x  .
.        .  x      x  .     .  x        x  .
.        .    WHITE   .  BLACK  .  x        x  .
.        .    QUEEN   .  PAWN   .  x        x  .
.        .  x      x  .     .  x        x  .
.        .  x      x  .     .  x        x  .
.        .  xxxxxxxx  .     .  xxxxxxxx  .
.  .  .  .  .  .  .  .  .  .  .  .  .  .  .  .
.        .        .         .        .
.        .        .         .        .
```

with the extra x's indicating a black square.

Problem 9.3.3 (*Fancy Chessboard*)

Modify the program written for Problem 9.3.2 to make it produce a picture of the required piece rather than just its name. For example, a pawn may be represented by

```
            0
         _     _
            .
            .
            .
         .     .
            .     .
```

Problem 9.3.4 (*Roman Numerals*)

One of the principal stumbling blocks in the early development of mathematics was the notation used for numbers before the "Arabic" or "decimal" number system was introduced, since some of the older number systems were quite unsuited for arithmetic. As an example, the Roman system of numbers makes use of the symbols M (with value 1000), D (value 500), C (value 100), L (value 50), X (value 10), V (value 5), and I (value 1).

In the "old Roman" system a number is a sequence of M's, D's, C's, L's, X's, V's, and I's in that order, the value of a number just being the sum of the values of the individual symbols.

In the "modern Roman" system a number is also a sequence of M's, D's, C's, L's, X's, V's, and I's. The symbols have to appear more or less in that order and the value of a number is obtained as before with one important exception: A symbol C, X, or I may precede a symbol of higher value, in which case the value of that symbol C, X, or I is taken to be negative.

EXAMPLE

Decimal	Old Roman	Modern Roman
4	IIII	IV
9	VIIII	IX
91	LXXXXI	XCI

Write a program to read five pairs of old Roman numbers and print their sum as old Roman numbers: (a) Perform the addition without converting the numbers to decimal; (b) perform the addition by converting the numbers to decimal, adding the decimal numbers, and converting the result to an old Roman number.

Problem 9.3.5 (*Roman Arithmetic*)

Write a program to read five pairs of modern Roman numbers, each pair separated by either $+$, $-$, or $\cdot$, indicating addition, subtraction, or multiplication. The program is to perform the operation indicated for each pair and then print the result as a modern Roman number.

Problem 9.3.6 (*Base Conversion*)

A number in a number system with base $b \geq 2$ (see Problem 4.3.1) is of the form $a_n a_{n-1} \cdots a_2 a_1 a_0$, where each of the symbols a_i $(i = 1, 2, \ldots, n)$ has a value between 0 and $b - 1$, the value of a_i usually being denoted by $v(a_i)$. The value of the number $a_n a_{n-1} \cdots a_2 a_1 a_0$ is given by $v(a_n) \cdot b^n + v(a_{n-1}) \cdot b^{n-1} + \cdots + v(a_2) \cdot b^2 + v(a_1) \cdot b + v(a_0)$.

If $b = 2$, the system is called a "binary number system" and it is common practice to use the symbols 0 and 1 with $v(0) = 0$ and $v(1) = 1$. The value of the binary number 10101 is thus $v(1) \cdot 2^4 + v(0) \cdot 2^3 + v(1) \cdot 2^2 + v(0) \cdot 2^1 + v(1) = 16 + 4 + 1 = 21$.

If $b = 3$, the system is called a "ternary number system" and using the symbols X, Y, and Z with $v(X) = 0$, $v(Y) = 1$, and $v(Z) = 2$, the value of the ternary number $YXXXZ$ is given by $v(Y) \cdot 3^4 + v(X) \cdot 3^3 + v(X) \cdot 3^2 + v(X) \cdot 3 + v(Z) = 81 + 2 = 83$.

If $b = 8$, the system is called an "octal number system" and one could use the symbols $0, 1, 2, \ldots, 7$ with $v(i) = i$ for $i = 0, 1, \ldots, 7$. The value of the octal number 322 is obtained as $v(3) \cdot 8^2 + v(2) \cdot 8 + v(2) = 3 \cdot 64 + 2 \cdot 8 + 2 = 210$.

If $b = 16$, the system is called a "hexadecimal number system" and one often uses the symbols $0, 1, 2, \ldots, 9, A, B, C, D, E, F$ with $v(i) = i$ for $i = 0, 1, 2, \ldots, 9$ and $v(A) = 10, v(B) = 11, v(C) = 12, v(D) = 13, v(E) = 14$, and $v(F) = 15$.

The following algorithm will find, for any given number $x > 0$, a number $a_n a_{n-1} \cdots a_2 a_1 a_0$ in a base b number system whose value agrees with the value of x.

Step 1. Let $i = 0$.

Step 2. Let $c = \mathrm{mod}(x,b)$.

Step 3. Let a_i be that symbol of the base b number system with $v(a_i) = c$.

Step 4. Let $x = \mathrm{floor}(x/b)$.

Step 5. If $x = 0$, then stop.

Step 6. Let $i = i + 1$ and go to Step 2.

A number of cards are available, each containing a three-letter code in card columns 1 to 3 and a character string x of unspecified length in some other unspecified position; x is a number in a base b number system, where b is 2, 3, 8, 10, or 16 depending on whether the three-letter code is BIN, TER, OCT, DEC, or HEX.

Write a program to read these cards and print each number as a number in a base $b = 2, 3, 8, 10, 16$ number system.

EXAMPLE

For the input DEC 27 the program should print
BIN ... 11011   TER ... YXXX   OCT ... 33   DEC ... 27   HEX ... 1B

Problem 9.3.7 (*Printing of Expressions, Version 1*)

A number m followed by m expressions consisting of integers, parentheses, and the "operators" $+$, $-$, $*$, $/$, and $**$ is available on punched cards, where $a + b$, $a - b$, and a/b have the usual meaning, $a*b$ means $a \cdot b$, and $a**b$ means a^b. If a,b,c are integers or expressions in parentheses, $a*b + c$ means $(a*b) + c$ rather than $a*(b+c)$: The operator $*$ is performed before the operation $+$; the "priority" of $*$ is higher than the priority of $+$. The "priority relation" between the five operators mentioned is as follows: $*$ and $/$ have the same priority, $+$ and $-$ have the same priority, $**$ has the highest priority, followed by $*$ and $/$, followed by $+$ and $-$. The meaning of $a**b*a+c*a+b$ is thus $((a**b)*a)+(c*a)+b$.

Write a program to print the m expressions in their usual mathematical form, i.e., with $*$ replaced by $\cdot$ and omitted except between integers, with $**$ expressed by printing the portion after $**$ a line higher, and with superfluous parentheses removed.

EXAMPLE

$3*2**(5*(3+2))-18$ should be printed as

$$5(3+2)$$
$$3\cdot2 \qquad -18$$

Problem 9.3.8 (*Printing of Expressions, Version 2*)

Expand the program for Problem 9.3.7 to also allow "identifiers" (any one of the single letters $A, B, \ldots, Z$) and "identifiers with subscripts" (identifiers followed by an expression in parentheses).

EXAMPLE

$3*R(I+2)**(2*Z+W)-3*A(2)$ should be printed as

$$2Z+W$$
$$3R \qquad -3A$$
$$I+2 \qquad 2$$

Problem 9.3.9 (*Reading of Expressions*)

A number of cards are available, each containing an arrangement of integers, blanks, parentheses, and the symbols $+$, $-$, $\cdot$, and $/$. The input information represents an expression in the usual mathematical notation, the first card being the top line of the expression, the second card the next line, etc. Write a program to print the expression using the operators $+$, $-$, $*$ (for multiplication), $/$, and $**$ (for exponentiation), $a**b$ meaning a^b.

Note: This problem is the converse of Problem 9.3.7. Given input of the form

Card 1:	$4+6$
Card 2:	$5(3+7)$ $\quad$ 3
Card 3:	$3\cdot2$ $\quad$ $-(2+4)$ $\quad$ -8

the program should print $3*2**(5*(3+7))-(2+4)**3**(4+6)-8$.

10

RECURSION

10.1 INTRODUCTION

"Recursion" is the name given to defining a function, an algorithm, or a collection of items in terms of itself. For the purposes of this book it suffices to illustrate the concept by a selection of typical examples.

EXAMPLE 1

For integers $n \geq 0$ a function fact(n)† can be defined in terms of itself as follows:

$$\text{fact}(n) = \begin{cases} 1, & \text{if } n \leq 1 \\ n \cdot \text{fact}(n-1), & \text{otherwise} \end{cases}$$

Alternatively, one can use an algorithm to define fact(n).

Definition of the function fact(n)

Step 1. If $n \leq 1$, then let fact(n) = 1 and stop.

Step 2. Let fact(n) = $n \cdot$ fact($n - 1$).

According to both definitions of fact(n), one can obtain fact(5) as follows: fact(5) = $5 \cdot$ fact(5 − 1) = $5 \cdot$ fact(4) = $5 \cdot 4 \cdot$ fact(4 − 1) = $5 \cdot 4 \cdot$ fact(3) = $5 \cdot 4 \cdot 3 \cdot$ fact(3 − 1) = $5 \cdot 4 \cdot 3 \cdot$ fact(2) = $5 \cdot 4 \cdot 3 \cdot 2 \cdot$ fact(2 − 1) = $5 \cdot 4 \cdot 3 \cdot 2 \cdot 1$ = 120.

†In mathematics and other parts of this book the symbol $n!$ is used rather than fact(n). In this chapter fact(n) is preferred to emphasize that fact(n) is a function.

EXAMPLE 2

For integers $n,m \geq 1$ one can define a function prod(n,m) in terms of itself as

$$\text{prod}(n,m) = \begin{cases} n, & \text{if } m = 1 \\ n + \text{prod}(n,m-1), & \text{otherwise} \end{cases}$$

According to this definition, prod(5,3) = 5 + prod(5,2) = 5 + 5 + prod(5,1) = 5 + 5 + 5 = 15. It is easily seen that prod(n,m) = $n \cdot m$, the usual product of n and m, for every pair of integers $n,m \geq 1$.

EXAMPLE 3

For integers $n,m \geq 1$ the largest common factor lcf(n,m) (see Problem 3.2.24) can be defined recursively by

$$\text{lcf}(n,m) = \begin{cases} n, & \text{if } m = 0 \\ \text{lcf}(m,\text{mod}(n,m)), & \text{otherwise} \end{cases}$$

According to this definition, lcf(36,90) = lcf(90,mod(36,90)) = lcf(90,36) = lcf(36,mod(90,36)) = lcf(36,18) = lcf(18,mod(36,18)) = lcf(18,0) = 18.

EXAMPLE 4

For nonnegative integers n,x,y one can define the "Ackermann function" $A(n,x,y)$ as follows:

$$A(n,x,y) = \begin{cases} x + 1, & \text{if } n = 0 \\ x, & \text{if } n = 1 \text{ and } y = 0 \\ 0, & \text{if } n = 2 \text{ and } y = 0 \\ 1, & \text{if } n = 3 \text{ and } y = 0 \\ 2, & \text{if } n \geq 4 \text{ and } y = 0 \\ A(n-1,A(n,x,y-1),x), & \text{otherwise} \end{cases}$$

Using an algorithm one could write

Definition of the function $A(n,x,y)$

Step 1. If $n = 0$, then let $A(n,x,y) = x + 1$ and stop.

Step 2. If $n = 1$ and $y = 0$, then let $A(n,x,y) = x$ and stop.

Step 3. If $n = 2$ and $y = 0$, then let $A(n,x,y) = 0$ and stop.

Step 4. If $n = 3$ and $y = 0$, then let $A(n,x,y) = 1$ and stop.

Step 5. If $n \geq 4$ and $y = 0$, then let $A(n,x,y) = 2$ and stop.

Step 6. Let $A(n,x,y) = A(n-1,A(n,x,y-1),x)$.

Step 7. Stop.

According to this definition, $A(2,3,2) = A(1,A(2,3,1),3) = A(1,A(1,A(2,3,0),3),3) = A(1,A(1,0,3),3)$. Now $A(1,0,3) = A(0,A(1,0,2),0) = A(1,0,2) + 1 = A(0,A(1,0,1),0) + 1 = A(1,0,1) + 1 + 1 = A(0,A(1,0,0),0) + 2 = A(0,0,0) + 2 = 1 + 2 = 3$. Thus $A(2,3,2) = A(1,A(1,0,3),3) = A(1,3,3) = A(0,A(1,3,2),3) = A(1,3,2) + 1 = A(0,A(1,3,1),3) + 1 = A(1,3,1) + 1 + 1 = A(0,A(1,3,0),3) + 2 = A(1,3,0) + 1 + 2 = 3 + 3 = 6$.

Note: The Ackermann function is used in the theory of recursive functions as an example of "nonprimitive" recursion, a subject beyond the scope of this book. It can be shown that the Ackermann function is a generalization of addition, multiplication, and exponentiation. For example,

$$A(1,x,y) = x + y$$
$$A(2,x,y) = x \cdot y$$
$$A(3,x,y) = x^y$$
$$A(4,x,y) = \underbrace{\left(\left(\cdots\left(\left(2^x\right)^x\right)^{x^{\cdot^{\cdot^{\cdot}}}}\right)\right)^x}_{y \text{ times}} = 2^{(x^y)}$$

EXAMPLE 5

An algorithm factor(n,m) that for integers $n \geq m \geq 1$ will print all factors of n not smaller than m can be defined in terms of itself as follows.

Definition of the algorithm factor(n,m)

Step 1. If $m > n$, then stop.

Step 2. If mod(n,m) = 0, then print m.

Step 3. Let $m = m + 1$.

Step 4. Perform the algorithm factor (n,m).

Step 5. Stop.

EXAMPLE 6

Consider a set *Prop* defined in terms of itself as follows:

1. 3 belongs to *Prop*.
2. 5 belongs to *Prop*.
3. If A and B belong to *Prop*, then the value of $A \cdot B$ belongs to *Prop*.
4. If A and B belong to *Prop*, then the value $A \cdot B + 2$ belongs to *Prop*.
5. Nothing but what can be obtained from rules 1–4 belongs to *Prop*.

To see that 257 belongs to *Prop* one can proceed as follows: 3 belongs to *Prop* by rule 1; 5 belongs to *Prop* by rule 2; thus $3 \cdot 5 + 2 = 17$ belongs to

Prop by rule 4; thus $17 \cdot 5 = 85$ belongs to *Prop* by rule 3; thus $85 \cdot 3 + 2 = 257$ belongs to *Prop* by rule 4.

It should be noted that the definition of *Prop* as given does not provide an obvious way to determine whether a given number n belongs to *Prop* or not. This is true in general: If a set s (of numbers, sequences of characters, etc.) is given by a recursive definition, it is often quite difficult to determine for a given item whether it is in s or not.† In most practical cases some obvious property of the given set s often helps to find out whether a given item x is in s or not. In the example of the set *Prop* one can note that application of both rules 3 and 4 to numbers A and B produces a number C with $C \geq 3 \cdot \min(A,B)$. Thus applying rules 3 and 4 k times, a number $D \geq 3^{k+1}$ is obtained. To find out whether a number $n < 3^{k+1}$, for some k, is in *Prop* or not it thus suffices to determine whether n can be generated by k or fewer applications of rules 3 and 4.

EXAMPLE 7

Many examples of recursion involve sequences of characters, usually called "character strings." Consider a set of characters called $\langle$digit$\rangle$‡ consisting of the ten characters 0, 1, 2, 3, 4, 5, 6, 7, 8, and 9 and a set of character strings called $\langle$integer$\rangle$ defined recursively by

1. Every element of $\langle$digit$\rangle$ is in $\langle$integer$\rangle$.
2. An element of $\langle$digit$\rangle$ followed by an element of $\langle$integer$\rangle$ is in $\langle$integer$\rangle$.
3. Nothing but what can be obtained using rules 1 and 2 is in $\langle$integer$\rangle$.

To see that 8329 is in $\langle$integer$\rangle$ one can proceed as follows: 9 is in $\langle$integer$\rangle$ by rule 1; thus 29 is in $\langle$integer$\rangle$ by rule 2; hence 329 is in $\langle$integer$\rangle$ by rule 2; and therefore 8329 is in $\langle$integer$\rangle$ as desired.

EXAMPLE 8

Consider the set $\langle$integer$\rangle$ of Example 7; a set of characters called $\langle$operator$\rangle$ consisting of the four characters $+$, $-$, $/$, and $\cdot$; and a set of character strings called $\langle$expression$\rangle$ defined recursively by

1. An element of $\langle$integer$\rangle$ is an element of $\langle$expression$\rangle$.
2. An element of $\langle$expression$\rangle$ followed by an element of $\langle$operator$\rangle$ followed by an element of $\langle$expression$\rangle$ is an element of $\langle$expression$\rangle$.
3. Nothing but what can be obtained from rules 1 and 2 belongs to $\langle$expression$\rangle$.

†Indeed, it is known from the theory of computability that sometimes it is not possible at all to determine whether an item x is in s or not.

‡The symbols $\langle$ and $\rangle$ are often found in the literature in connection with sets of character strings.

To see that $358+4\cdot83-{}^{11}/_2$ belongs to ⟨expression⟩ observe that 358, 4, 83, 11, and 2 are in ⟨expression⟩ by 1; thus $358+4$ is in ⟨expression⟩ by rule 2; $358+4\cdot83$ again by rule 2; thus $358+4\cdot83-11$ by rule 2; and finally $358+4\cdot83-{}^{11}/_2$ also by rule 2.

Note: For the definition of programming languages it is necessary to define terms such as "integer," "expression," "program," etc. This can be done by defining sets ⟨integer⟩, ⟨expression⟩, and ⟨program⟩ and agreeing that "integer" is anything that belongs to ⟨integer⟩, "expression" anything belonging to ⟨expression⟩, and so forth. For defining sets of character strings a symbolism called the "Backus Naur Form" (B.N.F.) is often used, B.N.F. just being a more compact way of writing definitions such as the ones in Examples 7 and 8. The definitions of the sets ⟨digit⟩, ⟨integer⟩, ⟨operator⟩, and ⟨expression⟩ using B.N.F. look like this:

⟨digit⟩:: = 0 | 1 | 2 | 3 | 4 | 5 | 6 | 7 | 8 | 9

⟨integer⟩:: = ⟨digit⟩ | ⟨digit⟩ ⟨integer⟩

⟨operator⟩:: = + | − | · | /

⟨expression⟩:: = ⟨integer⟩ | ⟨expression⟩ ⟨operator⟩ ⟨expression⟩

The vertical stroke is used to indicate alternatives. Instead of writing "an element of ⟨x⟩ followed by an element of ⟨y⟩," one just writes ⟨x⟩ and ⟨y⟩ in juxtaposition as ⟨x⟩ ⟨y⟩. Thus the first line means that the set ⟨digit⟩ consists of the characters 0, 1, 2, 3, 4, 5, 6, 7, 8, and 9; the second line means that an element of the set ⟨integer⟩ is either an element of ⟨digit⟩ or an element of ⟨digit⟩ followed by an element of ⟨integer⟩; etc.

10.2 PROBLEMS

A few of the following problems require that recursion is allowed in the programming language used for solving them. Thus many versions of FORTRAN are not applicable, but most versions of Algol 60, PL/1, Lisp, etc., can be used.

Problem 10.2.1 (*Recursive Factorial*)

Using the recursive formula in Example 1, write a program to calculate fact(n) for $n =$ 3, 6, 9, 12, 15. Note that fact(15) has 13 digits.

Problem 10.2.2 (*Recursive Largest Common Factor*)

Using the recursive formula given in Example 3, write a program to calculate lcf(n,m) for 15 pairs of seven-digit integers n and m, available on punched cards.

Problem 10.2.3 (*Ackermann's Function, Version 1*)

Using the recursive formula given in Example 4, write a program that attempts to calculate $A(n,x,y)$ for 15 triples of positive integers n, x, and y.

The program should determine the number d of times the recursive formula $A(n,x,y) = A(n - 1,A(n,x,y - 1),x)$ is used and should print both the value of $A(n,x,y)$ and the corresponding number d. The program is to discontinue the calculation of $A(n,x,y)$ and print a suitable message if d starts to exceed 2000.

Problem 10.2.4 (*Ackermann's Function, Version 2*)

Write a program that attempts to calculate $A(n,x,y)$ similar to Problem 10.2.3 for 15 triples of positive integers n, x, and y without using recursion.

Hint: Make use of a so-called "goal list" as follows: The goal list is a sequence of quadruples (r_1,n_1,x_1,y_1), (r_2,n_2,x_2,y_2), . . . , (r_k,n_k,x_k,y_k). Each quadruple (r_i,n_i,x_i,y_i) is called a "goal" and has the following meaning: If $r_i = -1$, then $A(n_i,x_i,y_i)$ has not been calculated yet and is needed for the calculation of $A(n_{i-1},x_{i-1},y_{i-1})$; if $r_i \neq -1$, then $r_i = A(n_i,x_i,y_i)$.

To calculate $A(n,x,y)$ for some triple of positive integers n, x, and y one starts with the goal list containing nothing but $(-1,n,x,y)$ (see Step 1 below) indicating that $A(n,x,y)$ has not been calculated yet. Then the following process is carried out repeatedly with the rightmost goal $(-1,n',x',y')$ on the goal list. *Case* (*a*): If $A(n',x',y')$ cannot be calculated directly (i.e., $n' \neq 0$, $y' \neq 0$), a new goal $(-1,n',x',y' - 1)$ is added to the right end of the goal list (see Step 9 below). *Case* (*b*): If $A(n',x',y')$ can be calculated directly (i.e., $n' = 0$ or $y' = 0$), then replace $(-1,n',x',y')$ by (r',n',x',y'), where $r' = A(n',x',y')$ (see Steps 3–7 below). If (r',n',x',y') is the only goal left on the goal list, then r' is the originally desired value of $A(n,x,y)$ and the algorithm terminates (see Step 10 below). Otherwise the goal (r',n',x',y') is removed from the goal list, and the preceding goal $(-1,n'',x'',y'')$ is replaced by $(-1,n'' - 1,r',x'')$ (see Steps 11–13 below).

Step 1. Let $r_1 = -1$, let $n_1 = n$, let $x_1 = x$, and let $y_1 = y$.

Step 2. Let $i = 1$.

Step 3. If $n_i = 0$, then let $r_i = x_i + 1$ and go to Step 10.

Step 4. If $n_i = 1$ and $y_i = 0$, then let $r_i = x_i$ and go to Step 10.

Step 5. If $n_i = 2$ and $y_i = 0$, then let $r_i = 0$ and go to Step 10.

Step 6. If $n_i = 3$ and $y_i = 0$, then let $r_i = 1$ and go to Step 10.

Step 7. If $n_i \geq 4$ and $y_i = 0$, then let $r_i = 2$ and go to Step 10.

Step 8. Let $i = i + 1$.

Step 9. Let $r_i = -1$, let $n_i = n_{i-1}$, let $x_i = x_{i-1}$, let $y_i = y_{i-1} - 1$, and go to Step 3.

Step 10. If $i = 1$, then print r_1 and stop.

Step 11. Let $i = i - 1$.

Step 12. Let $n_i = n_i - 1$ and let $z = x_i$.

Step 13. Let $x_i = r_{i+1}$, let $y_i = z$, and go to Step 3.

It is instructive to observe the changes of the goal list during the calculation of $A(2,3,2)$:

$$(-1,2,3,2)$$
$$(-1,2,3,2)(-1,2,3,1)$$
$$(-1,2,3,2)(-1,2,3,1)(-1,2,3,0)$$
$$(-1,2,3,2)(-1,2,3,1)(0,2,3,0)$$
$$(-1,2,3,2)(-1,1,0,3)$$
$$(-1,2,3,2)(-1,1,0,3)(-1,1,0,2)$$
$$(-1,2,3,2)(-1,1,0,3)(-1,1,0,2)(-1,1,0,1)$$
$$(-1,2,3,2)(-1,1,0,3)(-1,1,0,2)(-1,1,0,1)(-1,1,0,0)$$
$$(-1,2,3,2)(-1,1,0,3)(-1,1,0,2)(-1,1,0,1)(0,1,0,0)$$
$$(-1,2,3,2)(-1,1,0,3)(-1,1,0,2)(-1,0,0,0)$$
$$(-1,2,3,2)(-1,1,0,3)(-1,1,0,2)(1,0,0,0)$$
$$(-1,2,3,2)(-1,1,0,3)(-1,0,1,0)$$
$$(-1,2,3,2)(-1,1,0,3)(2,0,1,0)$$
$$(-1,2,3,2)(-1,0,2,0)$$
$$(-1,2,3,2)(3,0,2,0)$$
$$(-1,1,3,3)$$
$$(-1,1,3,3)(-1,1,3,2)$$
$$(-1,1,3,3)(-1,1,3,2)(-1,1,3,1)$$
$$(-1,1,3,3)(-1,1,3,2)(-1,1,3,1)(-1,1,3,0)$$
$$(-1,1,3,3)(-1,1,3,2)(-1,1,3,1)(3,1,3,0)$$
$$(-1,1,3,3)(-1,1,3,2)(-1,0,3,3)$$
$$(-1,1,3,3)(-1,1,3,2)(4,0,3,3)$$
$$(-1,1,3,3)(-1,0,4,3)$$
$$(-1,1,3,3)(5,0,4,3)$$
$$(-1,0,5,3)$$
$$(6,0,5,3)$$

A goal list $g_1, g_2, \ldots, g_k$ like the one above, where each g_i can be calculated as soon as g_{i+1} is known, is often called a "push-down list" or "push-down stack."

Problem 10.2.5 (*Partitions, Version 2*)

In Problem 3.2.2 $P(n)$, the number of ways one can write the integer n as the sum of positive integers, was determined for $n = 1, 2, \ldots, 12$. Write a program to determine $P(n)$ for $n = 1, 2, 3, \ldots, 35$ using the recursive formula known from combinatorics:

$$P(n) = \begin{cases} 1, & \text{if } n = 0 \\ 0, & \text{if } n < 0 \\ R(1) - R(2) + R(3) - R(4) + \cdots, & \text{otherwise} \end{cases}$$

where

$$R(k) = P\left(n - \frac{3k^2 - k}{2}\right) + P\left(n - \frac{3k^2 + k}{2}\right)$$

For example, $P(5) = P(4) + P(3) - P(0) = P(3) + P(2) + P(2) + P(1) - 1$
$= P(2) + P(1) + P(2) + P(2) + P(0) - 1 = 3 \cdot P(2) + P(1) = 3 \cdot P(1) +$
$3 \cdot P(0) + P(0) = 7 \cdot P(0) = 7.$

Note: Solve this problem either using a recursive algorithm or by systematically calculating $P(0)$, $P(1)$, $P(2)$, ...

Problem 10.2.6 (*Partitions, Version 3*)

The number $P(n)$ of Problem 10.2.5 can also be found by calculating the value $Q(n,n)$, where $Q(n,m)$ is defined recursively below. Write a program to determine $P(n)$ for $n = 1, 2, 3, \ldots, 35$ by determining the value of $Q(n,n)$.

$$Q(n,m) = \begin{cases} 1, & \text{if either } n = 1 \text{ and } m \geq 1, \\ & \quad \text{or if } m = 0, \text{ or if } m = 1 \\ 0, & \text{if } m < 0 \\ Q(n-1,m) + Q(n,m-n), & \text{otherwise} \end{cases}$$

For example, $P(5) = Q(5,5) = Q(4,5) + Q(5,0) = Q(3,5) + Q(4,1) + 1$
$= Q(2,5) + Q(3,2) + 2 = Q(1,5) + Q(2,3) + Q(2,2) + Q(3,-1) + 2$
$= 1 + Q(1,3) + Q(2,1) + Q(1,2) + Q(2,0) + 0 + 2 = 7.$

Note: Solve problem either by using recursive algorithm or by using a goal list analogous to Problem 10.2.4.

Problem 10.2.7

The quantity $Q(n,m)$ $(1 \leq n \leq m)$ defined in Problem 10.2.6 represents the number of ways m can be written as the sum of not more than n positive numbers. Thus $Q(2,6) = 4$ since 6 can be written in four ways as the sum of not more than two integers, $6 = 6 = 1 + 5 = 2 + 4 = 3 + 3$.

Write a program to calculate a table of $Q(n,m)$ for all integers n,m satisfying $1 \leq n < m \leq 20$.

Problem 10.2.8 (*Remainder*)

Ten triples of positive four-digit integers are available on punched cards. For each triple a,b,c calculate $\text{rem}(a^b,c)$ as follows:

$$\text{rem}(a^b,c) = \begin{cases} \text{rem}((a^2)^{b/2},c), & \text{if } a < c \text{ and } b \geq 2 \text{ is even} \\ \text{mod}(a \cdot \text{rem}((a^2)^{(b-1)/2},c),c), & \text{if } a < c \text{ and } b \geq 3 \text{ is odd} \\ a, & \text{if } a < c \text{ and } b = 1 \\ \text{rem}((\text{mod}(a,c))^b,c), & \text{if } a \geq c \end{cases}$$

Note: $\text{rem}(a^b,c)$ is the remainder of dividing a^b by c. For example, $\text{rem}(29^{48}, 11) = \text{rem}(7^{48}, 11) = \text{rem}(49^{24}, 11) = \text{rem}(5^{24}, 11) = \text{rem}(25^{12}, 11)$
$= \text{rem}(3^{12}, 11) = \text{rem}(9^6, 11) = \text{rem}(81^3, 11) = \text{rem}(4^3, 11) = \text{mod}(4 \cdot \text{rem}(16, 11), 11) = \text{mod}(4 \cdot \text{rem}(5,11),11) = \text{mod}(20,11) = 9.$

Problem 10.2.9 (*Binomial Coefficients*)

Write a program that reads five pairs of integers m,n with $0 \le m \le n \le 30$ and that calculates for each pair the binomial coefficient $b_{n,m}$ (see Problem 1.2.13) defined by the recursive formula:

$$b_{n,m} = \begin{cases} 1, & \text{if either } m = 0 \text{ or if } m = n \\ b_{n-1,m-1} + b_{n-1,m}, & \text{otherwise} \end{cases}$$

Note: Solve this problem using either a recursive algorithm or a goal list analogous to Problem 10.2.4.

Problem 10.2.10 (*Recursive Fibonacci Numbers*)

Write a program that reads five integers $1 \le n \le 40$ and that calculates for each integer n the number F_n (see Problem 1.2.17) using the recursive formula:

$$F_n = \begin{cases} 1, & \text{if } n \le 2 \\ F_{n-1} + F_{n-2}, & \text{otherwise} \end{cases} \quad .$$

Problem 10.2.11 (*Recursive Roots*)

Write a program that reads three triples of numbers n, a, and e with $1 \le n \le 300$, $a = 1$, and $0.0000001 \le e \le 0.001$ and that calculates for each triple n,a,e the number $r(n,a,e)$ using the recursive formula:

$$r(n,a,e) = \begin{cases} a, & \text{if abs}(a^2 - n) < e \\ r\left\{n, \dfrac{a^2 + n}{2a}, e\right\}, & \text{otherwise} \end{cases}$$

Note: $r(n,a,e)$ is an approximation of $\sqrt{n}$; see Problem 4.2.2. For $n = 2$, $a = 1$, and $e = 0.001$ one obtains $r(2,1,0.001) = r(2,1.5,0.001) = r(2,1.41666,0.001) = r(2,1.41421,0.001) = 1.41421$.

Problem 10.2.12 (*Tower of Hanoi*)

A stack of n discs of decreasing size (largest disc at the bottom) is held together by a pin (call it pin 1) passing through holes in the centre of the discs. Two further pins (call them pin 2 and pin 3), which are empty to start with, are available. The situation is depicted for $n = 5$ in the accompanying figure. The problem is to move the stack of discs from pin 1 to pin 2 in the following manner: (a) Only one disc can be moved at a time, (b) at no time must a disc be placed on top of a smaller one, and (c) at each stage each of the discs must be on either pin 1, pin 2, or pin 3.

Write a program that solves the problem for $n = 3, 4, 5$, and 6 and displays every move made. It is convenient to call the pins p_1, p_2, and p_3

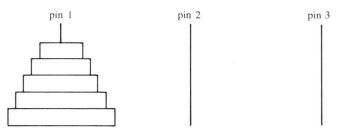

and to number the n discs $1, 2, 3, \ldots, n$. As an example, the program should print the following for $n = 3$:

p_1:	3,2,1	p_2:	nothing	p_3:	nothing
p_1:	3,2	p_2:	1	p_3:	nothing
p_1:	3	p_2:	1	p_3:	2
p_1:	3	p_2:	nothing	p_3:	2,1
p_1:	nothing	p_2:	3	p_3:	2,1
p_1:	1	p_2:	3	p_3:	2
p_1:	1	p_2:	3,2	p_3:	nothing
p_1:	nothing	p_2:	3,2,1	p_3:	nothing

Hint: The recursive algorithm move(i,j,m) defined below will move the topmost $m \geq 1$ discs of p_i to pin p_j using only the third pin p_k in accordance with (a)–(c) if the topmost discs of p_k and p_j are larger than the mth disc from the top of p_i. Thus, suppose that move (i,j,m) is applied to

$$p_i: \quad a_1, a_2, \ldots, a_n, b_1, b_2, \ldots, b_m$$
$$p_j: \quad c_1, c_2, \ldots, c_p$$
$$p_k: \quad d_1, d_2, \ldots, d_q$$

with disc c_p larger than disc b_1 or $p = 0$ and disc d_q larger than disc b_1 or $q = 0$; then move(i,j,m) will produce

$$p_i: \quad a_1, a_2, \ldots, a_n$$
$$p_j: \quad c_1, c_2, \ldots, c_p, b_1, b_2, \ldots, b_m$$
$$p_k: \quad d_1, d_2, \ldots, d_q$$

Definition of the recursive algorithm move(i,j,m)

Step 1. If $m = 1$, then move the topmost disc from p_i to p_j and stop.

Step 2. Perform the algorithm move($i,k,m-1$), where $i \neq k \neq j$.

Step 3. Move the topmost disc from p_i to p_j.

Step 4. Perform the algorithm move($k,j,m-1$), where $i \neq k \neq j$.

Step 5. Stop.

As an example, consider the application of move(1,2,3) to p_1: 3,2,1; p_2: nothing; p_3: nothing.
By Step 2 move(1,3,2) has to be performed first.
  By Step 2 move(1,2,1) has to be performed.
    By Step 1 the topmost disc of p_1 is moved to p_2, yielding p_1: 3,2; p_2: 1; p_3: nothing. Now move(1,2,1) is complete.
  By Step 3 the topmost disc of p_1 is moved to p_3, yielding p_1: 3; p_2: 1; p_3: 2.
  By Step 4 move(2,3,1) has to be performed.
    By Step 1 the topmost disc of p_2 is moved to p_3, yielding p_1: 3; p_2: nothing; p_3: 2,1. Now move(2,3,1) and thus move(1,3,2) is complete.
By Step 3 the topmost disc of p_1 is moved to p_2, yielding p_1: nothing; p_2: 3; p_3: 2,1.
By Step 4 move(3,2,2) has to be performed.
  By Step 2 move(3,1,1) has to be performed.
    By Step 1 the topmost disc of p_3 is moved to p_1, yielding p_1: 1; p_2: 3; p_3: 2. Now move(3,1,1) is complete.
  By Step 3 the topmost disc of p_3 is moved to p_2, yielding p_1: 1; p_2: 3,2; p_3: nothing.
  By Step 4 move(1,2,1) has to be performed.
    By Step 1 the topmost disc of p_1 is moved to p_2, yielding p_1: nothing; p_2: 3,2,1; p_3: nothing. Now move (1,2,1) is complete. Thus move(3,2,2) is complete. Thus move(1,2,3) is complete and the algorithm terminates.

Problem 10.2.13 (*The End of the Universe*)

The "tower of Hanoi" problem discussed in Problem 10.2.12 is known under many names and is part of many a myth and legend. One legend reports about a temple hidden in the jungles of India where priests have been working since the beginning of time to move a stack of 50 golden discs according to the rules described from one golden pin to another golden pin. When they will have finished their monumental task the end of the universe will have come.

Suppose that the priests are moving one disc per second. Suppose that they never make a mistake. Use the algorithm described in Problem 10.2.12 to write a program to determine how many years will pass between the beginning of time and the end of the universe.

Hint: Let $f(n)$ be the number of moves necessary for n discs; thus $f(1) = 1$, $f(2) = 3$, etc. By examining the algorithm given in Problem 10.2.12, construct a formula for $f(n)$ in terms of $f(n-1)$. Evaluate this formula for $n = 50$.

Problem 10.2.14 (*Tower of Saigon*)

Modify the program for Problem 10.2.12 for the case when one additional pin, pin 4, is available.

Problem 10.2.15 (*Winning Positions*)

For many games not involving chance between two players X and Y, player X wins if he can, on making his move, attain what can be called a "final winning position for X" [checkmate for chess, the position (0,0,0) for Nim (see Problem 5.2.5), no men of player Y remaining on the board for checkers, etc.]. One can define a set of "winning positions for X" as follows: (a) Every final winning position for X is a winning position for X. (b) A position p is a winning position for X, if, no matter what move is made by Y, player X can react with a move leading to a winning position for X.

As explained in Problem 5.2.5, once X can attain a winning position when making his move he can systematically win the game.

Write a program to determine all winning positions for the game Nim (see Problem 5.2.5) using the recursive definition given above.

Problem 10.2.16 (*Losing Positions*)

To determine all winning positions for a player X in some game (see Problem 10.2.15) it is often advisable also to use the concept of a "losing position": (a) Every final winning position for X is a winning position for X. (b) A position p is a losing position for Y if player X can make a move leading to a winning position for X. (c) A position p is a winning position for X if every move made by Y leads to a losing position for Y.

Write a program to determine all winning positions for (a) a game of Nim (see Problem 5.2.5) played with 25 counters arranged in five rows (1,3,5,7,9) and (b) a version of Nim played with 16 counters arranged in four rows (1,3,5,7) where the player who is forced to remove the last counter loses.

Problem 10.2.17 (*Chess End Game*)

For complicated games such as chess it is impossible to obtain all winning positions because of the computation effort involved. Still certain situations in chess can be handled successfully using the concept of winning and losing position.

Write a program to determine all winning positions for White in a game of chess played on a 4 by 4 board where the only pieces on the board are the kings and the white queen.

Problem 10.2.18 (*White Always Wins*)

Write a program to simulate two players, Black and White, playing a game of chess on a 4 by 4 board with only the kings and the white queen on the board. The starting positions of the three pieces are to be read from a punched card. Assume that White always starts to move. The strategies of Black and White are as follows: Black chooses moves at random (see

Chapter 8), and White makes use of the winning positions obtained in Problem 10.2.17.

Note: If interactive facilities are available, the program should simulate only White, Black's moves being made by a human opponent.

Problem 10.2.19 *(Prop)*

Write a program to find all positive integers not exceeding 2000 that belong to the set *Prop* defined in Example 6.

Problem 10.2.20

Write a program that reads ten character strings of up to 60 characters and determines for each character string whether it belongs to the set ⟨expression⟩ defined in Example 8.

Problem 10.2.21 *(Value of an Expression)*

Consider the sets ⟨integer⟩ and ⟨operator⟩ of Example 8, the set ⟨right⟩ consisting of the one character], and the set ⟨left⟩ consisting of the one character [. Let ⟨ex⟩ be a set defined as follows: (a) An element of ⟨integer⟩ is an element of ⟨ex⟩. (b) An element of ⟨left⟩ followed by an element of ⟨ex⟩ followed by an element of ⟨operator⟩ followed by an element of ⟨ex⟩ followed by an element of ⟨right⟩ is an element of ⟨ex⟩. (c) Nothing but what can be obtained from rules (a) and (b) is in ⟨ex⟩.

Write a program that reads ten character strings. For each character string x not in ⟨ex⟩ the program should print the word INVALID; for each character string x in ⟨ex⟩ the program should print the word VALID and the value of x, denoted by val(x), which is obtained as follows:

$$\text{val}(x) = \begin{cases} x, & \text{if } x \text{ is in } \langle\text{integer}\rangle \\ \text{val}(y) + \text{val}(z), & \text{if } x \text{ is of the form } [y + z] \\ \text{val}(y) - \text{val}(z), & \text{if } x \text{ is of the form } [y - z] \\ \text{val}(y) \cdot \text{val}(z), & \text{if } x \text{ is of the form } [y \cdot z] \\ \text{floor}\left(\dfrac{\text{val}(y)}{\text{val}(z)}\right), & \text{if } x \text{ is of the form } [y/z] \end{cases} \quad \begin{array}{l} \text{where both } y \text{ and} \\ z \text{ are in } \langle\text{ex}\rangle. \end{array}$$

EXAMPLE

The character string $x = [[[[3+14]/10]+2]\cdot[5 + [3\cdot2]]]$ is in ⟨ex⟩. val(x) = val($[[[3+14]/10]+2]$)·val($[5+[3\cdot2]]$). Since val($[[[3+14]/10]+2]$) = val($[[3+14]/10]$) + val(2) = floor(val($[3+14]$)/val(10)) + 2 = floor((val(3) + val(14))/val(10)) + 2 = floor((val(3) + val(14))/val(10)) + 2 = floor((3+14)/10) + 2 = 3 and val($[5+[3\cdot2]]$) = val(5) + val($[3\cdot2]$) = 5 + val(3)·val(2) = 11, one obtains val(x) = 3·11 = 33.

Problem 10.2.22 (*Polish Notation*)

Consider the sets ⟨integer⟩ and ⟨operator⟩ defined in Example 8 and let ⟨sep⟩ be a set consisting of the single character #. Define a set ⟨polish⟩ recursively as follows: (a) An element of ⟨integer⟩ is an element of ⟨polish⟩. (b) An element of ⟨polish⟩ followed by an element of ⟨sep⟩ followed by an element of ⟨polish⟩ followed by an element of ⟨operator⟩ is an element of ⟨polish⟩. (c) Nothing but what can be obtained from rules (a) and (b) is in ⟨polish⟩.

Write a program that reads 10 character strings. For each character string x not in ⟨polish⟩ the program should print the word INVALID; for each character string x in ⟨polish⟩ the program should print the word VALID and the value of x, denoted by res(x), which is obtained as follows:

$$\text{res}(x) = \begin{cases} x, & \text{if } x \text{ is in } \langle\text{integer}\rangle \\ \text{res}(y) + \text{res}(z), & \text{if } x \text{ is of the form } y\#z+ \\ \text{res}(y) - \text{res}(z), & \text{if } x \text{ is of the form } y\#z- \\ \text{res}(y)\cdot\text{res}(z), & \text{if } x \text{ is of the form } y\#z\cdot \\ \text{floor}\left(\dfrac{\text{res}(y)}{\text{res}(z)}\right), & \text{if } x \text{ is of the form } y\#z/ \end{cases} \quad \begin{matrix} \text{where } y \text{ and } z \text{ are} \\ \text{both in } \langle\text{polish}\rangle. \end{matrix}$$

EXAMPLE

The character string $x = 3\#14+\#10/\#2+\#5\#3\#2\cdot+\cdot$ is in ⟨polish⟩. res(x) = res(y)·res(z), where $y = 3\#14+\#10/\#2+$ and $z = 5\#3\#2\cdot+$. Since res($3\#14+\#10/\#2+$) = res($3\#14+\#10/$) + res(2) = floor(res($3\#14+$)/res(10)) + 2 = floor((res(3) + res(14))/10) + 2 = floor((3 + 14)/10) + 2 = 3 and res($5\#3\#2\cdot+$) = res(5) + res($3\#2\cdot$) = 5 + res(3)·res(2) = 11, one obtains $x = 3\cdot11 = 33$.

Note: An element of ⟨polish⟩ is called an "expression in reverse polish notation." The importance of reverse polish notation rests on two facts: (a) For every element x in ⟨ex⟩ an element y in ⟨polish⟩ can be found such that val(x) = res(y) (see Problem 10.2.23). (b) For every y in ⟨polish⟩ res(y) can be calculated easily without using recursion (see Problem 10.2.24). Thus one way of finding val(x) for some x in ⟨ex⟩ is first to determine a y in ⟨polish⟩ with val(x) = res(y) and then to calculate res(y). Many compilers actually transform all arithmetic expressions into reverse polish before processing them further.

Problem 10.2.23 (*Conversion to Polish Expressions*)

For any element x of ⟨ex⟩, $x = a_1a_2a_3\cdots a_n$ with a_i in either ⟨integer⟩, ⟨left⟩, ⟨right⟩, or ⟨operator⟩ ($1 \le i \le n$), the following algorithm will produce an element y of ⟨polish⟩, $y = b_1b_2\cdots b_m$ with b_j in either ⟨integer⟩, ⟨sep⟩, or ⟨operator⟩ ($1 \le j \le m$) such that val(x) = res(y).

Step 1. Let $i = 1$, let $j = 1$, and let $k = 1$.

Step 2. If $i > n$, then stop.

Step 3. If a_i is in $\langle$left$\rangle$, then let $i = i + 1$ and go to Step 2.

Step 4. If a_i is in $\langle$integer$\rangle$, then let $b_j = a_i$, let $j = j + 1$, let $i = i + 1$, and go to Step 2.

Step 5. If a_i is in $\langle$operator$\rangle$, then let $b_j = \#$, let $c_k = a_i$, let $j = j + 1$, let $k = k + 1$, let $i = i + 1$, and go to Step 2.

Step 6. If a_i is in $\langle$right$\rangle$, then let $b_j = c_{k-1}$, let $j = j + 1$, let $k = k - 1$, let $i = i + 1$, and go to Step 2.

The reader not familiar with reverse polish notation is urged to follow this algorithm step by step to see how $y = 3\#14+\#10/\#2+\#5\#3\#2\cdot+\cdot$ is produced from $x = [[[[3+14]/10]+2]\cdot[5+[3\cdot2]]]$.

Suppose that an integer m followed by m character strings is available on punched cards. Write a program that will determine for each character string x whether x is in $\langle$ex$\rangle$ or not. If x is in $\langle$ex$\rangle$, the program should determine a character string y in $\langle$polish$\rangle$ such that $\mathrm{val}(x) = \mathrm{res}(y)$.

Note: Rather than first checking whether x is in $\langle$ex$\rangle$ and then determining y, modify the algorithm given above such that both tasks are accomplished simultaneously.

Problem 10.2.24 (*Value of Polish Expressions*)

For any element y of $\langle$polish$\rangle$, $y = b_1 b_2 \cdots b_m$ with b_j in either $\langle$integer$\rangle$, $\langle$sep$\rangle$, or $\langle$operator$\rangle$ $(1 \le j \le m)$, the following algorithm will calculate a number r with $r = \mathrm{res}(y)$.

Step 1. Let $i = 1$ and let $j = 1$.

Step 2. If $j > m$, then let $r = c_i$ and stop.

Step 3. If b_j is in $\langle$integer$\rangle$, then let $c_i = b_j$, let $i = i + 1$, let $j = j + 1$, and go to Step 2.

Step 4. If b_j is in $\langle$sep$\rangle$, then let $j = j + 1$ and go to Step 2.

Step 5. If b_j is the character $+$, then let $c_{i-1} = c_{i-1} + c_i$, let $i = i - 1$, let $j = j + 1$, and go to Step 2.

Step 6. If b_j is the character $-$, then let $c_{i-1} = c_{i-1} - c_i$, let $i = i - 1$, let $j = j + 1$, and go to Step 2.

Step 7. If b_j is the character $\cdot$, then let $c_{i-1} = c_{i-1} \cdot c_i$, let $i = i - 1$, let $j = j + 1$, and go to Step 2.

Step 8. If b_j is the character $/$, then let $c_{i-1} = \mathrm{floor}(c_{i-1}/c_i)$, let $i = i - 1$, let $j = j + 1$, and go to Step 2.

The reader not familiar with reverse polish notation is urged to follow this

algorithm step by step to see how $r = 33$ is calculated for $y = 3\#14+$
$\#10/\#2+\#5\#3\#2\cdot+\cdot$.

Suppose that an integer m followed by m character strings is available
on punched cards. Write a program that will determine for each character
string y whether y is in $\langle$polish$\rangle$ or not. If y is in $\langle$polish$\rangle$, the program should
calculate res(y).

Note: Rather than first checking whether y is in $\langle$polish$\rangle$ and then
calculating res(y), modify the above algorithm such that both tasks are
accomplished simultaneously.

Problem 10.2.25 (*Closed Curves*)

Consider the drawing of n closed curves $c_1, c_2, \ldots, c_n$ in the plane subject to the following rules: (a) c_1 is drawn arbitrarily. (b) For every $i \geq 2$,
c_i intersects each of $c_1, c_2, \ldots, c_{i-1}$ in exactly two distinct points. (c) No
three curves ever meet in a single point. How many regions $f(n)$ in the plane
are defined by the n curves?

Clearly, $f(1) = 2$ since a single closed curve divides a plane into two
regions, one inside the curve and one outside; $f(2) = 4$, since two closed curves
subject to rules (b) and (c) divide the plane into four regions 1, 2, 3, and 4,
as shown in the accompanying figure. Indeed, it is easily seen that $f(n)$ can

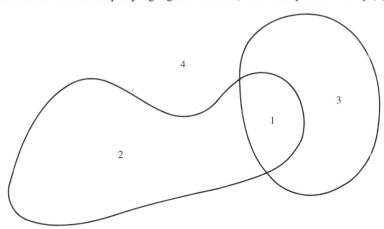

be found by the formula

$$f(n) = \begin{cases} 2, & \text{if } n = 1 \\ f(n-1) + 2\cdot(n-1), & \text{otherwise} \end{cases}$$

Write a program to determine $f(1), f(2), \ldots, f(20)$.

11

ASSORTED PROBLEMS

11.1 LARGE INTEGERS

When working with integers on a computer there is always some restriction on the size of the integers that can be used. Such a restriction might be "integers cannot have more than 15 digits" or "no integer must exceed $2^{31} - 1$," etc. To overcome limitations of the size of integers allowed one can work with the digits of a number individually (as is done in manual calculations) rather than considering all digits of a number as one entity.

As an example, suppose that two positive 20-digit numbers a and b are given as input and that their sum is to be computed. A program such as

Step 1. Read a.

Step 2. Read b.

Step 3. Let $c = a + b$.

Step 4. Print c.

will be illegal in many programming languages because of the size of the numbers involved. Instead, one can calculate the digits of c one by one by adding the corresponding digits of a and b and taking care of a possible carry, as is shown by the algorithm below. The digits of a, from left to right, are called $a_1, a_2, \ldots, a_{20}$ and similarly the digits of b and c are called $b_1, b_2, \ldots, b_{20}$ and $c_1, c_2, \ldots, c_{20}$. For simplicity it is assumed that the sum c of a and b does not have more than 20 digits.

Step 1. Read $a_1, a_2, \ldots, a_{20}$.

Step 2. Read $b_1, b_2, \ldots, b_{20}$.

Step 3. Let $i = 20$.

Step 4. Let $c_i = a_i + b_i$.

Step 5. If $i > 1$, then let $i = i - 1$ and go to Step 4.

Step 6. Let $i = 20$.

Step 7. Let $c_{i-1} = c_{i-1} + \text{floor}(c_i/10)$.

Step 8. Let $c_i = \text{mod}(c_i, 10)$.

Step 9. If $i > 2$, then let $i = i - 1$ and go to Step 7.

Step 10. Print $c_1, c_2, \ldots, c_{20}$.

It should be noted how the numbers are added digit by digit in Step 4, how care is taken of a possible carry in Step 7, and how the actual digits of the results are obtained in Step 8.

It is instructive to examine the above algorithm for a particular choice of values a and b. Suppose that $a = a_1 a_2 a_3 \cdots a_{20}$ and $b = b_1 b_2 b_3 \cdots b_{20}$ are the numbers given below:

a_1	a_2	a_3	a_4	a_5	a_6	a_7	a_8	a_9	a_{10}	a_{11}	a_{12}	a_{13}	a_{14}	a_{15}	a_{16}	a_{17}	a_{18}	a_{19}	a_{20}
0	6	3	8	9	5	2	1	4	6	3	8	7	7	2	6	4	9	9	1

b_1	b_2	b_3	b_4	b_5	b_6	b_7	b_8	b_9	b_{10}	b_{11}	b_{12}	b_{13}	b_{14}	b_{15}	b_{16}	b_{17}	b_{18}	b_{19}	b_{20}
1	2	3	4	5	9	8	7	6	5	4	3	2	1	7	8	4	9	5	5

Steps 3–5 will calculate $c_1 c_2 c_3 \cdots c_{20}$ as follows:

c_1	c_2	c_3	c_4	c_5	c_6	c_7	c_8	c_9	c_{10}	c_{11}	c_{12}	c_{13}	c_{14}	c_{15}	c_{16}	c_{17}	c_{18}	c_{19}	c_{20}
1	8	6	12	14	14	10	8	10	11	7	11	9	8	9	14	8	18	14	6

Thus $c_1, c_2, c_3, \ldots, c_{20}$ represents the result of a digit by digit addition. Now Steps 6–9 take care of carries and the desired result $c_1 c_2 c_3 \cdots c_{20}$ is obtained:

c_1	c_2	c_3	c_4	c_5	c_6	c_7	c_8	c_9	c_{10}	c_{11}	c_{12}	c_{13}	c_{14}	c_{15}	c_{16}	c_{17}	c_{18}	c_{19}	c_{20}
1	8	7	3	5	5	0	9	1	1	8	1	9	9	0	4	9	9	4	6

It is not really necessary to work with the digits individually. It suffices to consider sufficiently small groups of digits individually, e.g., groups of five digits. Thus the above problem could also be solved by calling the first five digits of a a_1, the next five a_2, etc., and similarly for b and c. Their sum could then be obtained by using an algorithm such as

Step 1. Read $a_1, a_2, \ldots, a_4$.

Step 2. Read $b_1, b_2, \ldots, b_4$.

Step 3. Let $i = 4$.

Step 4. Let $c_i = a_i + b_i$.

Step 5. If $i > 1$, then let $i = i - 1$ and go to Step 4.

Step 6. Let $i = 4$.

Step 7. Let $c_{i-1} = c_{i-1} + \text{floor}(c_i/100000)$.

Step 8. Let $c_i = \text{mod}(c_i, 100000)$.

Step 9. If $i > 2$, then let $i = i - 1$ and go to Step 7.

Step 10. Print $c_1, c_2, \ldots, c_4$.

Now the two numbers a and b considered before are added as follows:

a_1	a_2	a_3	a_4
06389	52146	38772	64991

b_1	b_2	b_3	b_4
12345	98765	43217	84955

Steps 3–5 yield

c_1	c_2	c_3	c_4
18734	150911	81989	149946

and Steps 7–9 give the desired result:

c_1	c_2	c_3	c_4
18735	50911	81990	49946

Problem 11.1.1 *(Large Sums)*

Write a program that, given a positive integer n followed by n pairs of positive 80-digit integers, determines for each pair a and b the sum $a + b$.

Problem 11.1.2 *(Large Differences)*

Write a program that, given a positive integer n followed by n pairs of positive 80-digit integers $a_1, b_1, a_2, b_2, \ldots, a_n, b_n$ with $a_i > b_i$ for all i, determines for each pair a_i and b_i the difference $a_i - b_i$.

Problem 11.1.3

Write a subroutine that, given any two 80-digit integers a and b (positive or negative), determines $a + b$.

Problem 11.1.4 *(Large Fibonacci Numbers)*

Write a program that calculates the first 100 Fibonacci numbers (see Problem 1.2.17).

Note: The 100th Fibonacci number has less than 40 digits.

Problem 11.1.5 *(Large Powers)*

Write a program that calculates the numbers $2, 2^2, 2^3, \ldots, 2^{110}$.

Note: 2^{110} has almost 50 digits.

Problem 11.1.6 (*Large Factorials*)

Write a program that calculates 1!, 2!, 3!, ... , 30! (see Problem 1.4.4).
Note: 30! has less than 50 digits.

Problem 11.1.7 (*Large Products*)

Given a positive integer n followed by n pairs of positive 20-digit integers, determine for each pair a and b the product ab.

Note: The product can have up to 40 digits.

Problem 11.1.8 (*Large Quotients*)

A number of cards are available containing a positive integer n followed by n pairs of positive 40-digit integers $a_1, b_1, a_2, b_2, \ldots, a_n, b_n$ with $b_i \neq 0$ for all i. Write a program to determine for each pair a_i and b_i the value of floor(a_i/b_i).

Problem 11.1.9 (*Large Remainder*)

Same as Problem 11.1.8 but determine mod(a_i,b_i).

Problem 11.1.10 (*Large Large Common Factors*)

Same as Problem 11.1.8 but determine lcf(a_i,b_i).

Hint: Use mod(a_i,b_i) as developed in Problem 11.1.9 and the algorithm for largest common factor as given in Problem 3.2.24.

Problem 11.1.11 (*Decimal Expansion*)

Given a positive integer n followed by n pairs of positive six-digit integers $a_1, b_1, a_2, b_2, \ldots, a_n, b_n$ with $10 > a_i/b_i > 1$ for all i, write a program to determine for each pair a_i and b_i the first 200 digits of the decimal value of a_i/b_i.

Problem 11.1.12 (*Periodic Decimal Expansions*)

Same as Problem 11.1.11 but determine additionally if the decimal expansion of a_i/b_i starts to get periodical. If this is the case, also print the sequence of digits that repeats.

Hint: To determine the decimal expansion $d_0 \cdot d_1 d_2 \cdots d_m$ of a fraction a/b with $10 > a/b > 1$ to m decimal places and to determine if the expansion is periodical one can proceed as follows:

Step 1. Let $i = 0$ and let $r_0 = a$.

Step 2. Let $d_i = $ floor(r_i/b).

Step 3. Let $i = i + 1$.

Step 4. Let $r_i = 10$ mod(r_{i-1},b).

Step 5. If $i \leq m$, go to Step 2.

Step 6. Stop.

The sequence $d_0, d_1, d_2, \ldots, d_m$ represents the desired decimal expansion $d_0 \cdot d_1 d_2 \cdots d_m$. It is periodic if and only if for two values s and t $(0 \leq s < t \leq m) \, r_s = r_t$ and the sequence of digits $d_s, d_{s+1}, \ldots, d_{t-1}$ is the sequence of repeating digits.

11.2 FRACTIONS

The numbers that can be used for calculations in most programming languages are the usual decimal numbers or variations thereof, such as $10, -3.6, 18.982, 0.0005$, etc. Fractions such as $\frac{3}{4}, \frac{1}{2}, \frac{2}{3}$, etc., are used in their decimal forms 0.75, 0.5, and 0.6666..., respectively. Since fractions cannot always be converted exactly to decimal form using a finite number of digits, this conversion can occasionally introduce undesirable errors. In such situations it is the programmer's responsibility to ensure that calculations are indeed performed using fractions rather than their decimal form. This can be done by interpreting each fraction as a pair of numbers, the fraction $\frac{3}{4}$ as (3,4), $\frac{1}{2}$ as (1,2), $\frac{2}{3}$ as (2,3) and, more generally, a/b as (a,b). To perform a certain computation involving such pairs (fractions) the programmer has to specify how to obtain the pair (fraction) that is to be the result of the computation. The basic rules for manipulating fractions are

1. $\dfrac{a}{b} + \dfrac{c}{d} = \dfrac{ad + cb}{bd}$,   i.e., $(a,b) + (c,d) = (ad + cb, bd)$.

2. $\dfrac{a}{b} - \dfrac{c}{d} = \dfrac{ad - cb}{bd}$,   i.e., $(a,b) - (c,d) = (ad - cb, bd)$.

3. $\dfrac{a}{b} \cdot \dfrac{c}{d} = \dfrac{ac}{bd}$,   i.e., $(a,b) \cdot (c,d) = (ac, bd)$.

4. $\dfrac{a}{b} \bigg/ \dfrac{c}{d} = \dfrac{ad}{bc}$,   i.e., $(a,b)/(c,d) = (ad, bc)$.

When working with fractions (a,b) it is convenient to keep both the "numerator" a and the "denominator" b as small as possible. This is achieved by working with "reduced" fractions, i.e., with fractions (a,b) with $\mathrm{lcf}(a,b) = 1$. Given any fraction (c,d), a reduced fraction (a,b) of same value is given by $a = c/\mathrm{lcf}(c,d)$, $b = d/\mathrm{lcf}(c,d)$. Note that adding, subtracting, multiplying, or dividing reduced fractions according to formulae 1, 2, 3, and 4 does not always yield a reduced fraction.

Problem 11.2.1 (*Sum of Fractions*)

Write a program that, given a positive integer n followed by n pairs of fractions (a_i, b_i) and (c_i, d_i) $(i = 1, 2, \ldots, n)$, finds for each i the sum of the fractions (a_i, b_i) and (c_i, d_i) as a fraction in reduced form.

Problem 11.2.2 (*Mean of Fractions*)

Write a program that, given a positive integer n ($5 \leq n \leq 10$) followed by n fractions $a_1/b_1, a_2/b_2, \ldots, a_n/b_n$ with $0 < a_i, b_i < 20$ for all i, finds the sum $s = (a_1/b_1) + (a_2/b_2) + \cdots + (a_n/b_n)$ and the arithmetic mean $m = s/n$ as fractions in reduced form.

Problem 11.2.3 (*Sorting of Fractions*)

Write a program that, given a positive integer n ($5 \leq n \leq 50$) followed by n fractions $a_1/b_1, a_2/b_2, \ldots, a_n/b_n$, sorts them into ascending order using one of the methods described in Chapter 7. For simplicity assume that all a_i and b_i are positive.

Note: For two fractions a/b and c/d ($a,b,c,d \geq 0$) $a/b < c/d$ if and only if $ad < bc$.

Problem 11.2.4

Using the formula $x_1 = 1, x_{n+1} = (x_n^2 + a)/2x_n$ ($n \geq 1$), write a program to calculate for $a = 2, 3, 4$, and 5 the numbers x_1, x_2, x_3, x_4, and x_5 as fractions in reduced form.

Note: $x_1, x_2, \ldots, x_5$ are fractions approximating $\sqrt{a}$. (See Problem 4.2.2.) The numerators and denominators can get as large as 15 digits.

Problem 11.2.5

Same as Problem 11.2.4 but calculate $x_1, x_2, \ldots, x_8$.

Note: The numerators and denominators can get as large as 150 digits, so the method for dealing with large integers suggested in Section 11.1 has to be used.

Problem 11.2.6 (*Linear Equations Using Fractions*)

Given a positive integer n and n systems of two linear equations in two variables

$$a_{11}x_1 + a_{12}x_2 = b_1$$
$$a_{21}x_1 + a_{22}x_2 = b_2$$

where $a_{11}, a_{12}, a_{21}, a_{22}, b_1$, and b_2 are fractions, write a program to find a solution of the system in the form of reduced fractions using Cramer's rule of Chapter 13.

Problem 11.2.7

Same as Problem 11.2.6 but for systems of three linear equations in three variables and using Gaussian elimination as described in Chapter 13.

Problem 11.2.8 (*Harmonic Series*)

Write a program to determine $1 + \frac{1}{2} + \frac{1}{3} + \cdots + 1/n$ for $n = 1, 2, 3,$ ..., 20 in the form of reduced fractions.

Problem 11.2.9

Same as Problem 11.2.8 but for $n = 21, 22, \ldots, 50$.

Note: Numerators and denominators can get as large as 50 digits, so the method for dealing with large integers suggested in Section 11.1 has to be used.

Problem 11.2.10

Same as Problem 2.2.4 but use the formula

$$n \text{ degrees Fahrenheit} = \frac{5(n - 32)}{9} \text{ degrees centigrade}$$

and compute the table using reduced fractions.

11.3 CONTINUED FRACTIONS

An expression of the form

$$a_1 + \cfrac{1}{a_2 + \cfrac{1}{a_3 + \cfrac{1}{a_4 + \cdots}}}$$

where the a_i's are positive integers is called a "continued fraction" and is symbolically written as $[a_1, a_2, a_3, a_4, \ldots]$.

As an example, the continued fraction [1,2,6,5] is the expression

$$1 + \cfrac{1}{2 + \cfrac{1}{6 + \cfrac{1}{5}}}$$

and can be converted to a fraction in the obvious manner as follows:

$$1 + \cfrac{1}{2 + \cfrac{1}{6 + \cfrac{1}{5}}} = 1 + \cfrac{1}{2 + \cfrac{1}{\frac{31}{5}}} = 1 + \cfrac{1}{2 + \frac{5}{31}} = 1 + \cfrac{1}{\frac{67}{31}} = 1 + \frac{31}{67} = \frac{98}{67}$$

Given any continued fraction $[a_1, a_2, \ldots, a_n, \ldots]$, the fraction corresponding to the finite continued fraction $[a_1, a_2, \ldots, a_n]$ is called the "*n*th approximation of $[a_1, a_2, \ldots, a_n, \ldots]$," is usually denoted by p_n/q_n, and can be computed as follows:

$$p_0 = 1, \quad q_0 = 0, \quad p_1 = a_1, \quad q_1 = 1 \quad \text{and} \quad p_i = a_i p_{i-1} + p_{i-2},$$
$$q_i = a_i q_{i-1} + q_{i-2} \quad \text{for } i \geq 2$$

As an example, consider again the continued fraction [1,2,6,5]. Using the above formulae, one finds $p_0 = 1$, $p_1 = 1$, $p_2 = 3$, $p_3 = 19$, $p_4 = 98$ and $q_0 = 0$, $q_1 = 1$, $q_2 = 2$, $q_3 = 13$, $q_4 = 67$.

It is known from the theory of continued fractions that every positive number a can be written as a continued fraction $a = [a_1, a_2, a_3, a_4, \ldots]$, that this continued fraction is finite if a is rational, and that it is "periodic" if a is a real root of a quadratic equation $b_1 x^2 + b_2 x + b_3 = 0$, b_1, b_2, and b_3 integers.

Given an arbitrary positive number a, the continued fraction $a = [a_1, a_2, a_3, \ldots]$ can be found as follows:

Step 1. Let $i = 1$.

Step 2. Let $a_i = \text{floor}(a)$.

Step 3. If $a = a_i$, then stop.

Step 4. Let $a = 1/(a - a_i)$, let $i = i + 1$, and go to Step 2.

EXAMPLE 1

Consider $a = \frac{98}{67}$. By Step 2, $a_1 = 1$. Since $a_1 \neq a$, the process continues. By Step 4, $a = 1/(\frac{98}{67} - 1) = 1/\frac{31}{67} = \frac{67}{31}$. By Step 2, $a_2 = 2$. Since $a_2 \neq a$, the process continues. By Step 4, $a = 1/(\frac{67}{31} - 2) = 1/\frac{5}{31} = \frac{31}{5}$. By Step 2, $a_3 = 6$. Since $a_3 \neq a$, the process continues. By Step 4, $a = 1/(\frac{31}{5} - 6) = 1/\frac{1}{5} = 5$. By Step 2, $a_4 = 5$. Since $a_4 = a$, the process terminates. One has obtained $\frac{98}{67} = [a_1, a_2, a_3, a_4] = [1,2,6,5]$ in agreement with earlier calculations.

EXAMPLE 2

Consider $a = \sqrt{2}$. By Step 2, $a_1 = 1$. Since $a_1 \neq a$, the process continues. By Step 4, $a = 1/(\sqrt{2} - 1) = (\sqrt{2} + 1)/(2 - 1) = \sqrt{2} + 1$. By Step 2, $a_2 = 2$. Since $a_2 \neq a$, the process continues. By Step 4, $a = 1/(\sqrt{2} + 1 - 2) = 1/(\sqrt{2} - 1) = \sqrt{2} + 1$. This agrees with what has been obtained in a previous Step 4. Thus $a_2 = a_3 = a_4 = \cdots = 2$ and one has obtained $\sqrt{2} = [1,2,2,2, \ldots]$.

It is important to note that in both examples the calculations in Step 4 have been carried out using integers only. Otherwise, errors due to truncation will pose a serious problem. The recommended process for finding the continued fraction $[a_1, a_2, \ldots]$ of any expression of the form $(b + c\sqrt{d})/e$

(b, c, d, and e integers, $d,e > 0$) using integers only is the following:

Step 1. Let $b_0 = b$, let $c_0 = c$, let $e_0 = e$, and let $i = 1$.

Step 2. Let $a_i = \text{floor}((b_{i-1} + c_{i-1}\sqrt{d})/e_{i-1})$.

Step 3. Let $b_i = -e_{i-1}b_{i-1} + a_i e_{i-1}^2$.

Step 4. Let $c_i = c_{i-1}e_{i-1}$.

Step 5. Let $e_i = -(b_{i-1} - a_i e_{i-1})^2 + c_{i-1}^2 d$.

Step 6. If $e_i < 0$, then let $e_i = -e_i$, let $b_i = -b_i$, and let $c_i = -c_i$.

Step 7. Let $g = \text{lcf}(b_i,c_i,e_i)$.

Step 8. Let $b_i = b_i/g$, let $c_i = c_i/g$, and let $e_i = e_i/g$.

Step 9. Let $i = i + 1$ and go to Step 2.

The reader unfamiliar with continued fractions is urged to carry out this algorithm manually step by step for both $\frac{98}{67}$ (i.e., $b = 98$, $c = 0$, $d = 1$, $e = 67$) and $\sqrt{2}$ (i.e., $b = 0$, $c = 1$, $d = 2$, $e = 1$).

The importance of continued fractions lies in the fact that given a number a and its continued fraction $a = [a_1,a_2, \ldots]$, the values of p_i/q_i are very good approximations of a. Indeed, it can be shown that

1. $\text{abs}(a - (p_i/q_i)) < 1/q_i^2$ for every i.
2. $\text{abs}(a - (p_i/q_i)) > \text{abs}(a - (p/q))$ for some integers p/q implies that $q > q_i$. Thus the fractions p_i/q_i are the "best possible rational approximations of the given number a with denominator not exceeding q_i."

Problem 11.3.1 (*Continued Fractions, Version 1*)

Write a program that will read a positive integer n followed by n positive integers $a_1, a_2, \ldots, a_n$ and will determine the value of each of the continued fractions $[a_1,a_2, \ldots, a_i]$ with $i = 1, 2, \ldots, n$ both as fractions $(p_i,q_i) = p_i/q_i$ and as decimal numbers.

Problem 11.3.2 (*Approximations*)

Write a program to calculate p_i/q_i for the continued fraction $[1,2,2,2, \ldots]$ for $i = 1, 2, \ldots, 25$.

Note: By Example 2 above the values p_i/q_i are approximate values of $\sqrt{2}$.

Problem 11.3.3 (*Continued Fractions, Version 2*)

A positive integer n and n pairs of integers $a_1, b_1, a_2, b_2, \ldots, a_n, b_n$ with $a_i > b_i > 0$ are available on punched cards. Write a program to find the continued fraction for each fraction a_i/b_i ($i = 1, 2, \ldots, n$).

Problem 11.3.4 (*Cogwheels*)

When trying to synchronize the movement of a telescope with the apparent movement of stars, two cogwheels with a and b teeth, respectively, are required, where a and b are large integers depending on celestial constants and the mechanism used to power the telescope. Since a and b are often very large (e.g., 12-digit integers), it is not feasible to actually use cogwheels with that many teeth. Rather, one has to design cogwheels with c and d teeth, respectively, such that the difference of c/d and a/b is less than a permissible tolerance e (e.g., $e = 0.00001$) and such that c and d are as small as possible. The first systematic investigation of this problem was done by Huygens in 1703 and led to the development of continued fractions. According to the property 1 of continued fractions mentioned earlier, the problem can be solved by determining the continued fraction $a/b = [a_1,a_2, \ldots]$ by calculating the fractions p_1/q_1, p_2/q_2, ... by finding the smallest i for which $1/q_i^2 < e$ and then using $c = p_i$, $d = q_i$. Indeed, abs$((a/b) - (c/d))$ $=$ abs$((a/b) - (p_i/q_i)) < 1/q_i^2 < e$, as desired.

Write a program that will determine for each of five triples (a,b,e) available on punched cards $(a > b > 100000)$ a fraction c/d such that abs$((a/b) - (c/d)) < e$.

Problem 11.3.5 (*Continued Fractions, Version 3*)

Six groups of four integers b, c, d, and e $(d,e > 0)$ are available on punched cards. Write a program that will find for each group b, c, d, and e the numbers $a_1, a_2, \ldots, a_{100}$ of the continued fraction $[a_1,a_2,\ldots] = (b + c\sqrt{d})/e$.

Note: The finite continued fraction $[a_1,a_2,\ldots,a_{100}]$ thus obtained permits the calculation of fractions p_i/q_i, which are very close to the more complicated number $(b + \sqrt{d})/e$. These fractions can be used in solving problems analogous to the one explained in Problem 11.3.4.

Problem 11.3.6

Write a program that will read ten pairs of numbers b and e (b a positive integer, e a positive number less than 0.001) and that will determine for each pair b,e that fraction $(c,d) = c/d$ for which d is as small as possible and abs$(\sqrt{b} - (c/d)) < e$.

Hint: Proceed as in Problem 11.3.4 using the continued fraction $[a_1,a_2,a_3,\ldots] = \sqrt{b}$.

Problem 11.3.7 (*Pellian Equation*)

Write a program to determine all pairs of integers (x,y) with $y < 9999999$ satisfying the equation $x^2 - 13y^2 = 1$.

Hint: Equations of the form $x^2 - dy^2 = 1$ are called "Pellian equations." Solutions of such equations can be found by determining the continued fraction $\sqrt{d} = [a_1, a_2, \ldots]$ by calculating the fractions $p_1/q_1, p_2/q_2, \ldots$ and examining the pairs $(x,y) = (p_i,q_i)$ for $i = 1, 2, \ldots$.

Problem 11.3.8 (*Linear Diophantine Equations*)

A positive integer m and m groups of three integers (b_1, c_1, d_1), (b_2, c_2, d_2), ..., (b_m, c_m, d_m) are available on punched cards. Write a program that tries to determine for each triple (b_i, c_i, d_i) two integers s_1 and s_2 such that $b_i s_1 + c_i s_2 = d_i$.

Note: From the theory of so-called "diophantine" equations it is well known that an equation of the form

$$bx_1 + cx_2 = d \qquad (b, c, \text{ and } d \text{ positive integers}) \qquad (1)$$

has no integer solutions if lcf(b,c) is not a factor of d, and has infinitely many solutions if lcf(b,c) is a factor of d. In the latter case a solution (s_1, s_2) of Equation (1) can be obtained as follows:

Step 1. Let $b' = b/\text{lcf}(b,c)$ and let $c' = c/\text{lcf}(b,c)$.

Step 2. Find the continued fraction $b'/c' = [a_1, a_2, \ldots, a_n]$.

Step 3. Let $s_1' = (-1)^n q_{n-1}$ and let $s_2' = (-1)^{n+1} p_{n-1}$, where p_{n-1}/q_{n-1} is the $(n-1)$th approximation of the continued fraction $[a_1, a_2, \ldots, a_n]$, as usual.

Step 4. Let $s_2 = (d/\text{lcf}(b,c))s_1'$ and $s_2 = (d/\text{lcf}(b,c))s_2'$.

It is easy to see that all infinitely many solutions of Equation (1) can be obtained from the one solution (s_1, s_2) by taking

$$\left(s_1 + \frac{c}{\text{lcf}(b,c)}t, \quad s_2 - \frac{b}{\text{lcf}(b,c)}t\right)$$

for $t = 0, \pm1, \pm2, \pm3, \ldots$.

EXAMPLE 3

Consider $52x_1 + 28x_2 = 20$. Since lcf(52,28) = 4 is a factor of 20, there are infinitely many integer solutions. By Step 1, $b' = 13$ and $c' = 7$. Step 2 yields $\frac{13}{7} = [1,1,6]$; i.e., $n = 3$. Therefore $p_0 = 1$, $p_1 = 1$, $p_2 = 2$ and $q_0 = 0$, $q_1 = 1$, $q_2 = 1$. Thus by Step 3 $s_1' = (-1)^3 q_2 = -1$ and $s_2' = (-1)^4 p_2 = 2$. By Step 4 one finally obtains $s_1 = \frac{20}{4}(-1) = -5$ and $s_2 = \frac{20}{4}(2) = 10$.

Indeed, $52(-5) + 28(10) = -260 + 280 = 20$. All solutions are given by $(-5 + 7t, 10 - 13t)$ for $t = 0, \pm1, \pm2, \ldots$.

Problem 11.3.9 (*Transporting Spaghetti*)

The unique location of Venice in northeastern Italy poses a transportation problem in many cases. To transport large quantities of spaghetti from Milano to Venice a company uses trucks capable of carrying A tons from Milano to Mestre, the city on the mainland closest to Venice, and boats capable of carrying B tons from Mestre to Venice. One day the depot in Venice requests an arbitrary amount of spaghetti but not less than C tons and the depot in Mestre requests exactly D tons. For ten different integer choices of A, B, C, and D determine the smallest number of trucks to be sent from Milano to satisfy both orders such that every truck and boat used for the transport is loaded to capacity.

Hint: Calling the number of trucks s_1 and the number of boats s_2, positive integer values for s_1 and s_2 have to be determined such that $As_1 - Bs_2 = D$ and $Bs_2 \geq C$.

11.4 SOME IMPORTANT NUMBERS AND FUNCTIONS

Draw a circle with centre C, radius 1, and a halfline l_1 starting in centre C as shown in Fig. 11-1. Drawing any other halfline l_2 starting in centre C creates an "angle" α, as shown in Fig. 11-2. The size of such an angle α can be measured in terms of the length of the arc of the circle that is swept when rotating l_1 counterclockwise until it coincides with l_2. Since the circumference of the whole circle is $2\pi = 6.282\ldots$, the circumference of a quartercircle and thus the size of the angle α shown in Fig. 11-3 is $\pi/2 = 1.57079\ldots$

Measuring the size of an angle in such a manner is called measuring an angle in "radians." This is different from measuring an angle in "degrees" as is customary in high school, where the circumference of a circle is divided into 360 equal parts called "degrees." The relation between degrees and radians is given by the formula

$$2\pi \text{ radians} = 360 \text{ degrees,} \quad \text{i.e., } 1 \text{ radian} = 57.2957\ldots \text{ degrees}$$

Throughout the rest of this section it will be assumed for convenience that all angles are measured in radians and do not exceed 2π.

Consider once more Fig. 11-2. Call the point of intersection of l_2 with the circle A, draw a line l_3 perpendicular to l_1 through A, and call the intersection of l_3 with l_1 B, as indicated in Fig. 11-4.

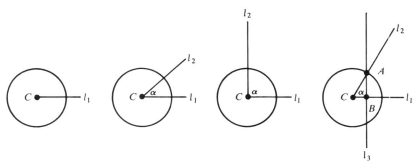

Figure 11-1   Figure 11-2   Figure 11-3   Figure 11-4

One can now define two values sin(α) and cos(α) that depend on the size of α as follows:

sin(α) is the length of the line segment *A* to *B*.

cos(α) is the length of the line segment *C* to *B*.

For many problems (see, e.g., Section 11.5) it is necessary to know the values sin(α) and cos(α) given the size of α. For this reason many programming languages have some built-in mechanism for finding sin(α) or cos(α) given α. It is instructive, however, to see how sin(α) or cos(α) can be determined without relying on such a built-in mechanism.

It is known from calculus that

$$\cos(\alpha) = 1 - \frac{\alpha^2}{2!} + \frac{\alpha^4}{4!} - \frac{\alpha^6}{6!} + \frac{\alpha^8}{8!} \cdots \tag{1}$$

$$\sin(\alpha) = \alpha - \frac{\alpha^3}{3!} + \frac{\alpha^5}{5!} - \frac{\alpha^7}{7!} + \frac{\alpha^9}{9!} \cdots \tag{2}$$

Since both infinite series are alternating, the error committed when considering the first $(n - 1)$ terms only does not exceed the nth term (see Problem 1.2.12). The infinite series (1) and (2) thus provide a simple method for calculating sin(α) and cos(α) with reasonable accuracy, in particular if α is small. It is always possible to reduce the size of α to at least $\pi/4 = 0.785...$ according to the rules below, which are known from trigonometry.

1. If $2\pi > \alpha > \pi$, then $\sin(\alpha) = -\sin(\alpha - \pi)$ and $\cos(\alpha) = -\cos(\alpha - \pi)$.
2. If $\pi > \alpha > \pi/2$, then $\sin(\alpha) = \sin(\pi - \alpha)$ and $\cos(\alpha) = -\cos(\pi - \alpha)$.
3. If $\pi/2 \geq \alpha \geq \pi/4$, then $\sin(\alpha) = \cos((\pi/2) - \alpha)$ and $\cos(\alpha) = \sin((\pi/2) - \alpha)$.

Thus, e.g., $\sin(5\pi/3) = -\sin((5\pi/3) - \pi) = -\sin(2\pi/3)$ $= -\sin(\pi - (2\pi/3)) = -\sin(\pi/3) = -\cos((\pi/2) - (\pi/3)) = -\cos(\pi/6)$.

It is easy to see that for values $0 \leq \alpha \leq \pi/4$ the formulae cos(α) = 1 $- (\alpha^2/2!) + (\alpha^4/4!) - (\alpha^6/6!) + (\alpha^8/8!)$ and sin(α) = $\alpha - (\alpha^3/3!) + (\alpha^5/5!)$ $- (\alpha^7/7!)$ are accurate up to six decimal places. Using an additional term $-\alpha^{10}/10!$ ($\alpha^9/9!$, respectively) gives two extra decimal places. Other important quantities associated with an angle α are tan(α), defined as tan(α) = sin(α)/cos(α), and the "inverse" function arctan(x) of tan(α), defined by the relation arctan(x) = α if and only if tan(α) = x. It is known from calculus that for every $n \geq 1$

$$\arctan(x) = x - \frac{x^3}{3} + \frac{x^5}{5} - \frac{x^7}{7} + \cdots + (-1)^n \frac{x^{2n+1}}{2n+1} + R_n,$$

where

$$\text{abs}(R) \leq \frac{(\text{abs}(x))^{2n+3}}{2n+3}$$

One of the most fascinating numbers to be found when studying calculus is the number $e = 2.718\ldots$, defined by the infinite series

$$e = 1 + \frac{1}{1!} + \frac{1}{2!} + \frac{1}{3!} + \cdots \dagger \tag{3}$$

It can be shown that given any number x one can write

$$e^x = 1 + \frac{x}{1!} + \frac{x^2}{2!} + \frac{x^3}{3!} + \cdots \tag{4}$$

of which Equation (3) is a special case for $x = 1$. A straightforward calculation shows that for $\text{abs}(x) < n + 1$

$$\text{abs}\left(e^x - \left(1 + \frac{x}{1!} + \frac{x}{2!} + \cdots + \frac{x^n}{n!}\right)\right) < \frac{(\text{abs}(x))^{n+1}}{n!(n + 1 - x)}$$

and thus Equation (4) can be used to calculate e^x for small values of x, say $\text{abs}(x) \leq 1$.

It is also possible to calculate e with high accuracy using the fact established by Euler that e can be written as a continued fraction $e = [2,1,2,1, 1,4,1,1,6,1,1,8,1,\ldots]$.

In contrast to the simple pattern in the continued fraction of e no pattern has been found to date for the continued fraction of the number π. The beginning of the continued fraction of π is

$$\pi = [3,7,15,1,292,1,1,1,2,1,3,1,14,2,1,1,2,2,2,2,1,84,2,1,1,15,3,13,1,4,$$
$$2,6,6,99,1,2,2,6,3,5,1,1,6,8,1,\ldots]$$

Given a positive number x, the number y for which $e^y = x$ is called the "natural logarithm of x" and is denoted by $\ln(x)$. It is known from calculus that for every $n \geq 1$ and every $x > 0$

$$\ln(x) = 2\left(a + \frac{a^3}{3} + \frac{a^5}{5} + \frac{a^7}{7} + \cdots + \frac{a^{2n-1}}{2n - 1} + R_n\right)$$

with

$$a = \frac{x - 1}{x + 1},$$

where

$$\text{abs}(R_n) < \text{abs}\left(\frac{a^{2n+1}}{n(1 - a)}\right)$$

Problem 11.4.1 (Cos)

Using Equation (1) and rules 1–3, write a program to calculate a table of $\cos(\alpha)$ for $\alpha = 0.01, 0.02, \ldots, 6.28$ radians with six decimal places of accuracy.

$\dagger e$ is called "Euler's number." It is the base of the natural logarithm. Some outstanding properties of e are that the derivative of e^x is e^x, that $\lim_{n\to\infty}(1 + (1/n))^n = e$, and that $e^{iz} = \cos(z) + i\sin(z)$, where $i = \sqrt{-1}$.

Problem 11.4.2 (Sin)

Same as Problem 11.4.1 but for sin(α) and eight decimal places accuracy.

Problem 11.4.3

Using Equations (1) and (2) and rules 1–3, write a program to prepare a table of sin(α) and cos(α) for $\alpha = 0, 1, 2, \ldots, 359$ degrees using the relation 1 radian $= 57.2957$ degrees.

Problem 11.4.4 (*e*)

Calculate the value of *e* using Equation (3) with eight decimal places of accuracy.

Problem 11.4.5 (e^x)

Write a program to prepare a table of the values of e^x for $x = 0, 0.01, 0.02, \ldots, 1.99, 2$ with four decimal places of accuracy.

Hint: For $x > 1$, use the fact that $e^x = ee^{x-1}$.

Problem 11.4.6 (*e by Continued Fractions*)

Write a program to calculate the values of $(p_1, q_1), (p_2, q_2), \ldots, (p_{10}, q_{10})$ for the continued fraction of *e*. (See Section 11.3.)

Problem 11.4.7

Write a program to calculate the value of *e* to 18 decimal places using continued fractions.

Hint: Determine an approximation p_n/q_n of the continued fraction of *e* such that q_n has at least nine digits. By converting p_n/q_n to decimal, using a method as in Problem 11.1.11, the desired number is found.

Problem 11.4.8 (Pi, *Version 5*)

Write a program to calculate the value of π to 18 decimal places of accuracy using continued fractions.

Problem 11.4.9 (*Best* Pi, *Version 6*)

Throughout this book a number of methods for the calculation of π are discussed. To calculate π efficiently with high accuracy one generally depends on the series for the arctan(x) function given earlier in this section. Thus, e.g., using the fact that arctan(1) $= \pi/4$, one obtains the formula stated in Problem 1.2.12.

Using the fact that $\pi/4 = \arctan(\frac{1}{2}) + \arctan(\frac{1}{3})$ or the fact that $\pi/4 = 4\arctan(\frac{1}{5}) - \arctan(\frac{1}{239})$, write a program to find the value of π with 35 digits of accuracy.

Note: With the help of the above formulae, the value of π has been calculated with more than 100,000 digits of accuracy.

Problem 11.4.10 (*Accurate e*)

It is known from the theory of continued fractions that the number a given by $e = (1 + a)/(a - 1)$ has the continued fraction $a = [2,6,10,14,18, \ldots]$. Write a program based on this fact to compute the value of e to 100 decimal places of accuracy.

Hint: Calculate a fraction p/q that coincides with a up to 101 decimal places. It can be shown that by calculating

$$e = \frac{1 + (p/q)}{(p/q) - 1} = \frac{(p + q)/q}{(p - q)/q} = \frac{p + q}{p - q}$$

one does indeed obtain e up to 100 decimal places of accuracy.

Problem 11.4.11 (*nth Roots*)

Based on the fact that $\sqrt[n]{b} = e^{ln(b)/n}$, write a program to calculate $\sqrt[n]{b}$ for $b = 1, 1.5, 2, 2.5,$ and 3 and $n = 2, 3, 4, 5,$ and 6. For both the calculation of $\ln(x)$ and e^x, use the series given earlier in this section.

11.5 TRIANGLES

Problem 11.5.1 (*Triangle?*)

Given an integer n and n triples (a_i,b_i,c_i) $(i = 1, 2, \ldots, n)$ of positive numbers, write a program to determine for each triple (a_i,b_i,c_i) whether there exists a triangle with sides a_i, b_i, and c_i, respectively.

Hint: Three numbers a, b, and c are the sides of a triangle if and only if the sum of any two is larger than the third. This is the case if and only if $a + b + c > 2 \max(a,b,c)$.

Problem 11.5.2 (*Area, Version 1*)

Given an integer n and n triples (a_i,b_i,c_i) as in Problem 11.5.1, write a program to determine for each triple (a_i,b_i,c_i) the area of the triangle with sides a_i, b_i, and c_i.

Hint: If a, b, and c are the sides of a triangle, the area V of the triangle is given by $V = \sqrt{s(s - a)(s - b)(s - c)}$, where $s = (a + b + c)/2$.

Problem 11.5.3 (*Right Triangles*)

Write a program to determine all triangles with sides a, b, and c such that (a) a, b, and c are integers > 0; (b) the triangle has a right angle opposite side c; (c) $b = c - 1$; and (d) $c < 2000$.

Hint: Use the fact that for every such tringle $a^2 = 2c - 1$ and $a > 1$.

Problem 11.5.4 (*Line Segment*)

Given an integer n and the coordinates of n pairs of points (A_i, B_i) $(i = 1, 2, \ldots, n)$ in a rectangular coordinate system in the plane, write a program to determine the length of the line segment between A_i and B_i for every i.

Hint: The length of a line segment between a point with coordinates (x_1, y_1) and a point with coordinates (x_2, y_2) is given by

$$\sqrt{(x_1 - x_2)^2 + (y_1 - y_2)^2}.$$

Problem 11.5.5 (*Three-Dimensional Line Segment*)

Given an integer n and the coordinates of n pairs of points (A_i, B_i) $(i = 1, 2, \ldots, n)$ in a rectangular coordinate system in 3-space, write a program to determine the length of the line segment between A_i and B_i for every i.

Hint: A point in 3-space is given by a triple of numbers. The length of a line segment between a point with coordinates (x_1, y_1, z_1) and a point with coordinates (x_2, y_2, z_2) is given by $\sqrt{(x_1 - x_2)^2 + (y_1 - y_2)^2 + (z_1 - z_2)^2}$.

Problem 11.5.6 (*Area, Version 2*)

Given an integer n and the coordinates of n triples of points (A_i, B_i, C_i) $(i = 1, 2, \ldots, n)$ in a rectangular coordinate system in the plane, write a program to determine for every i the area of the triangle determined by the three points A_i, B_i, and C_i.

Hint: Calculate the three sides of the triangle using the formula given in Problem 11.5.4 and then proceed as in Problem 11.5.2.

Problem 11.5.7 (*Area, Version 3*)

Given an integer n and the coordinates of n triples of points (A_i, B_i, C_i) $(i = 1, 2, \ldots, n)$ in a rectangular coordinate system in 3-space, write a program to determine for every i the area of the triangle determined by the three points A_i, B_i, and C_i.

Hint: Calculate the three sides of the triangle using the formula given in Problem 11.5.5 and then proceed as in Problem 11.5.2.

Problem 11.5.8 (*Area, Version 4*)

Same as Problem 11.5.6 but use the fact known from analytic geometry that a triangle whose vertices have the coordinates (x_1, y_1), (x_2, y_2), and (x_3, y_3), respectively, has the area $\frac{1}{2} \operatorname{abs}(x_1 y_2 + x_2 y_3 + x_3 y_1 - x_2 y_1 - x_3 y_2 - x_1 y_3)$.

Problem 11.5.9 (*Area, Version 5*)

Same as Problem 11.5.7 but use the fact known from analytic geometry that a triangle whose vertices have the coordinates (x_1, y_1, z_1), (x_2, y_2, z_2), and

(x_3, y_3, z_3), respectively, has the area

$$\tfrac{1}{2}\sqrt{(a_2 b_3 - a_3 b_2)^2 + (a_3 b_1 - a_1 b_3)^2 + (a_1 b_2 - a_2 b_1)^2}$$

where $a_1 = x_2 - x_1$, $a_2 = y_2 - y_1$, and $a_3 = z_2 - z_1$ and where $b_1 = x_3 - x_1$, $b_2 = y_3 - y_1$, and $b_3 = z_3 - z_1$.

Problem 11.5.10 (*Law of Cosines*)

Given an integer n and n triples of numbers (a_i, b_i, γ_i) $(i = 1, 2, \ldots, n)$ representing triangles with sides a_i and b_i $(a_i, b_i > 0)$ and enclosed angle γ_i $(0 < \gamma_i < \pi)$, write a program to find for every i the missing side c_i.

Hint: Use the "law of cosines" $c_i = \sqrt{a_i^2 + b_i^2 - 2a_i b_i \cos(\gamma_i)}$.

Problem 11.5.11 (*Law of Sines*)

Given an integer n and n triples of numbers (a_i, β_i, γ_i) $(i = 1, 2, \ldots, n)$ representing triangles with sides a_i $(a_i > 0)$ and adjacent angles β_i and γ_i $(0 < \beta_i, \gamma_i < \pi/2)$, write a program to find the missing angle α_i and the missing sides b_i and c_i opposite the angles β_i and γ_i, respectively.

Hint: Use the fact that $\alpha_i = \pi - \beta_i - \gamma_i$ and the "law of sines"

$$c_i = \frac{a_i \sin(\gamma_i)}{\sin(\alpha_i)}, \quad b_i = \frac{a_i \sin(\beta_i)}{\sin(\alpha_i)}$$

Problem 11.5.12 (*Heights*)

Given an integer n and n triples (a_i, b_i, c_i) as in Problem 11.5.1, write a program to determine for each triple representing a triangle the shortest distance of each of the three vertices of the triangle from the opposite side of the triangle.

Hint: Let a triangle with vertices A, B, and C and area V have the sides a, b, and c (opposite to A, B, and C, respectively); then the distance of A from a is given by $2V/a$, where V can be calculated as in Problem 11.5.2.

11.6 SEARCHING

One of the most basic problems encountered in data processing is to locate a given item (e.g., account number, book title, value of a function) in a given collection of such items (e.g., a file of account numbers, a collection of book titles, a table of values of a function).

The problem can be formulated as follows: Given a collection of items $a_1, a_2, a_3, \ldots, a_n$ and a single item b, "locate" the item b in the collection; i.e., find that integer i (if it exists) for which $a_i = b$.

If the collection of items $a_1, a_2, \ldots, a_n$ is not ordered (not in ascending order, not in alphabetical order, etc.), the best one can do is to compare b one by one with $a_1, a_2, \ldots, a_n$ until a matching item is found or until the collection is exhausted. It will then take on the order of n steps to locate the given item b. If, however, the collection of items is ordered in some sense (e.g., in alphabetical or in ascending order), more efficient methods of locating a given item can be used, as outlined below. For the sake of simplicity it is assumed in the following that the collection of items $a_1, a_2, \ldots, a_n$ is a collection of numbers in ascending order and that the given item b is indeed in the collection. Suitable modifications can be made for other cases.

The best-known method for locating b under such conditions is the "interval halving method": The given number b is compared with a number a_m in the "middle" of the collection. If $b < a_m$, the search continues in the "left half" of the collection; if $b = a_m$, the search is completed; if $b > a_m$, the search continues in the "right half" of the collection. Since the size of the collection still to be searched is reduced at each step by a factor of 2, it will take on the order of $\log(n)$ steps to locate the given item b. A detailed algorithm follows.

Interval halving method for finding an integer i such that given a collection of numbers $a_1, a_2, \ldots, a_n$ in ascending order and a number b in this collection, $a_i = b$

Step 1. Let $l = 1$ and let $r = n$.

Step 2. Let $m = \text{floor}((l + r)/2)$.

Step 3. If $b = a_m$, then let $i = m$ and stop.

Step 4. If $b < a_m$, then let $r = m - 1$ and go to Step 2.

Step 5. Let $l = m + 1$ and go to Step 2.

The similarity of the method above with the interval halving method for finding the zeroes of functions in Chapter 6 is no coincidence. Let $a_1, a_2, \ldots, a_n$ be a collection of numbers in ascending order. Define a function $f(x)$ by $f(x) = a_t + (a_{t+1} - a_t)(x - t)$ for $t = \text{floor}(x)$. Note that $f(j) = a_j$ for $j = 1, 2, \ldots, n$. Let b be that number in the collection $a_1, a_2, \ldots, a_n$ to be located. The function $g(x) = f(x) - b$ is continuous and clearly $g(1) \leq 0$ and $g(n) \geq 0$. Thus the interval halving method of Chapter 6 can be used to find a value s for which $g(s) = f(s) - b = 0$. Now s must be an integer; hence $f(s) = a_s$. Thus $a_s = b$ as desired. It should be clear from the above that methods for finding a zero of a function can often be adapted to searching problems. It should also be noted that there is a close connection between some sorting and searching methods: As an example, the ideas developed in Method 8 (sorting by distribution) and Problem 7.2.6 of Chapter 7 can be used to construct highly efficient search algorithms.

Given a function $f(x)$ and two numbers a,b with $a < b$, a function $g(x)$ is called the "inverse" function of $f(x)$ for x between a and b if $g(f(x)) = x$ for every x between a and b. Thus $\ln(x)$ is the inverse function of e^x for every x since $\ln(e^x) = x$ for every x (see Section 11.4), $\sqrt{x}$ is the inverse function of x^2 for every $x \geq 0$ since $\sqrt{x^2} = x$ for $x \geq 0$, etc.

Consider a function $f(x)$ with an inverse function $g(x)$ and an arbitrary value y. The value of $g(y)$ can be calculated by finding a zero of the equation $f(x) - y = 0$ in one variable x according to methods discussed in Chapter 6. For if s is a zero of the equation $f(x) - y = 0$, i.e., if $f(s) - y = 0$, then $f(s) = y$; i.e., $g(f(s)) = g(y)$; i.e., $s = g(y)$.

A rough table of the inverse function $g(x)$ of a given function $f(x)$ can be obtained from a table of the function $f(x)$ by the method of "linear interpolation." Given values $x_1 < x_2 < \cdots < x_n$, a function $f(x)$ and the corresponding function values $b_1 = f(x_1)$, $b_2 = f(x_2), \ldots, b_n = f(x_n)$ with $b_1 < b_2 < b_3 \cdots < b_n$† and given values $y_1 < y_2 < \cdots < y_m$, with $b_1 \leq y_1$ and $y_m \leq b_n$, approximate values $c_1 = g(y_1), c_2 = g(y_2), \ldots, c_m = g(y_m)$ of the inverse function $g(x)$ of $f(x)$ can be found by the method of linear interpolation as follows:

Step 1. Let $j = 1$.

Step 2. If there exists an integer i with $b_i = y_j$, then let $c_j = x_i$ and go to Step 5.

Step 3. Determine an integer i such that $b_i < y_j < b_{i+1}$.

Step 4. Let $c_j = x_i + ((x_{i+1} - x_i)(y_j - b_i)/(b_{i+1} - b_i))$.

Step 5. If $j < m$, then let $j = j + 1$ and go to Step 2.

EXAMPLE

Consider the function $f(x) = x^2$ with the inverse function $g(x) = \sqrt{x}$. Given $x_1 = 20$, $x_2 = 21$, $x_3 = 22$, $x_4 = 23$, $b_1 = f(x_1) = 400$, $b_2 = f(x_2) = 441$, $b_3 = f(x_3) = 484$, and $b_4 = f(x_4) = 529$, approximate values of $c_1 = g(443) = \sqrt{443} = \sqrt{y_1}$, $c_2 = g(456) = \sqrt{456} = \sqrt{y_2}$, and $c_3 = g(489) = \sqrt{489} = \sqrt{y_3}$ can be obtained using the above algorithm. By Step 1, $j = 1$. Step 2 does not yield a result since no integer i with $f(x_i) = 443$ exists. By Step 3 one obtains $i = 2$ since $f(x_2) = 441 < 443 < f(x_3) = 484$. Thus Step 4 yields $c_1 = x_2 + ((x_3 - x_2)(y_1 - b_2)/(b_3 - b_2)) = 21 + \frac{2}{43} = 21.046. \ldots$ By Step 5, j is increased to 2 and the process is repeated, yielding $c_2 = 21.349 \ldots$ and $c_3 = 22.111 \ldots$ (For comparison, the exact values are $c_1 = 21.047563 \ldots$, $c_2 = 21.35415 \ldots$, and $c_3 = 22.11334 \ldots$)

Problem 11.6.1 (*Telephone Book*)

A telephone company has arranged its file of customers according to phone numbers. Each entry (record) of the file consists of a seven-digit phone number followed by a sequence of up to 40 characters representing name and address of the customer. Every day a number of requests are received for the name and address of a customer that corresponds to a phone number. Assume that both the customer file (in ascending order by phone

---

†The situation is similar for the case $b_1 > b_2 > \cdots > b_n$.

number) and the requests (consisting of just a phone number) are available on punched cards. Write a program that will determine for each request (i.e., phone number given) the name and address of the customer. Use interval halving for locating the phone number, and make sure to take care of phone numbers that have not been assigned to any customer. For simplicity assume that the customer file does not have more than 200 entries.

Problem 11.6.2 (*Key-Word Index, Version 3*)

A key-word index (see Problem 7.2.11) is available on punched cards. It is followed by a number of "request" cards, each containing a single key word. Write a program that will determine for each key word all titles in which the key word occurs. Use interval halving for locating the key words and make sure to take care of key words that do not occur in any title. For simplicity assume that the key-word index does not contain more than 200 entries.

Problem 11.6.3 (*Roots by Interpolation*)

Write a program to generate x^2 for $x = 1, 1.1, 1.2, \ldots, 29.9, 30$ and then use linear interpolation to calculate approximate values of $\sqrt{1}, \sqrt{2}, \ldots, \sqrt{900}$.

Problem 11.6.4 (ln(*x*) *by Interpolation*)

Write a program to generate e^x for $x = 0, 0.01, 0.02, \ldots, 0.99, 1$ and then use linear interpolation to calculate approximate values for $\ln(1)$, $\ln(1.1), \ldots, \ln(2.7)$.

Problem 11.6.5 (arcsin(*x*))

The inverse function of $\sin(x)$ is usually called $\arcsin(x)$; i.e., $\arcsin(a)$ is that angle α (in radians) with $\sin(\alpha) = a$. Write a program to generate $\sin(x)$ for $x = 0, 0.01, 0.02, \ldots, 1.57$ and then use linear interpolation to calculate $\arcsin(0)$, $\arcsin(.01), \ldots, \arcsin(0.99)$.

Problem 11.6.6 (*Law of Sines and Cosines*)

Given an integer n and n triples of numbers (a_i, b_i, β_i) $(i = 1, 2, \ldots, n)$ representing triangles with sides a_i and b_i $(a_i, b_i > 0)$ and angle β_i $(0 < \beta_i < \pi/2)$ opposite b_i, find the missing angles α_i $(0 < \alpha_i < \pi/2)$ and γ_i $(\alpha_i$ opposite $a_i)$ and the missing side c_i.

Hint: Use the "law of sines" $\alpha_i = \arcsin((a_i \sin(\beta_i))/b_i)$ and calculate α_i by finding a zero of the equation $\sin(x) - (a_i \sin(\beta_i))/b_i = 0$ using the interval halving method of Chapter 6. Then calculate γ_i using $\gamma_i = \pi - \alpha_i - \beta_i$ and calculate c_i using the "law of cosines" as explained in Problem 11.5.10.

Problem 11.6.7 *(Three Angles)*

Given an integer n and n triples (a_i, b_i, c_i) as in Problem 11.5.1, determine for each triangle with sides a_i, b_i, and c_i the angle α_i opposite side a_i, β_i opposite b_i, and γ_i opposite c_i.

Hint: Use the "law of cosines" $\gamma_i = \arccos((a_i^2 + b_i^2 - c_i^2)/2a_i b_i)$, $\beta_i = \arccos((a_i^2 + c_i^2 - b_i^2)/2a_i c_i)$, and $\alpha_i = \pi - \beta_i - \gamma_i$ and calculate $\arccos(x)$, the inverse function of $\cos(x)$, similar to $\arcsin(x)$ in Problem 11.6.6.

11.7 NUMERICAL INTEGRATION

A basic problem in mathematics is to determine for a given function $f(x)$ and two numbers a and b $(a < b)$ the area bounded by the graph of the function $f(x)$, by the x-axis of the coordinate system and two lines parallel to the $f(x)$-axis with a distance of a units and b units, respectively, from the $f(x)$-axis. This area is shaded in Fig. 11-5. The area determined in this manner is usually denoted by $\int_a^b f(x)\,dx$. It is read as either "the area determined by $f(x)$ between a and b" or "the definite integral of $f(x)$ from a to b."

For some functions $f(x)$ methods derived in calculus allow the calculation of a function $g(x)$ such that $\int_a^b f(x)\,dx = g(b) - g(a)$ for every choice of a and b. In all cases where it is impossible or difficult to find such a function $g(x)$ one can still calculate an approximate value of $\int_a^b f(x)\,dx$ by dividing the area into small pieces whose area can be approximately calculated.

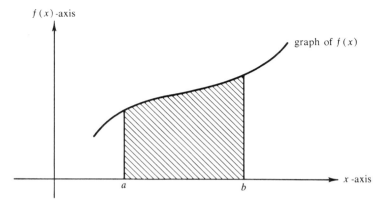

Figure 11-5

In the following discussion $f(x)$ is assumed to be both continuous (see Chapter 6) and nonnegative.

Given a function $f(x)$ and two values $a < b$, the area $\int_a^b f(x)\, dx$ can be found approximately by dividing it into strips of equal width and approximating the area of each strip by a rectangle, as indicated in Fig. 11-6. Dividing the area into n strips (four in Fig. 11-6) as shown in Fig. 11-6 and using the area of the n rectangles as approximation A of $\int_a^b f(x)\, dx$, one obtains the "rectangle formula":

$$A = c(f(a) + f(a + c) + f(a + 2c) + \cdots + f(a + (n - 1)c))$$

where

$$c = \frac{b - a}{n}$$

It is easily seen that $\mathrm{abs}\left(\int_a^b f(x)\, dx - A\right) < c\,\mathrm{abs}(f(b) - f(a))$ if $f(x)$ is either steadily increasing or decreasing between a and b.

Similarly one can obtain the "trapezoidal formula"

$$A = \frac{c}{2}(f(a) + 2f(a + c) + 2f(a + 2c) + \cdots + 2f(a + (n - 1)c) + f(b))$$

with

$$\mathrm{abs}\left(\int_a^b f(x)\, dx - A\right) \le \frac{c^2(b - a)g_2}{6}$$

the "tangent formula"

$$A = c\left(f\left(a + \frac{c}{2}\right) + f\left(a + c + \frac{c}{2}\right) + \cdots + f\left(a + (n - 1)c + \frac{c}{2}\right)\right)$$

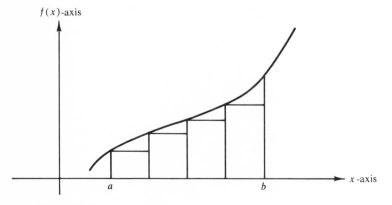

Figure 11-6

with

$$\text{abs}\left(\int_a^b f(x)\,dx - A\right) \le \frac{c^2(b-a)g_2}{24}$$

and "Simpson's formula"

$$A = \frac{c}{6}\left(f(a) + 4f\left(a + \frac{c}{2}\right) + 2f(a + c) + 4f\left(a + c + \frac{c}{2}\right) + 2f(a + 2c)\right.$$

$$\left. + \cdots + 2f(a + (n-1)c) + 4f\left(a + (n-1)c + \frac{c}{2}\right) + f(b)\right)$$

with

$$\text{abs}\left(\int_a^b f(x)\,dx - A\right) \le \frac{c^4(b-a)g_4}{720}$$

In the above, g_2 is a number such that $\text{abs}(f''(x)) \le g_2$ for every x between a and b and g_4 is a number such that $\text{abs}(f^{iv}(x)) \le g_4$ for every x between a and b, where $f''(x)$ and $f^{iv}(x)$ are the second derivative† and fourth derivative, respectively, of $f(x)$.

Problem 11.7.1 (*Rectangle Formula*)

Write a program to determine $\int_4^t ((\sqrt{x+1} + x^2)/\sqrt{x^3 - 1})\,dx$ for $t = 5, 6, 7, \ldots, 15$ with two decimal places of accuracy using the rectangle formula.

Hint: $f(x) = (\sqrt{x+1} + x^2)/\sqrt{x^3 - 1}$ increases steadily between 4 and 15, $f(4) = 2.297528.\ldots, f(15) = 3.942420.\ldots$

Problem 11.7.2 (*Comparison, Version 1*)

Write a program to determine approximate values for $\int_0^1 (x^3 + 2x^2)\,dx$ using the rectangle formula, the trapezoidal formula, the tangent formula, and Simpson's formula by dividing the area into $n = 2, 10, 20$, and 50 strips.

Problem 11.7.3 (*Comparison, Version 2*)

For $t = 0.2, 0.4, 0.6, 0.8$, and 1, write a program to determine $\int_0^t e^{(x^2)}\,dx$ using the method and accuracy indicated: (a) rectangle formula, two decimal places; (b) trapezoidal formula, four decimal places, $g_2 = 20$; (c) tangent formula, four decimal places, $g_2 = 20$; and (d) Simpson's formula, eight decimal places, $g_4 = 120$.

Problem 11.7.4 (*Simpson's Formula*)

Write a program to determine $\int_2^8 x(4 + x^2)^{-1/3}\,dx$ by Simpson's formula, dividing the area into 10, 20, 30, $\ldots$, 80 strips.

†See any book on calculus.

Problem 11.7.5 (*Trapezoidal Formula*)

It is known from calculus that $\int_0^t (1/(1 + x^2))\, dx = \arctan(t)$. Write a program to determine $\arctan(t)$ for $t = 0.2, 0.4, 0.6, 0.8,$ and 1 by the trapezoidal formula choosing $n = 1000$.

Problem 11.7.6 (*Logarithm*)

It is known from calculus that $\int_1^t (1/x)\, dx = \ln(t)$. Write a program to determine $\ln(2)$, $\ln(2.5)$, and $\ln(3)$ by the trapezoidal formula choosing $n = 500$.

Problem 11.7.7 (Pi, *Version 7*)

Write a program to determine π to three decimals using numerical integration and the rectangle formula.

Hint: The quartercircle with radius 1 in Fig. 11-7 is the graph of the function $f(x) = \sqrt{1 - x^2}$. Thus the shaded area is given by $\int_0^1 \sqrt{1 - x^2}\, dx$. Since the area of a quartercircle with radius 1 is $\pi/4$, one obtains $\pi = 4 \int_0^1 \sqrt{1 - x^2}\, dx$.

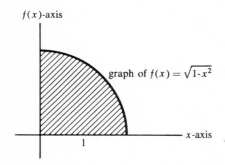

f(x)-axis

graph of $f(x) = \sqrt{1-x^2}$

x-axis

1

Figure 11-7

Problem 11.7.8 (Pi, *Version 8*)

Write a program to determine π to eight decimal places by numerical integration and Simpson's formula.

Hint: The method of Problem 11.7.7 has to be modified since no value g_4 with $\text{abs}(f^{iv}(x)) \leq g_4$ for x between 0 and 1 can be found. However, the shaded area A in Fig. 11-8 is given by $2\left(\int_0^{\sqrt{2}/2} \sqrt{1 - x^2}\, dx\right) - 1$ and thus $\pi = 8 \int_0^{\sqrt{2}/2} \sqrt{1 - x^2}\, dx - 2$. A somewhat tedious calculation shows that g_4

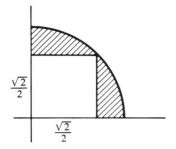

$\dfrac{\sqrt{2}}{2}$

$\dfrac{\sqrt{2}}{2}$

Figure 11-8

$= 120$ can be used between 0 and $\sqrt{2}/2$. To calculate π to eight decimal places it suffices to calculate $\int_{0}^{\sqrt{2}/2} \sqrt{1 - x^2}\, dx$ to nine decimal places. Using $g_4 = 120$, it is easy to see that Simpson's formula for $n = 100$ will give the desired accuracy.

12

STATISTICS

12.1 ELEMENTARY COMPUTATIONS

If you are given a large table of data, it is almost impossible to extract the relevant facts from this table without some knowledge of statistics. This chapter will not attempt to present a course in statistics, but rather concentrate on the computational problems arising from statistics. Statistical tables such as

Heights of University of Alberta First-Year Male Students 1946–1958

Height (to nearest inch)	Frequency	Height (to nearest inch)	Frequency
56	2	68	311
57	0	69	317
58	0	70	332
59	1	71	280
60	1	72	228
61	3	73	135
62	4	74	74
63	16	75	26
64	35	76	16
65	70	77	4
66	154	78	1
67	203		2213

are easy to follow, but they tell only the bare facts about the first-year students and leave the reader to draw his own conclusions. In the following, entries in such a table will be denoted by $x_1, x_2, x_3, x_4, \ldots, x_n$. For the above table x_1 is the height of the first man (i.e., 56 inches), x_2 is the height of the second man (i.e., 56 inches), x_3 is the height of the third man (i.e., 59 inches), etc.

The first question that normally arises out of such a table of measurements is "what is the average height of the first-year male student?" There are essentially two different methods of finding this out. The first is to line up all the 2213 men in order of height and then take the man in the middle (i.e., man 1107). His height is known as the "median" height:

$$\text{Median} = \begin{cases} x_{(n+1)/2} & \text{if } n \text{ is odd} \\ \dfrac{x_{n/2} + x_{(n/2)+1}}{2} & \text{if } n \text{ is even} \end{cases}$$

The median is a very useful item of information and, in most cases, can be found by hand because there is little computation involved. On the other hand, the median does not consider the heights of any but the middleman in the sequence and, if the population happened to contain a large number of midgets or giants, may not accurately reflect the height that is most common. For this reason the measure that is most widely used for the average height is the "mean." The mean, which is usually denoted by $\bar{x}$, is given by

$$\bar{x} = \frac{x_1 + x_2 + x_3 + \cdots + x_n}{n}$$

The mean will tell something about the data under consideration but it will not tell anything about how wide the distribution is in the population. For example, if the population included some midgets and giants, then the distribution of heights would be over a wide range; on the other hand, if the population consisted of people who were only 1 or 2 inches above or below the average, then the distribution would be narrow. One elementary measure of distribution is the "range" of heights (i.e., the difference between the smallest and largest person in the population). However, this is not a good indication of the distribution because the inclusion of one midget or one giant can cause drastic changes in the range.

One reasonable measure of distribution is to compute the distance, or "deviation," of each individual from the average, and then find the average of these distances. This "average deviation" from the mean is acceptable as a measure of deviation within the group under consideration. If the purpose of the statistics is just to study a small group, then the average deviation is sufficient; the purpose of most statistical surveys is, however, to inquire about the properties of a small sample of the population and then to use this to make predictions about the population as a whole. Because of taking only a small sample, it is necessary to weight the deviations falling at extreme distances from the mean more than deviations close to the mean.

This gives another measure of deviation called the "standard deviation," which is generally denoted by the Greek letter σ (sigma):

$$\sigma = \sqrt{\frac{(\bar{x} - x_1)^2 + (\bar{x} - x_2)^2 + (\bar{x} - x_3)^2 + \cdots + (\bar{x} - x_n)^2}{n}}$$

Average deviation

$$= \frac{\text{abs}(\bar{x} - a_1) + \text{abs}(\bar{x} - a_2) + \text{abs}(\bar{x} - a_3) + \cdots + \text{abs}(\bar{x} - a_n)}{n}$$

At times it is necessary to answer questions such as

Do men vary in height more than women?

Do men vary in weight more than women?

Do men vary in weight more than elephants?

Do men vary in height more than in weight?

To compare variations between two populations of items, it is possible to compute a "coefficient of variation," which is $\sigma/\bar{x}$. If population 1 has a greater coefficient of variation than population 2, then population 1 varies more than population 2.

Another fact that is useful to know is if this distribution about the mean is "even" or if it is a "skew" distribution. For example, if there were more tall people than short people, then it would be nice to find that this situation existed. This can be done by calculating a number known as "Pearson's measure of skewness":

$$\text{Skewness} = \frac{3(\text{mean} - \text{median})}{\sigma}$$

If the skewness is a positive number, then it indicates that there were a large number of tall people (i.e., the mean was greater than the median); and if the skewness is negative, then there were a larger number of short people in our sample.

Problem 12.1.1 *(Average)*

Write a program to read in data, such as in the table given above, and compute the median and mean of the population.

Problem 12.1.2 *(Deviation)*

Write a program that will read in data, such as the table of heights above, and then compute the mean, range, average deviation, and standard deviation of the items.

Problem 12.1.3 *(Coefficient of Variation)*

Write a program to compute means, standard deviations, and coefficients of variation from statistical tables. Use this program to investigate variation among several different populations.

Problem 12.1.4 (*Skewness*)

Write a program to produce, from a statistical table, the median, mean, standard deviation, and skewness of a population.

Problem 12.1.5 (*Authorship*)

The study of ancient literature often involves attempting to determine whether a piece of prose was written by person A or B. For example, it is often thought that Bacon may have written some of the plays attributed to Shakespeare or that St. Paul was not the author of all the epistles attributed to him. It has been observed that, after reaching maturity, the literary style of an author does not change substantially with passing years. It is very difficult to discuss something as subtle as literary style with any exactness, so students of literature have resorted to some simple statistical tests to help them determine authorship. The early Greek versions of the epistles of St. Paul have been subjected to very intensive study. It seems that Paul only wrote a few and that the others should be attributed to several early Christian leaders.

Some very simple statistical tests will easily show style differences between authors. For example, the number of letters in each word is very characteristic of certain authors. The average word length, standard deviation of word length, and skewness for one author may differ considerably from the same quantities for a different author. The same may be true for the number of words in each sentence.

This book has two authors. Write a program that will read at least one page of text from each of Chapters 1, 2, 7, and 12 and apply the statistical tests to word length and sentence length. From the results, attempt to determine which chapters were written by the same author.

Problem 12.1.6 (*Random Test, Version 1*)

Write a program to generate 1000 random integers between 1 and 50 (see Chapter 8) and count how many times each number occurs. From this table the program should determine the average random number, the standard deviation, and the skewness. More will be said about tests for randomness later.

12.2 OTHER STATISTICAL COMPUTATIONS

One of the most useful tests in statistical theory is called the χ^2 test (pronounced "chi-square," where chi rhymes with eye). This test is used to determine if the frequency of occurrence of some item differs significantly from what might have been expected in theory.

$$\chi^2 = \frac{(F_1 - T_1)^2}{F_1} + \frac{(F_2 - T_2)^2}{F_2} + \frac{(F_3 - T_3)^2}{F_3} \cdots$$

where F_i is the frequency of occurrence of the ith item (e.g., the number of men of a certain height) and T_i is the number that should have occurred according to theory.

Take a very simple example. Assume that a coin is thrown 100 times and that heads occurs 35 times and tails 65 times. In theory, each should have occurred 50 times. If the test had gone according to theory, then the value of χ^2 should be zero; however,

$$\chi^2 = \frac{(35 - 50)^2}{35} + \frac{(65 - 50)^2}{65}$$

$$= \frac{225}{35} + \frac{225}{65}$$

$$= 6.42 + 3.46 = 9.88$$

Before finding what is meant by $\chi^2 = 9.88$, it is necessary to discuss the notion of "degrees of freedom." In tossing a coin 100 times it is necessary only to know that heads occurred 35 times to have all the information about the test. The number of times tails came up is just $100 - 35$. Once the frequency of occurrence of one item is known, the other is fixed. Thus tossing a coin is known as having one degree of freedom. When throwing a six-sided die, it is only necessary to know how often a 1, a 2, a 3, a 4, and a 5 have come up to calculate the number of times a 6 must have come up. Thus a die has five degrees of freedom. In general, if there are n possible outcomes of an experiment, then the experiment has $n - 1$ degrees of freedom.

An examination of the χ^2 graph in Fig. 12-1 shows that a situation having

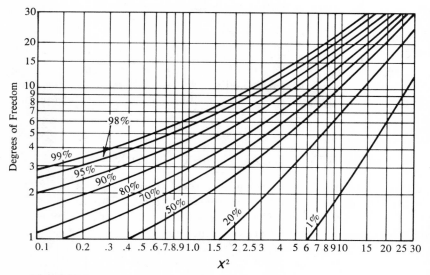

Figure 12-1

one degree of freedom and a χ^2 value of 9.88 has less than 1% chance of occurring by accident. Thus the coin is likely to have been biased.

When given a table of statistical data it is often the case that it is incomplete. For example, 20 salesmen were given intelligence tests and the results of these tests were recorded with their sales records as follows:

Test scores:	40	70	50	60	80	50	90	40	60	60
Sales:	25	60	45	50	45	20	55	30	45	30

Test scores:	55	70	40	35	85	60	58	76	42	75
Sales:	47	62	27	25	62	42	40	52	27	53

If one now wishes to determine how many sales should be expected from a salesman scoring 72 on his tests, a method must be found to "interpolate" between the values for 70 and 75 that are found in the table. It is always possible to construct a "scattergram" of the data and try to find a straight line $y = a + bx$ that best approximates the situation and then read off the expected sales from this straight line.

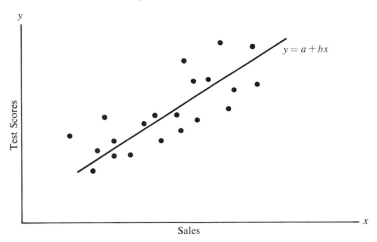

It is not always obvious what values of a and b will give the line that best fits the observed data. It is known that the coefficients a and b can be calculated according to the formula

$$Sxy = x_1 y_1 + x_2 y_2 + x_3 y_3 + \cdots + x_n y_n$$
$$Sx = x_1 + x_2 + x_3 + \cdots + x_n$$
$$Sy = y_1 + y_2 + y_3 + \cdots + y_n$$
$$SSx = x_1^2 + x_2^2 + x_3^2 + \cdots + x_n^2$$
$$b = \frac{n(Sxy) - (Sx)(Sy)}{n(SSx) - (Sx)^2}$$
$$a = \frac{Sy}{n} - b\left(\frac{Sx}{n}\right)$$

Not only is it interesting to note the nature of the relationship between two items (e.g., intelligence scores and sales ability), but it is often essential to know if it is a strong relationship. If the scores on an intelligence test were strongly "correlated" to sales ability, then there is no point in hiring someone to sell a product unless he scores well on the intelligence test. On the other hand, if the correlation is weak, then someone who scored only 30 on the intelligence test may be able to outsell a person who scored 70.

It is possible to define a "correlation coefficient"

$$r = \frac{n \cdot Sxy - Sx \cdot Sy}{\sqrt{n \cdot SSx - (Sx)^2} \sqrt{n \cdot SSy - (Sy)^2}}$$

where Sxy, Sx, Sy, and SSx are the same as defined previously and

$$SSy = y_1^2 + y_2^2 + y_3^2 + \cdots + y_n^2$$

n = number of observations

If r is close to $+1$ or -1, then there is a very strong correlation between x and y; if r is close to 0, then there is a very weak correlation of x and y.

Problem 12.2.1 (*Random Test, Version 2*)

The χ^2 test makes an excellent test for randomness of a series of random numbers. Write a program to generate 1000 random integers between 1 and 10 (see Chapter 8). If the random number generator is uniform, then, in theory, it will give the value 1 100 times, the value 2 100 times, etc. The whole process has nine degrees of freedom. The program should calculate and print the value of χ^2 and the graph of χ^2 should be consulted to determine if this particular distribution of random numbers could have occurred by accident. If the value, found from the χ^2 graph, is over 90%, then it is a good random number generator.

Problem 12.2.2 (*Serial Correlation*)

The χ^2 test used in Problem 12.2.1 provides a test to determine if the numbers are distributed according to theory. The test does not indicate if there is anything amiss with the order in which the numbers are produced. A random number generator may produce a good distribution but have a very bad "serial correlation." Write a program using random numbers (see Chapter 8) to simulate 501 throws of a five-sided die. For each pair (x,y) with $1 \leq x,y \leq 5$, determine how often the program simulated the occurrence of the number x followed by the occurrence of the number y. The theoretically expected value is 20 for each pair (x,y). Calculate the value of χ^2 and determine if the random number generator has a good serial correlation. (There are 24 degrees of freedom.)

Problem 12.2.3 (*Serial Correlation, Version 2*)

Write a program using random numbers to simulate 542 throws of a three-sided die. For each triple (x,y,z) with $1 \leq x,y,z \leq 3$, determine how often a run of x,y,z has occurred. The theoretically expected value is 20. Calculate the value of χ^2 and thus determine the effectiveness of the serial correlation in groups of three. (There are 26 degrees of freedom.)

Problem 12.2.4 (*Random Test, Version 3*)

Write a program to produce several different sets of 1000 random numbers. Each set should be produced by a different random number generator or by the same generator using different numbers to start the process (see Chapter 8). The program should compute the χ^2 value for each set and then indicate which set is the best (i.e., has the lowest χ^2 value). (See Problem 12.2.1.)

Problem 12.2.5 (*Biased Coins*)

Seven coins were tossed 1280 times and the observed frequency of the number of heads were noted after each step. The results of the experiment were as follows:

Number of heads	0	1	2	3	4	5	6	7
Observed frequency	10	61	198	335	363	219	79	15
Theoretically expected	10	70	210	350	350	210	70	10

Write a program to calculate χ^2 from this set of data and then compare the value obtained to the graph of χ^2 to determine if the seven coins were more than 1% biased.

Problem 12.2.6 (*Intelligent Salesman*)

Determine the equation of the straight line that best fits the data given for salesmen in the introduction to this section. Use this equation to print out a table of scores in the intelligence test and expected number of sales for each value of intelligence test scores from 30 to 100.

Problem 12.2.7 (*Chi-Square Test*)

Assuming that there is a direct relationship between intelligence and sales ability, write a program to compute a value for χ^2 using the actual observed results and the results predicted by the straight line obtained in Problem 12.2.6.

Problem 12.2.8 (*Correlation Coefficient*)

Write a program to find the correlation coefficient for the scores on the intelligence test and sales ability for the data given in the introduction to this section.

13

SYSTEMS OF LINEAR EQUATIONS

13.1 INTRODUCTION

A system of n linear equations in n variables $x_1, x_2, x_3, \ldots, x_n$ is of the form

$$
\begin{aligned}
a_{11}x_1 + a_{12}x_2 + a_{13}x_3 + \cdots + a_{1n}x_n &= b_1 \\
a_{21}x_1 + a_{22}x_2 + a_{23}x_3 + \cdots + a_{2n}x_n &= b_2 \\
&\ \vdots \\
a_{n1}x_1 + a_{n2}x_2 + a_{n3}x_3 + \cdots + a_{nn}x_n &= b_n
\end{aligned}
\tag{1}
$$

where the a_{ij}'s and b_i's ($1 \leq i \leq n$, $1 \leq j \leq n$) are real numbers. The problem to be considered in this chapter is to find values $s_1, s_2, \ldots, s_n$ such that

$$
\begin{aligned}
a_{11}s_1 + a_{12}s_2 + \cdots + a_{1n}s_n &= b_1 \\
a_{21}s_1 + a_{22}s_2 + \cdots + a_{2n}s_n &= b_2 \\
&\ \vdots \\
a_{n1}s_1 + a_{n2}s_2 + \cdots + a_{nn}s_n &= b_n
\end{aligned}
$$

Such an n-tuple of values $(s_1, s_2, \ldots, s_n)$ is called a "solution" of the given system of equations.

To start with, consider the following three systems of three linear equations in three variables x_1, x_2, x_3:

$$\left.\begin{array}{l} 3x_1 + 7x_2 - x_3 = 7 \\ x_1 + 3x_2 + 3x_3 = 1 \\ 2x_1 + 5x_2 + x_3 = 4 \end{array}\right\} \quad (2)$$

$$\left.\begin{array}{l} 3x_1 + 7x_2 - x_3 = 7 \\ x_1 + 3x_2 + 3x_3 = 1 \\ 2x_1 + 5x_2 + x_3 = 5 \end{array}\right\} \quad (3)$$

$$\left.\begin{array}{l} x_1 + 2x_2 - x_3 = 1 \\ -x_1 + 3x_2 + 2x_3 = -1 \\ x_1 + 11x_2 + x_3 = 3 \end{array}\right\} \quad (4)$$

Consider first system (2). The third equation is obtained by adding one half of the first equation and one half of the second equation. Thus the third equation does not provide additional information and the solutions of (2) must be the same as the solutions of

$$\begin{array}{l} 3x_1 + 7x_2 - x_3 = 7 \\ x_1 + 3x_2 + 3x_3 = 1 \end{array} \quad (2')$$

It is now easy to see that for every number t, $s_1 = 12t + 7$, $s_2 = -5t - 2$, and $s_3 = t$ are a solution of (2') and therefore of (2). Indeed, $3(12t + 7) + 7(-5t - 2) - t = 7$, $(12t + 7) + 3(-5t - 2) + 3t = 1$, and $2(12t + 7) + 5(-5t - 2) + t = 4$. Thus system (2) has infinitely many solutions.

Consider now system (3). By adding one half of the first and one half of the second equations one obtains $2x_1 + 5x_2 + x_3 = 4$. This is in contradiction to the third equation of system (3): $2x_1 + 5x_2 + x_3 = 5$. For no choice of x_1, x_2, or x_3 can both equations be satisfied. Thus system (3) has no solution at all.

Consider finally system (4). By adding the first equation to the second equation and subtracting the first equation from the third equation, one obtains a system evidently having the same solutions as (4):

$$\begin{array}{l} x_1 + 2x_2 - x_3 = 1 \\ 5x_2 + x_3 = 0 \\ 9x_2 + 2x_3 = 2 \end{array} \quad (4')$$

Now one can add 9 times the second equation of (4') to -5 times the third equation of (4'), obtaining a system with still the same solutions as (4):

$$\begin{array}{l} x_1 + 2x_2 - x_3 = 1 \\ 5x_2 + x_3 = 0 \\ - x_3 = -10 \end{array} \quad (4'')$$

But (4″) has clearly exactly one solution, namely, $s_3 = 10$, $s_2 = -2$, and $s_1 = 15$. This must be the only solution of (4) and thus system (4) has exactly one solution.

The three examples given above are typical of the general situation. It is indeed known from linear algebra that, given a system of n equations in n variables, three situations are possible:

Situation 1. The given system has infinitely many solutions. This occurs if the following two conditions (a) and (b) are satisfied: (a) One of the equations of the system can be obtained by adding up multiples of other equations of the system and (b) if by adding up multiples of equations of the system, an equation A can be obtained whose left-hand side is equal to the left-hand side of an equation B of the system, then the right-hand sides of A and B are also the same.

Situation 2. The given system has no solutions. This occurs if by adding up multiples of equations of the system, an equation A can be obtained whose left-hand side is equal to the left-hand side of an equation B of the system, but the right-hand sides of A and B are different.

Situation 3. The given system has exactly one (a "unique") solution. This is the case if the left-hand side of no equation of the system can be obtained by adding up multiples of left-hand sides of other equations of the system.

When solving a system of linear equations related to some practical problem one generally encounters Situation 3. Therefore it is the aim of this chapter to discuss methods that allow the determination, given a system of linear equations, of whether that system has a unique solution and if so, allow the determination of a solution or approximate solution of the system.

There are essentially three types of methods available for doing this: (a) methods using elimination of variables, (b) methods using determinants, and (c) iterative methods. In what follows one prominent representative for each type of method will be discussed.

13.2 GAUSSIAN ELIMINATION

One of the most efficient methods for solving a system of linear equations is the "Gaussian elimination." It rests on the fact that given a system of n linear equations in n variables

$$
\begin{aligned}
a_{11}x_1 + a_{12}x_2 + \cdots + a_{1n}x_n &= b_1 \\
a_{21}x_1 + a_{22}x_2 + \cdots + a_{2n}x_n &= b_2 \\
&\vdots \\
a_{n1}x_1 + a_{n2}x_2 + \cdots + a_{nn}x_n &= b_n
\end{aligned}
\tag{5}
$$

a "triangular" system

$$c_{11}x_1 + c_{12}x_2 + \cdots + c_{1n}x_n = d_1$$
$$c_{22}x_2 + \cdots + c_{2n}x_n = d_2$$
$$\cdot \qquad \cdot \qquad \cdot \qquad \qquad \qquad (6)$$
$$\cdot \qquad \cdot$$
$$\cdot \qquad \cdot$$
$$c_{nn}x_n = d_n$$

with $c_{11} \neq 0$, $c_{22} \neq 0$, ..., $c_{nn} \neq 0$, can be found that has the same solution as (5) provided that (5) has a unique solution. It clearly is easy to determine the solution of a system of the form (6).

To obtain a system of the form (6) from a given system of the form (5) one repeatedly uses a process that, given a system with, say, m equations in m variables,

$$e_{11}x_1 + e_{12}x_2 + \cdots + e_{1m}x_m = f_1$$
$$e_{21}x_1 + e_{22}x_2 + \cdots + e_{2m}x_m = f_2$$
$$\cdot \qquad \cdot \qquad \qquad \cdot \qquad \cdot$$
$$\cdot \qquad \cdot \qquad \qquad \cdot \qquad \cdot \qquad (7)$$
$$\cdot \qquad \cdot \qquad \qquad \cdot \qquad \cdot$$
$$e_{m1}x_1 + e_{m2}x_2 + \cdots + e_{mm}x_m = f_m$$

produces a system

$$g_{11}x_1 + g_{12}x_2 + g_{13}x_3 + \cdots + g_{1m}x_m = h_1$$
$$g_{22}x_2 + g_{23}x_3 + \cdots + g_{2m}x_m = h_2$$
$$\cdot \qquad \cdot \qquad \qquad \cdot \qquad \cdot$$
$$\cdot \qquad \cdot \qquad \qquad \cdot \qquad \cdot \qquad (8)$$
$$\cdot \qquad \cdot \qquad \qquad \cdot \qquad \cdot$$
$$g_{m2}x_2 + g_{m3}x_3 + \cdots + g_{mm}x_m = h_m$$

consisting of a single equation in m variables and a system of $m - 1$ linear equations in $m - 1$ variables such that $g_{11} \neq 0$ and system (8) has the same solution as system (7). The crucial transition from system (7) to system (8) is performed as follows:

Step 1. Reorder the equations in system (7) to a system

$$g_{11}x_1 + g_{12}x_2 + \cdots + g_{1m}x_m = h_1$$
$$i_{21}x_1 + i_{22}x_2 + \cdots + i_{2m}x_m = j_2$$
$$i_{31}x_1 + i_{32}x_2 + \cdots + i_{3m}x_m = j_3$$
$$\cdot \qquad \cdot \qquad \qquad \cdot \qquad \cdot$$
$$\cdot \qquad \cdot \qquad \qquad \cdot \qquad \cdot \qquad (9)$$
$$\cdot \qquad \cdot \qquad \qquad \cdot \qquad \cdot$$
$$i_{m1}x_1 + i_{m2}x_2 + \cdots + i_{mm}x_m = j_m$$

such that $g_{11} = \max(\text{abs}(e_{11}), \text{abs}(e_{21}), \text{abs}(e_{31}), \ldots, \text{abs}(e_{m1}))$, i.e., such that the first number in the first equation is the largest number in absolute value of all numbers occuring as first number in any equation.

Step 2. If the first number in the first equation (i.e., g_{11}) is zero, then stop. *Note:* In this case the original system has no unique solution.

Step 3. For $k = 2, 3, 4, \ldots, m$, replace the kth equation by subtracting from it c times the first equation, where $c = i_{k1}/g_{11}$. *Note:* i_{k1} is the first number in the kth equation; g_{11} is the first number in the first equation.

To illustrate Gaussian elimination as described it is now applied to system (4)

$$x_1 + 2x_2 - x_3 = 1$$
$$-x_1 + 3x_2 + 2x_3 = -1$$
$$x_1 + 11x_2 + x_3 = 3$$

by tracing the method step by step.

Applying Step 1: No reordering is necessary. Applying Step 2: The first number in the first equation is 1, i.e., not equal to zero; thus the process can be continued. Applying Step 3: The second equation is to be replaced by subtracting from it $c = (-1)/1 = -1$ times the first equation, i.e., by adding the first equation; the third equation is to be replaced by subtracting from it $c = {}^1/_1 = 1$ times the first equation. Thus one obtains

$$x_1 + 2x_2 - x_3 = 1$$
$$5x_2 + x_3 = 0$$
$$9x_2 + 2x_3 = 2$$

Now the process described by Steps 1–3 has to be applied again to the system

$$5x_2 + x_3 = 0$$
$$9x_2 + 2x_3 = 2$$

Applying Step 1: Reordering is necessary and yields

$$9x_2 + 2x_3 = 2$$
$$5x_2 + x_3 = 0$$

Applying Step 2: The first number in the first equation is 9, i.e., not equal to zero; thus the process can be continued. Applying Step 3: The second equation is to be replaced by subtracting from it $c = \frac{5}{9}$ times the first equation. Thus one obtains

$$9x_2 + 2x_3 = 2$$
$$-\tfrac{1}{9}x_3 = -\tfrac{10}{9}$$

In total one has obtained

$$x_1 + 2x_2 - x_3 = 1$$
$$9x_2 + 2x_3 = 2$$
$$-\tfrac{1}{9}x_3 = -\tfrac{10}{9}$$

which is of the desired form (6). The solution $s_3 = 10$, $s_2 = -2$, and $s_1 = 15$ is now obtained readily.

Gaussian elimination will always transform a system of the form (5) successfully into a system of the form (6) if system (5) has a unique solution. If the original system (5) has no unique solution, Gaussian elimination breaks down for one of two reasons: (a) Either a zero is encountered in Step 2 of the algorithm given above or (b) when the final system (6) is obtained the left-hand side of the last equation (i.e., c_{nn}) is zero. Case (a) is illustrated by, e.g.,

$$2x_1 + 3x_2 - x_3 = 5$$
$$4x_1 + 6x_2 - x_3 = 9$$
$$-2x_1 - 3x_2 + 5x_3 = -5$$

Case (b) is illustrated by, e.g.,

$$-x_1 - x_2 - x_3 = 2$$
$$x_1 + 2x_2 + 2x_3 = 1$$
$$x_1 + 3x_2 + 3x_3 = 2$$

as can be easily verified by the reader.

Gaussian elimination is one of the most commonly used methods for solving a system of n linear equations in n variables. It requires on the order of n^3 calculations and can be used advantageously for systems of up to about 50 equations.

13.3 DETERMINANTS AND CRAMER'S RULE

An arrangement of n rows of n numbers each, set between vertical strokes, is called an "n by n determinant." Thus

$$A = \begin{vmatrix} a_{11} a_{12} a_{13} & \cdots & a_{1n} \\ a_{21} a_{22} a_{23} & \cdots & a_{2n} \\ \cdot & \cdot & \cdot & \cdot \\ \cdot & \cdot & \cdot & \cdot \\ \cdot & \cdot & \cdot & \cdot \\ a_{n1} a_{n2} a_{n3} & \cdots & a_{nn} \end{vmatrix}$$

where the a_{ij}'s ($1 \leq i \leq n$, $1 \leq j \leq n$) are real numbers, is an n by n determinant of real numbers called A. The first row of A consists of the n numbers $a_{11}, a_{12}, a_{13}, \ldots, a_{1n}$; the second row consists of the numbers $a_{21}, a_{22}, a_{23}, \ldots, a_{2n}$; etc. Reading the numbers downward rather than left to right one speaks of "columns" of the determinant. Thus the n numbers $a_{13}, a_{23}, \ldots, a_{n3}$ make up the third column of the determinant A. Note that the two subscripts of each "element" of the determinant determine the position of the element in the determinant. The element a_{ij} is in the ith row and jth column of the determinant; thus, e.g., a_{28} is in row 2 and column 8 of determinant A.

If A is an n by n determinant and i is an integer between 1 and n, then the "ith minor of A," which is usually denoted by A_i, is that $n-1$ by $n-1$ determinant obtained from A by deleting the first row and the ith column.

As an example, consider the 4 by 4 determinant B:

$$B = \begin{vmatrix} 3 & 0 & -1 & 0 \\ 6 & 8 & 1 & 0 \\ 0 & 3 & -1 & 2 \\ -1 & 2.3 & 18 & 0 \end{vmatrix}$$

The element in row 3 and column 2 of B is 3, in row 4 and column 2 is 2.3, etc. Row 2 of B consists of the four numbers 6, 8, 1, and 0; column 3 of B consists of the four numbers -1, 1, -1, and 18. The third minor of B, denoted by B_3, is obtained by deleting row 1 and column 3 of B and is thus the determinant

$$B_3 = \begin{vmatrix} 6 & 8 & 0 \\ 0 & 3 & 2 \\ -1 & 2.3 & 0 \end{vmatrix}$$

Similarly,

$$B_2 = \begin{vmatrix} 6 & 1 & 0 \\ 0 & -1 & 2 \\ -1 & 18 & 0 \end{vmatrix}$$

Every determinant A has a value, denoted by val(A). The value of a 2 by 2 determinant

$$A = \begin{vmatrix} a_{11} & a_{12} \\ a_{21} & a_{22} \end{vmatrix}$$

is defined by val(A) $= a_{11}a_{22} - a_{12}a_{21}$. The value of an n by n determinant ($n \geq 3$)

$$\begin{vmatrix} a_{11}a_{12}a_{13} & \cdots & a_{1n} \\ a_{21}a_{22}a_{23} & \cdots & a_{2n} \\ \cdot & \cdot & \cdot & \cdot \\ \cdot & \cdot & \cdot & \cdot \\ \cdot & \cdot & \cdot & \cdot \\ a_{n1}a_{n2}a_{n3} & \cdots & a_{nn} \end{vmatrix}$$

is defined in terms of the values of certain $n-1$ by $n-1$ determinants as follows:

val(A) $= a_{11}$ val(A_1) $- a_{12}$ val(A_2) $+ a_{13}$ val(A_3) $- \cdots - (-1)^n a_{1n}$ val(A_n)

In this formula A_i is the ith minor of A. Note that the formula given is "recursive" in the sense of Chapter 10 and can be used to calculate the value of any n by n determinant.

EXAMPLE 1

$$\text{val}\left(\begin{vmatrix} 2 & 6 \\ -1 & 2 \end{vmatrix}\right) = (2)(2) - (6)(-1) = 10$$

EXAMPLE 2

$$\text{val}\left(\begin{vmatrix} 2 & 1 & 0 & -1 \\ 0 & 1 & 3 & 2 \\ 0 & 0 & 2 & 1 \\ 0 & -5 & 0 & 0 \end{vmatrix}\right) = 2\,\text{val}\left(\begin{vmatrix} 1 & 3 & 2 \\ 0 & 2 & 1 \\ -5 & 0 & 0 \end{vmatrix}\right) - \text{val}\left(\begin{vmatrix} 0 & 3 & 2 \\ 0 & 2 & 1 \\ 0 & 0 & 0 \end{vmatrix}\right)$$

$$+ \text{val}\left(\begin{vmatrix} 0 & 1 & 3 \\ 0 & 0 & 2 \\ 0 & -5 & 0 \end{vmatrix}\right) = 2\,\text{val}\left(\begin{vmatrix} 2 & 1 \\ 0 & 0 \end{vmatrix}\right) - 6\,\text{val}\left(\begin{vmatrix} 0 & 1 \\ -5 & 0 \end{vmatrix}\right) + 4\,\text{val}\left(\begin{vmatrix} 0 & 2 \\ -5 & 0 \end{vmatrix}\right)$$

$$+ 3\,\text{val}\left(\begin{vmatrix} 0 & 1 \\ 0 & 0 \end{vmatrix}\right) - 2\,\text{val}\left(\begin{vmatrix} 0 & 2 \\ 0 & 0 \end{vmatrix}\right) - \text{val}\left(\begin{vmatrix} 0 & 2 \\ 0 & 0 \end{vmatrix}\right) + 3\,\text{val}\left(\begin{vmatrix} 0 & 0 \\ 0 & -5 \end{vmatrix}\right)$$

$$= -30 + 40 = 10$$

The fundamental result, known as "Cramer's rule," which establishes the connection between the solution of system of linear equations and the theory of determinants, is this: Let

$$\begin{aligned}
a_{11}x_1 + a_{12}x_2 + \cdots + a_{1n}x_n &= b_1 \\
a_{21}x_1 + a_{22}x_2 + \cdots + a_{2n}x_n &= b_2 \\
& \qquad\qquad\qquad\qquad\qquad (10) \\
a_{n1}x_1 + a_{n2}x_2 + \cdots + a_{nn}x_n &= b_n
\end{aligned}$$

be a system of n equations in n variables. Let D be the n by n determinant

$$D = \begin{vmatrix} a_{11}a_{12} & \cdots & a_{1n} \\ a_{21}a_{22} & \cdots & a_{2n} \\ \vdots & & \vdots \\ a_{n1}a_{n2} & \cdots & a_{nn} \end{vmatrix}$$

The system (10) has a unique solution if and only if $\text{val}(D) \neq 0$. Further, if B_i is the n by n determinant obtained from D by replacing the ith column

$$\begin{aligned}
& a_{1i} \\
& a_{2i} \\
& \vdots \\
& a_{ni}
\end{aligned}$$

of D by the right-hand side

$$b_1$$
$$b_2$$
$$\cdot$$
$$\cdot$$
$$\cdot$$
$$b_n$$

of (10), then the solution s_i $(1 \leq i \leq n)$ is

$$s_i = \frac{\text{val}(B_i)}{\text{val}(D)}$$

Thus Cramer's rule not only provides for a test whether a system (10) has a unique solution—it even gives a compact formula for the solution of the system.

Consider the system (4) examined earlier:

$$x_1 + 2x_2 - x_3 = 1$$
$$-x_1 + 3x_2 + 2x_3 = -1$$
$$x_1 + 11x_2 + x_3 = 3$$

It is easy to see that

$$\text{val}(D) = \text{val}\left(\begin{vmatrix} 1 & 2 & -1 \\ -1 & 3 & 2 \\ 1 & 11 & 1 \end{vmatrix}\right) = 1$$

Substituting into the formula one obtains for s_i $(i = 1, 2, 3)$

$$s_1 = \text{val}(B_1) = \text{val}\left(\begin{vmatrix} 1 & 2 & -1 \\ -1 & 3 & 2 \\ 3 & 11 & 1 \end{vmatrix}\right) = 15$$

$$s_2 = \text{val}(B_2) = \text{val}\left(\begin{vmatrix} 1 & 1 & -1 \\ -1 & -1 & 2 \\ 1 & 3 & 1 \end{vmatrix}\right) = -2$$

$$s_3 = \text{val}(B_3) = \text{val}\left(\begin{vmatrix} 1 & 2 & 1 \\ -1 & 3 & -1 \\ 1 & 11 & 3 \end{vmatrix}\right) = 10$$

in agreement with the solution obtained before.

The main drawback of Cramer's rule is the complicated calculation necessary for finding the value of a determinant. Despite the fact that the calculation of the value of a determinant can be greatly simplified by using rules known from the theory of determinants such as those given below, Cramer's rule cannot be recommended for large systems of equations.

Rule 1. Adding a multiple of some row to some other row or adding a multiple of some column to some other column does not change the value of a determinant.

Rule 2. Switching two rows or two columns of a determinant means multiplying its value by -1.

Rule 3. Multiplying a row or a column of a determinant by a number c means multiplying its value by c.

Rule 4. Inverting rows and columns of a determinant does not change its value.

Rule 5. If a row or column contains only zeroes, the value of the determinant is zero.

Rule 6.

$$\text{val}\begin{pmatrix}\begin{vmatrix} a_{11}a_{12} \cdots a_{1n} \\ 0 \quad a_{22} \cdots a_{2n} \\ \cdot \quad \cdot \qquad \cdot \\ \cdot \quad \cdot \qquad \cdot \\ \cdot \quad \cdot \qquad \cdot \\ 0 \quad a_{n2} \cdots a_{nn} \end{vmatrix}\end{pmatrix} = a_{11}\,\text{val}\begin{pmatrix}\begin{vmatrix} a_{22} \cdots a_{2n} \\ \cdot \qquad \cdot \\ \cdot \qquad \cdot \\ a_{n2} \cdots a_{nn} \end{vmatrix}\end{pmatrix}$$

Note that Rules 1, 2, 3, and 6 allow the calculation of the value of a determinant using a process analogous to Gaussian elimination.

This section is concluded by showing how the above rules can be used to calculate the value of the determinant in Example 2:

$$\text{val}\begin{pmatrix}\begin{vmatrix} 2 & 1 & 0 & -1 \\ 0 & 1 & 3 & 2 \\ 0 & 0 & 2 & 1 \\ 0 & -5 & 0 & 0 \end{vmatrix}\end{pmatrix} \overset{\text{(Rule 6)}}{=} 2\,\text{val}\begin{pmatrix}\begin{vmatrix} 1 & 3 & 2 \\ 0 & 2 & 1 \\ -5 & 0 & 0 \end{vmatrix}\end{pmatrix} \overset{\text{(Rule 3)}}{=} 10\,\text{val}\begin{pmatrix}\begin{vmatrix} 1 & 3 & 2 \\ 0 & 2 & 1 \\ -1 & 0 & 0 \end{vmatrix}\end{pmatrix}$$

$$\overset{\text{(Rule 1)}}{=} 10\,\text{val}\begin{pmatrix}\begin{vmatrix} 0 & 3 & 2 \\ 0 & 2 & 1 \\ -1 & 0 & 0 \end{vmatrix}\end{pmatrix} \overset{\text{(Rule 2)}}{=} -10\,\text{val}\begin{pmatrix}\begin{vmatrix} -1 & 0 & 0 \\ 0 & 2 & 1 \\ 0 & 3 & 2 \end{vmatrix}\end{pmatrix} \overset{\text{(Rule 6)}}{=} 10\,\text{val}\begin{pmatrix}\begin{vmatrix} 2 & 1 \\ 3 & 2 \end{vmatrix}\end{pmatrix} = 10$$

13.4 GAUSS–SEIDEL ITERATION

The Gauss–Seidel method described below is the best-known iterative process for solving systems of n linear equations in n variables. For each iteration on the order of n^2 steps are necessary. The Gauss–Seidel method is thus generally superior to Gaussian elimination for large systems of equations, that is, for systems with more than about 50 equations.

Consider a system of n linear equations in n variables

$$a_{11}x_1 + a_{12}x_2 + \cdots + a_{1n}x_n = b_1$$
$$a_{21}x_1 + a_{22}x_2 + \cdots + a_{2n}x_n = b_2$$
$$\vdots \qquad \vdots \qquad\qquad \vdots \qquad \vdots \qquad\qquad (11)$$
$$a_{n1}x_1 + a_{n2}x_2 + \cdots + a_{nn}x_n = b_n$$

which satisfies for every i ($1 \le i \le n$) the "convergence condition":

$$2\,\mathrm{abs}(a_{ii}) > \mathrm{abs}(a_{i1}) + \mathrm{abs}(a_{i2}) + \mathrm{abs}(a_{i3}) + \cdots + \mathrm{abs}(a_{in}) \qquad (12)$$

Given an arbitrary initial estimate of the solution $(s_1, s_2, \ldots, s_n)$ of system (11) and a positive number $e > 0$, the following algorithm will determine n values $s_1, s_2, \ldots, s_n$ such that

$$\mathrm{abs}(a_{11}s_1 + a_{12}s_2 + \cdots + a_{1n}s_n - b_1) + \mathrm{abs}(a_{21}s_1 + a_{22}s_2 + \cdots$$
$$+ a_{2n}s_n - b_2) + \cdots + \mathrm{abs}(a_{n1}s_1 + a_{n2}s_2 + \cdots + a_{nn}s_n - b_n) < e$$

Step 1. Let $i = 1$.

Step 2. Let $s_i = (b_i + a_{ii}s_i - (a_{i1}s_1 + a_{i2}s_2 + \cdots + a_{in}s_n))/a_{ii}$.

Step 3. If $i < n$, then let $i = i + 1$ and go to Step 2.

Step 4. If $\mathrm{abs}(a_{11}s_1 + a_{12}s_2 + \cdots + a_{1n}s_n - b_1) + \mathrm{abs}(a_{21}s_1 + a_{22}s_2 + \cdots + a_{2n}s_n - b_2) + \cdots + \mathrm{abs}(a_{n1}s_1 + a_{n2}s_2 + \cdots + a_{nn}s_n - b_n) < e$, then stop.

Step 5. Go to Step 1.

How fast the values obtained for $s_1, s_2, \ldots, s_n$ approach the actual solution of system (11) depends both on the choice of the initial estimate and on the system. The method always works if (12) is satisfied but works particularly well if $a_{11}, a_{22}, \ldots, a_{nn}$ are very large compared with all other a_{ij}'s. Note that condition (12) may not be satisfied for some system (11) but that a rearrangement of the equations can give a system that satisfies condition (12).

As an example, consider the system

$$x_1 - 3x_2 = 1$$
$$2x_1 - x_2 = 0 \qquad\qquad (13)$$

Condition (12) is not satisfied. Indeed, starting with $s_1 = 0$ and $s_2 = 0$ the following values are obtained successively for (s_1, s_2): (0,0), (1,2), (7,14), (43,86), ... Rearranging system (13) into

$$2x_1 - x_2 = 0$$
$$x_1 - 3x_2 = 1 \qquad\qquad (14)$$

condition (12) is satisfied. Starting with $s_1 = 0$ and $s_2 = 0$ the following values are obtained successively for

$$(s_1, s_2): \quad (0,0), \quad \left(0, \frac{-1}{3}\right), \quad \left(\frac{-1}{6}, \frac{-7}{18}\right), \quad \left(\frac{-7}{36}, \frac{-43}{108}\right), \quad \left(\frac{-43}{216}, \frac{-259}{648}\right), \quad \dots$$

These values approach rapidly the actual solution of (13), which is (s_1, s_2) = $(-1/5, -2/5)$.

The Gauss–Seidel method can provide correct answers even if (12) is not satisfied. If it is used in such a case it is imperative to incorporate in the program a check to determine whether successive n-tuples $(s_1, s_2, \dots, s_n)$ do indeed approach a solution.

13.5 PROBLEMS

Problem 13.5.1 (*Small Systems*)

As input data a system of (a) three equations in three variables, (b) four equations in four variables, and (c) eight equations in eight variables is given on punched cards. Using (1) Gaussian elimination and (2) Cramer's rule, write a program to determine if the given system has a unique solution. If none exists, the program should print a suitable message; otherwise it should find and print the solution.

Problem 13.5.2 (*Gaussian Elimination for a System of n Linear Equations in n Variables*)

As input data an integer n with $2 \leq n \leq 20$ is given, followed by n linear equations in n variables. It is not known whether the system has a unique solution. Write a program that uses Gaussian elimination to determine whether it has, and if so, determine the solution.

Problem 13.5.3 (*Small Determinants*)

As input data a (a) 3 by 3 determinant, (b) 4 by 4 determinant, and (c) 8 by 8 determinant is given on punched cards. Write a program to determine the value of the given determinant using (1) the definition of the value of a determinant and (2) a method analogous to Gaussian elimination.

Problem 13.5.4 (*General Program for Determining the Value of an n by n Determinant*)

As input data an integer n with $2 \leq n \leq 20$ is given, followed by an n by n determinant. Write a program that uses a method analogous to Gaussian elimination to calculate the value of the given determinant.

Problem 13.5.5 (*Travel in Europe*)

A person has decided to travel a total of 1800 miles by rented car, plane, train, and bus in Europe. The person wants to spend $158 on transportation, to spend 19 hours traveling altogether, and to make sure that the distance traveled by rented car and plane is equal to the distance traveled by train and bus.

A mile costs 12 cents using a rented car, 10 cents flying, 8 cents when going by train, and 5 cents when going by bus. Ten miles are covered in 3 minutes when flying, 10 minutes when driving a car, 12 minutes by bus, and 8 minutes by train.

Write a program to determine how many miles should be traveled by car, plane, bus, and train, respectively.

Problem 13.5.6 (*Iteration, Version 1*)

A system of three linear equations in three variables is given on punched cards. Write a program that uses as initial estimate $s_1 = s_2 = s_3 = 0$ and determines s_1, s_2, and s_3 after 1, 2, 3, . . . , 10 iterations of the Gauss–Seidel process.

Problem 13.5.7 (*Iteration, Version 2*)

A positive number $e > 0$ followed by a system of three linear equations in three variables

$$a_{11}x_1 + a_{12}x_2 + a_{13}x_3 = b_1$$
$$a_{21}x_1 + a_{22}x_2 + a_{23}x_3 = b_2$$
$$a_{31}x_1 + a_{32}x_2 + a_{33}x_3 = b_3$$

is given on punched cards. Write a program using Gauss–Seidel iteration with initial estimate $s_1 = s_2 = s_3 = 0$ to find s_1, s_2, and s_3 such that abs($a_{11}s_1 + a_{12}s_2 + a_{13}s_3 - b_1$) + abs($a_{21}s_1 + a_{22}s_2 + a_{23}s_3 - b_2$) + abs($a_{31}s_1 + a_{32}s_2 + a_{33}s_3 - b_3$) $< e$. Record the number of iterations necessary. It can be assumed that the convergence condition (12) of Section 13.4 is satisfied.

Problem 13.5.8 (*Iteration, Version 3*)

A positive number $e > 0$ followed by a system of four linear equations in four variables

$$a_{11}x_1 + a_{12}x_2 + a_{13}x_3 + a_{14}x_4 = b_1$$
$$a_{21}x_1 + a_{22}x_2 + a_{23}x_3 + a_{24}x_4 = b_2$$
$$a_{31}x_1 + a_{32}x_2 + a_{33}x_3 + a_{34}x_4 = b_3$$
$$a_{41}x_1 + a_{42}x_2 + a_{43}x_3 + a_{44}x_4 = b_4$$

is given on punched cards. Write a program using Gauss–Seidel iteration with initial estimate $s_1 = s_2 = s_3 = s_4 = 0$ to find s_1, s_2, s_3, and s_4 such that abs($a_{i1}x_1 + a_{i2}x_2 + a_{i3}x_3 + a_{i4}x_4 - b_i$) $< e$ for $i = 1, 2, 3, 4$. If the given system does not satisfy the convergence condition (12) of Section 13.4, reordering of the equations should be tried. If this fails, a suitable message should be printed.

Problem 13.5.9 (*Gauss–Seidel Iteration for a System of n Linear Equations in n Variables*)

As input data a number $e > 0$, an integer n with $2 \le n \le 60$, and a system of n linear equations in n variables

$$a_{11}x_1 + a_{12}x_2 + \cdots + a_{1n}x_n = b_1$$
$$a_{21}x_1 + a_{22}x_2 + \cdots + a_{2n}x_n = b_2$$
$$\vdots \qquad \vdots \qquad \qquad \vdots$$
$$a_{n1}x_1 + a_{n2}x_2 + \cdots + a_{nn}x_n = b_n$$

are given. Write a program using Gauss–Seidel iteration with initial estimate $s_1 = s_2 = \cdots = s_n = 0$ to find values $s_1, s_2, \ldots, s_n$ such that $\mathrm{abs}(a_{11}s_1 + a_{12}s_2 + \cdots + a_{1n}s_n - b_1) + \mathrm{abs}(a_{21}s_1 + a_{22}s_2 + \cdots + a_{2n}s_n - b_2) + \cdots + \mathrm{abs}(a_{n1}s_1 + a_{n2}s_2 + \cdots + a_{nn}s_n - b_n) < e$. Record the number of iterations required. If the convergence condition (12) of Section 13.4 is not satisfied, try reordering to make sure that it is indeed satisfied. If this fails, proceed with Gauss–Seidel iteration nevertheless, but incorporate into the program a test whether successive n-tuples $(s_1, s_2, \ldots, s_n)$ do approach the solution of the system. If this is not the case, the program should print an appropriate message.

Problem 13.5.10 (*Dietary Requirements*)

The following table shows the recommended daily dietary requirement for a 40-year-old man and the content of some nutrients in some common foods:

	Calories	Calcium (grams)	Protein (grams)	Vitamin C (milligrams)
Daily requirement	2600	0.8	70	70
Spinach—100 g	20	0.065	2	45
Milk—100 g	70	0.12	3.4	1.7
Cabbage with butter—100 g	75	0.036	1.6	16
Meat—100 g	350	0.01	21	0

Write a program to determine the amounts of spinach, milk, cabbage, and meat needed to satisfy the daily dietary requirement for calcium, protein, and vitamin C and yielding 1400 calories.

Problem 13.5.11 (*Electrical Networks*)

Consider the electrical network with wires $1, 2, 3, \ldots, 13$, as shown below. Write a program to read numbers $x_1, r_2, r_3, \ldots, r_{12}$ (x_1 indicating the current entering the network through wire 1 and leaving the network through wire 13; r_i indicating the resistance of wire i for $i = 2, 3, \ldots, 12$) and determine the current x_i flowing through wire i, $i = 2, 3, \ldots, 12$.

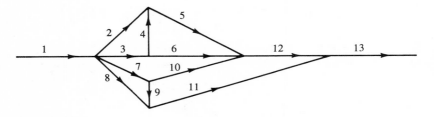

Figure 13-1

Hint: By Kirchhoff's first law the sum of the inflowing currents is equal to the sum of the outflowing currents for each junction, yielding†

$$x_1 = x_2 + x_3 + x_7 + x_8$$
$$x_2 + x_4 = x_5$$
$$x_3 = x_4 + x_6$$
$$x_7 = x_9 + x_{10}$$
$$x_8 + x_9 = x_{11}$$
$$x_5 + x_6 + x_{10} = x_{12}$$

By Ohm's law the voltage drop between two points is equal to the product of resistance and current, yielding

$$r_2 x_2 = r_3 x_3 + r_4 x_4$$
$$r_6 x_6 = r_4 x_4 + r_5 x_5$$
$$r_3 x_3 + r_6 x_6 = r_7 x_7 + r_{10} x_{10}$$
$$r_8 x_8 = r_7 x_7 + r_9 x_9$$
$$r_9 x_9 + r_{11} x_{11} = r_{10} x_{10} + r_{12} x_{12}$$

The above 11 equations determine the currents $x_2, x_3, \ldots, x_{12}$. If an x_i. turns out to have a negative value, it just means that the current flows opposite to the direction shown in the network.

†The equation $x_{12} + x_{11} = x_1$, which is also obtained, is easily seen not to provide any additional information.

14

PLOTTING

14.1 INTRODUCTION

If a person wishes to plot the graph of a function such as $f(x) = 3x^3 + 9x^2 - 2x - 54$, he must evaluate $f(x)$ for a large number of values of x and, having then obtained the coordinates of some of the points, sketch the graph by hand.

There are a number of ways that a computer can help in plotting graphs of functions. It can help in evaluating the function at a large number of points and may also be used to obtain simple plots on the line printer or typewriter. These plots may take the form of "histograms" (commonly called "bar graphs"), with each bar being represented by a series of x's or $*$'s, or they may take the form of an approximation to a continuous line by printing a set of axes on the page and printing asterisks in positions given by x and $f(x)$. A number of computing installations have graph plotters, which consist of a movable pen, controlled by the computer, for drawing continuous lines. Other installations may have television-like cathode ray tube displays for producing graphs and line drawings.

When plotting the graph of a function, particularly when plotting with a line printer, it is best to build up a complete representation of the output within the computer's memory and, after all computations are finished, print out the result. If the plotting surface (normally a page of line printer paper) has room for 120 positions in each of 60 lines, then an array of 120 columns and 60 rows will suffice to represent the plot. Initially the elements of this

175

array should be set to some code that represents a blank space; then as the coordinates of each point (x,y) of the plot are determined, a suitable character code may be stored in the array at the element in row x and column y. After this process has been carried out for all points to be printed, the array can be easily printed row by row. This method is particularly useful when the graph under consideration has more than one point in some of the lines to be printed, or if the graphs of several functions have to be plotted in the same coordinate system.

14.2 PLOTTING WITH THE LINE PRINTER

Problem 14.2.1 (*Logarithmic Histogram*)

Write a program that will read in a series of integers (each integer in the range 1–9,999,999,999) and compute and print their "logarithmic histogram." A logarithmic histogram of a set of integers is a histogram showing how many of the integers are single-digit numbers, two-digit numbers, three-digit numbers, . . . , ten-digit numbers.

Problem 14.2.2

Write a program that will evaluate the function $f(x) = x^2 + x - 50$ for $x = -10, -9, -8, \ldots, -1, 0, 1, \ldots, 9, 10$ and then plot the resulting values on the line printer. The line printer sheet should have the $f(x)$-axis running down the page and the x-axis running across the middle of the page. The plot should indicate where the two axes are by printing out two rows of dots, a horizontal one representing the x-axis and a vertical one representing the $f(x)$-axis. The graph of the function should be represented by a collection of asterisks printed at the coordinates $(x, f(x))$ $-10 \le x \le 10$. The actual value of $f(x)$ should be printed to the right of each asterisk. For example, a small part of the graph should look like

```
*(40)                   .
                        .
  *(22)                 .
                        .
    *(6)                .
                        .                                      (1)
 . . . . . . . . . . . . . . . . . . . . . x-axis
                        .
      *(−8)             .
                        .
        f(x)-axis
```

Problem 14.2.3 (*Scaled Plot*)

At times it is necessary to compute all the values of $f(x)$ that are to be plotted, then search through these values to find both the largest value and the smallest value, and then scale all the values of $f(x)$ so that they will fit on the paper. This is obviously necessary to plot (for $x = -30, -29, -28, \ldots,$ $+28, +29, +30$) the function $f(x) = 3x^2 + 9x - 120$ because $f(x)$ is very large for some values of x. However, it is also necessary if the values of a function are all very close to each other. For example, the values of $f(x)$ for

$$f(x) = \frac{1}{\sqrt{2\pi}} e^{(-x^2/2)} \qquad \text{(for } x = -10 \text{ to } +10\text{)}$$

are all in the range $0 < f(x) \leq 0.4$. To obtain a plot of this function the values of $f(x)$ must be scaled up to show anything except a straight line. If one has enough paper to make the $f(x)$-axis h units long, then two numbers, a and b, should be found such that $a < f(x) < b$ for every value of $f(x)$ in the interval under consideration. To plot the graph of $f(x)$ in the space available, one should actually plot a graph of $g(x)$, where $g(x) = h((f(x) - a)/(b - a))$. The x-axis may be scaled in a similar fashion if necessary.

Write a program to produce a scaled plot of the two functions mentioned above. The output should indicate the formula used for scaling and also show a table of the true values for x and $f(x)$ for each function.

Problem 14.2.4 (*Circle, Version 1*)

Write a program that will read three numbers, a, b, and r, and then produce a set of axes on a page of line printer paper with a circle (of radius r units) plotted so that its centre has the coordinates (a,b).

Hint: The equation of a circle with centre (a,b) is $(x - a)^2 + (y - b)^2 = r^2$.

Problem 14.2.5 (*Folium, Version 1*)

When plotting a circle it is necessary to remember the fact that for each value of x, with abs$(x - a) < r$, there are two values, y_1 and y_2, such that both (x,y_1) and (x,y_2) are points of the circle—one on the top part of the circle and one on the lower portion. For some graphs there may be many values of y that correspond to a single value of x.

Write a program that will plot, on the line printer, the graph of $f(x) = 0$, where $f(x) = \pm\sqrt{x^2((10 - x)/(10 + x))}$, for $x = -10, -9.5, -9, \ldots, 9,$ 9.5, 10.

Problem 14.2.6 (*Tiles*)

A person may tend to express his individuality by attempting to obtain a house, car, etc., that is, in some way, different from what all his friends have. He may attempt to decorate his house with shiny black walls and gold ceilings or produce some equally uncommon, yet pleasing, design to reflect his interests or profession. For example, several computer scientists and mathematicians have abandoned the traditional pattern for laying a tile floor (alternating white and black tiles) for a floor that has a red tile in the middle and then a seemingly random arrangement of light and dark tiles over the rest of the floor. A closer inspection reveals that the red tile is actually the center of a coordinate system. The tile with coordinates (a,b) represents the complex number $a + ib$. The dark tiles correspond to complex prime numbers and the light-colored tiles to complex numbers that are not complex prime numbers. (See Problem 3.2.11)

Write a program that will produce a picture of such a tile floor for a room 39 feet by 39 feet (each tile is 1 foot square). The red tile should be represented by an asterisk in the middle of a page of paper, the dark tiles by x's, and the light tiles by 0's.

Problem 14.2.7 (*Big Tiles*)

The same as Problem 14.2.6 but print the tile layout for a room 201 feet by 201 feet. Think carefully before you start because it will be necessary to produce several pieces of line printer paper, which will be taped together to produce the desired pattern.

Hint: This pattern has several axes of symmetry so it is not necessary to compute more than one-eighth of the total pattern; then fill in the rest by symmetry.

Problem 14.2.8 (*Plotting Pictures*)

Pictures in newspapers are composed of tens of thousands of small dots that vary from almost white to dense black in color. By printing the dots in appropriate combinations any desired gray tone may be obtained. Pictures may be "plotted" on the line printer, in the same way, by using various characters to obtain the correct gray tones. For example, when viewed from a distance, the character $ appears very dark and a period appears very light. Line printers have been used to produce very acceptable (when viewed from a distance of 6 feet or more) reproductions of the Madonna and Child, the Mona Lisa, and the middle fold out of *Playboy*.

Write a program that will produce a line printer picture (subject matter unspecified).

Problem 14.2.9 (*Making a Decoration*)

Write a program to produce a line printer picture (see Problem 14.2.8), along with a relevant message, that could be used as a suitable decoration. For example, at Christmas time, a picture of a winter scene with Santa, his sleigh, and reindeer in the foreground, and in the sky, in Old English script, a message wishing everyone a Merry Christmas and Happy New Year; or in the spring, a picture of a flower garden with an exhortation to the local populace to beautify the neighborhood.

Problem 14.2.10 (*Intersection*)

One of the favorite questions in an elementary mathematics course is "Given two equations $g(x,y) = 0$ and $h(x,y) = 0$, find the point (or points) at which the graphs of the equations intersect, i.e., find all the points (x,y) for which $g(x,y) = h(x,y) = 0$."

Write a program that will plot in one coordinate system the graphs of $g(x,y) = x^2 - 8x + y^2 + 11 = 0$ (a circle) and $h(x,y) = x + y - 5 = 0$ (a straight line). From this plot determine the two points at which these graphs intersect.

Hint: Plot the axes as periods, the circle as asterisks, and the straight line as x's. To determine pairs of numbers (x,y) satisfying an equation $g(x,y) = 0$ one chooses various values $a_1, a_2, \ldots$ for x, and for each value a_i of x one determines a zero of the function $g(a_i,y) = f(y) = 0$ using one of the methods described in Chapter 6.

Problem 14.2.11 (*Parabola*)

The general equation that describes a parabola is $y = ax^2 + bx + c$. A "tangent line" (at the point $x = t$) to this parabola has the equation $y = (2at + b)(x - t) + at^2 + bt + c$. A "normal line" (at the point $x = t$) is a line perpendicular to the tangent and is given by the equation $y = (t - x)/(2at + b) + at^2 + bt + c$.

Write a program that will read in values of a, b, c, and t, as well as the range of x that the plot should span (this should include t), and then plot, on the line printer, the parabola with tangent line and normal line at the point $x = t$.

Problem 14.2.12 (*Zeroes*)

One of the uses of a graph of a function $f(x)$ is to obtain rough estimates of the zeroes of the function [the values of x for which $f(x) = 0$]. This is often not a very accurate procedure when using the line printer as a plotting device. However, it is often possible to produce a plot that will indicate something about the position of the zeroes.

Given a polynomial, $P(x) = a_0 + a_1x + a_2x^2 + \cdots + a_nx^n$, it is possible to plot a series of points, (x,y), where $x = pa_1 \sin(z) + p^2a_2 \sin(2z) + \cdots + p^na_n \sin(nz)$, $y = a_0 + pa_1 \cos(z) + p^2a_2 \cos(2z) + \cdots + p^na_n \cos(nz)$ for $z = 0, \ldots, 2\pi$ radians. If the curve of this plot wraps around the origin $((x,y) = (0,0))$ k times, then there are k zeroes, $x_1, x_2, x_3, \ldots, x_k$, of $P(x) = 0$ such that $\text{abs}(x_i) < p$, for $i = 1, 2, 3, \ldots, k$.

Write a program to plot, on the line printer, the curve described above for the polynomial $P(x) = -1.9 - x + 2.3x^2 + x^3$ using two values of p, $p = 3.6$ and $p = 1.6$. By checking how many times the two curves wrap around the point $(0,0)$, determine how many zeroes x of $P(x)$ there are with $1.6 \leq \text{abs}(x) \leq 3.6$.

Problem 14.2.13 (*Circle, Version 2*)

Write a program to plot, on the line printer, the points (x,y) for $x = 25 \cos(z)$ and $y = 25 \sin(z)$, where z takes on the values $0, 0.1, 0.2, \ldots, 6.3$ radians.

Problem 14.2.14 (*Lemniscate*)

Write a program to plot, on the line printer, the curve defined by the equation $x^2 = -(y^2 - 1) \pm \sqrt{(y^2 - 1)^2 - (y^4 + 2y^2)}$. The plot should include all values of x for $-0.5 \leq y \leq 0.5$. Remember that, in general, there will be four values of x for each value of y. This curve is known as a "lemniscate."

Problem 14.2.15 (*Folium, Version 2*)

Write a program to plot, on the line printer, the curve defined by the equation $x^5 + y^5 + 5xy = 0$. The plot should include values of x from -2 to $+2$ in steps of 0.01. Each value of y may be determined by the binary search technique described in Chapter 13. This curve is known as a "folium."

14.3 USING A GRAPH PLOTTER

Most graph plotters are of the "step" variety; that is, they can move the pen only in discreet steps (generally of 0.01 inch or 0.005 inch) in one of eight basic directions, i.e.,

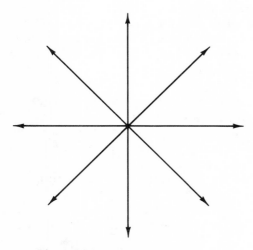

Figure 14-1

Because the size of each step is so small, the resulting curve looks very much like a smooth line. Although all the problems in Section 14.1 involved plotting on a line printer, they can, for the most part, be used as problems for a graph plotter. The problems in this section are designed to take advantage of the continuous nature of the line produced and the increased accuracy obtainable on the graph plotter.

Problem 14.3.1 *(Straight Line)*

Write a program that will read in four numbers (a, b, c, and d). These four numbers define two points—point 1 has coordinates (a,b) and point 2 has coordinates (c,d). The program should compute the best possible series of steps for a pen to take in order that it will draw as straight a line as possible between point 1 and point 2. You should assume that the plotter's pen moves in steps of 0.01 units whenever it travels "north," "south," "east," or "west" and that it moves in steps of 0.01414 units (i.e., $0.01\sqrt{2}$) when moving "northeast," "southeast," "southwest", or "northwest."

Hint: The equation of a line passing through the two points is

$$y = \frac{d-b}{c-a}(x-a) + b$$

The distance D between two points (a,b) and (c,d) is

$$D = \sqrt{(c-a)^2 + (d-b)^2}$$

Assume that the two points are (0,0) and (1,3). A single step from (0,0) in any of the eight possible directions would result in the pen moving to either (0,0.01) or (0.01,0.01), or (0.01,0), or (0.01,−0.01), or (0,−0.01), or (−0.01, −0.01), or (−0.01,0), or (−0.01,0.01) depending on its direction. Three of these moves will take the pen closer to the point (1,3) and five will take it farther away. These three "good" moves may be found from the distance formula. Of the three "good" moves, only one is allowable, and that should be the one that brings the pen closest to the straight line passing through the two points.

Problem 14.3.2 *(Nonexistent Zeroes)*

Write a program that will use the graph plotter to plot the two functions described in Problem 14.2.3. From an inspection of the graphs, attempt to determine the zeroes (if any) of the two functions.

Problem 14.3.3 *(Signature)*

Write your signature on a piece of finely ruled graph paper. Draw a set of axes on the graph paper and record all the points that your pen passed through when writing your signature. Write a program that will read in this list of points and reproduce your signature on the graph plotter.

Hint: Make your signature (on the graph paper) very large.

Problem 14.3.4 (*Archimedes*)

The Greeks had a method of determining the volume of any given solid figure. It was to carve a model of the figure and then immerse the figure in water and note the volume of water displaced. A similar process will give a rough approximation of any area A determined by the graph of a function $y = f(x)$, the x-axis, and two lines $x = a$ and $x = b$ drawn parallel to the y-axis. This area is usually denoted by $A = \int_a^b f(x)\, dx$ (see Section 11.7). The method consists of plotting the graph of $y = f(x)$, of cutting out the area A, and of dividing the weight of the area A by the weight of a unit square.

Write a program using the method described to find an approximate value of the area A defined by the x-axis and (a) the function $f(x) = 1/x$ and the lines $x = 0.01$ and $x = 100$ and (b) the function $f(x) = 100 + x - x^2$ and the lines $x = 3$ and $x = 11$.

Hint: To gain the greatest accuracy one should use the heaviest paper available and a very sensitive chemical balance.

15

ADVANCED PROBLEMS

15.1 NETWORK PROBLEMS

Problem 15.1.1 (*Shortest Road Connection*)

Punched cards are available containing a number of triples (A,B,d). Each triple represents two cities A and B and the mileage d of the shortest direct road connection (without other cities in between) from city A to city B. The last triple is of the form (END,END,0), indicating that no more direct road connections exist. Following this last triple a number m and m pairs (C,D) of cities C,D are punched on cards.

Write a program to find the shortest road connection from city C to city D for each pair (C,D) given and print both the total mileage and the route to be taken. You may assume that there are not more than 150 cities and that there are at most 10 roads leaving each city.

Note: Because of the number of cities involved it is not feasible to store the direct connections between the cities using a matrix such as in Problem 4.2.6. A method for storing the connections in a more compact manner has to be devised. One possible way of solving the problem for two cities C and D is to find for each $i = 1, 2, \ldots$ all cities that can be reached from C by visiting at most i cities and by calculating for each such city E the minimum mileage between C and E.

Problem 15.1.2 (*Air Distance*)

Punched cards are available giving the mileage between various cities and m pairs of cities (C, D) similar to Problem 15.1.1. Assuming that every road between two cities is a straight line, write a program to calculate the air distance $d(C, D)$ for each pair of cities given.

For simplicity the following assumptions may be made: (a) There are not more than 100 cities; (b) there are at most ten roads leaving each city; (c) if two cities B and C have a direct road connection with a city A, then either B and C have a direct connection or there exists a city D such that B and C have both a direct connection with D and the cities A, B, C, and D form a rectangle; (d) each city has a direct connection with at least two other cities; (e) there is a route leading from each city to each other city; (f) for each city A, each city B directly connected with A, and each city C not directly connected with A, the relation $d(A,B) < d(A,C)$ holds.

Note: The mileage information available does not always determine a unique road map. The program is to determine the air distances for one possible road map but should indicate whether other road maps are possible or not.

Problem 15.1.3 (*Drawing a Map*)

Punched cards are available containing information giving the mileage between various cities similar to Problem 15.1.1.

Write a program to plot a road map in accordance with the mileage information, assuming that every road between two cities is a straight line. The map should show the relative position of the various cities with distances proportional to the given ones. For simplicity you may assume that there are not more than 50 cities, that at most six roads are leaving each city, and that conditions (c)–(f) of Problem 15.1.2 are satisfied.

Note: If more than one road map fits the mileage information given, the program should print a message to that extent and plot one of the possible road maps.

Problem 15.1.4 (*The Road Inspector*)

Punched cards are available containing a number of pairs (A,B). Each pair (A,B) represents two cities A and B and the fact that a direct road connects them. The last pair is of the form (END,END) and indicates that no more direct road connections exist.

A road inspector has to examine the whole network of roads every month. To minimize his efforts he wants to make a tour covering every road segment exactly once and, of course, wants to end up in the city from which he starts his inspection tour. Assuming that there is an even number of roads leaving every city and that there is some route leading from each city to each other city, it is known from graph theory that such a tour, called a "Euler line," exists.

Write a program to find such a Euler line assuming that the above conditions are met.

Hint: A sequence of road sections $s_1, s_2, \ldots, s_n$ is called a "circuit" if no two are the same and if there exist n different cities $A_1, A_2, \ldots, A_n$ such that s_i leads from A_i to A_{i+1} for $i = 1, 2, \ldots, n-1$ and s_n leads from A_n to A_1. Using the following method, one can find a Euler line D given a road map with cities B and road sections S.

Step 1. Let $i = 1$.

Step 2. Find an arbitrary circuit C_i in S.

Step 3. Remove all road sections in C_i from S.

Step 4. If there are road sections left in S, then let $i = i + 1$ and go to Step 2.

Step 5. Let $C = \{C_1, C_2, \ldots, C_i\}$ be the set of circuits determined above.

Step 6. Let D be the circuit C_1.

Step 7. Remove C_1 from C.

Step 8. If C contains no further circuit, then stop.

Step 9. Determine a circuit E in C such that E and D have a city, say A, in common.

Step 10. Let D be the circuit obtained by combining E and D at the city A.

Step 11. Remove E from C and go to Step 8.

EXAMPLE

Consider the map of nine cities $1, 2, 3, \ldots, 9$ shown in Fig. 15-1. A typical set C of circuits that can be determined by Steps 1–5 is $C = (C_1, C_2, C_3)$ with C_1: s_1, s_2, s_9, s_4; C_2: $s_{14}, s_{11}, s_{13}, s_7, s_6$; and C_3: $s_3, s_{10}, s_{15}, s_{16}, s_{12}, s_8, s_5$. By Step 6 D: s_1, s_2, s_9, s_4. Since D and C_3 have city 3 in common, Step 10 yields D: $s_1, s_2, s_{10}, s_{15}, s_{16}, s_{12}, s_8, s_5, s_3, s_9, s_4$. Since D and C_2 now have city 8 in common, Step 10 yields D: $s_1, s_2, s_{10}, s_{11}, s_{13}, s_7, s_6, s_{14}, s_{15}, s_{16}, s_{12}, s_8, s_5, s_3, s_9, s_4$, which is indeed a Euler line: D describes a tour of the road network covering each road section exactly once.

Problem 15.1.5 (*Hamiltonian Circuit*)

Punched cards are available containing information similar to Problem 15.1.4 indicating how some cities are interconnected. Write a program that attempts to find a route passing through each city exactly once. Such a route is called a "Hamiltonian circuit."

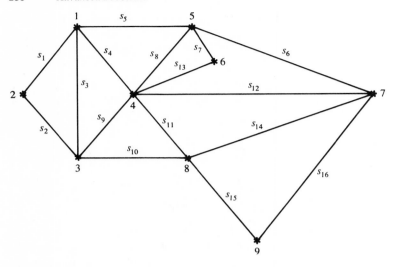

Figure 15-1

Note: It is much harder to find a Hamiltonian circuit than to find a Euler line (see Problem 15.1.4). Indeed, given a road map, it is often difficult to determine whether a Hamiltonian circuit exists. One often used method for finding a Hamiltonian circuit is a combination of backtracking (see Problem 5.1.6) and heuristics (see Problem 5.1.9). For each city A and positive integer i, let $p_i(A)$ be the number of cities that can be visited from A passing through not more than $i - 1$ cities, not counting cities already visited.

In trying to find a Hamiltonian circuit always choose as next city a city B not yet visited such that $p_1(B)$ is "minimal," i.e., is as small as possible. If there are two or more cities $B_1, B_2, \ldots, B_k$ such that $p_1(B_1) = p_1(B_2) = \cdots = p_1(B_k)$ is minimal, base the choice on $p_2(B_t), p_3(B_t), \ldots$ ($t = 1, 2, \ldots$, k). Continue this process until all cities have been visited or until some city is found without exit to some other still unvisited city. In the latter case a step of backtracking is necessary.

For simplicity you may assume that not more than 70 cities are available, with not more than eight roads leaving each city. Note the connection of finding a Hamiltonian circuit with finding a knight's tour on a chessboard; see Problem 5.1.9: Interpreting each square of the chessboard as a city and connecting two cities by a direct road, if a knight can go from the square corresponding to the one city to the square corresponding to the other city in one move, the problem of finding a knight's tour on the chessboard is equivalent to finding a Hamiltonian circuit in the road network described.

Test your program by applying it to some road networks for which Hamiltonian circuits are known to exist. Such road networks for n cities $1, 2, \ldots, n$ can be found as follows: Connect city i with city $i + 1$ ($i = 1, 2$,

..., $n - 1$) and city n with city 1. (This guarantees the existence of a Hamiltonian circuit.) Then add as many direct connections between any two cities you like to make the road network more complicated.

Problem 15.1.6 *(Traveling Salesman Problem)*

Punched cards are available containing information giving the mileage between various cities similar to Problem 15.1.1. It is often important not only to find a route passing through each city exactly once but to find such a route with minimal mileage. This problem is known as the "traveling salesman problem."

Write a program that attempts to solve the traveling salesman problem for up to 30 cities with up to six roads leaving each city.

Hint: First try to determine a Hamiltonian circuit H and the mileage of that Hamiltonian circuit $m(H)$. Next consider four cities, A, B, C, and D, such that A and B, C and D, A and C, and B and D have a direct road connection and such that the connections A to B and C to D are part of H. Construct a new Hamiltonian circuit H' from H by removing the connections A to B and C to D, and adding the connections A to C and B to D. If $m(H') < m(H)$, then use H' instead of H.

Continue the process described until the mileage does not decrease in 100 consecutive trials. To test your program choose a road map of about 15 cities that is known to have a Hamiltonian circuit (see Problem 15.1.5) and choose any mileages between the cities involved.

Problem 15.1.7 *(Maximum Flow in a Network)*

Consider a network N of one-way roads between n cities $1, 2, 3, \ldots, n$. Assume that for each road section i,j from a city i to a city j an integer $c(i,j)$ represents the "capacity" of the road section, i.e., gives the number of cars that can flow through the road section from i to j per second. If $c(i,j) = 0$, then there is no direct road from city i to city j.

Suppose that a certain "flow" of cars is given in this network. For any two cities i,j with $c(i,j) > 0$, let $f(i,j)$ be the current flow from city i to city j, $0 \leq f(i,j) \leq c(i,j)$. It is often important to determine the maximum number of cars that can flow from city 1 to city n using the given network N and to determine for which values of $f(i,j)$ the network N can accommodate this maximal flow.

Punched cards are available containing triples of positive integers (i,j,k), each triple representing the fact that $c(i,j) = k$. The last triple, indicating the end of input information, is $(0,0,0)$. Write a program to determine the maximal flow from city 1 to city n, assuming that the cities are numbered $1, 2, \ldots, n$ and determine $f(i,j)$ for the maximal flow for each road section i,j in the given network N. You may assume that $n \leq 80$.

Hint: To obtain a maximal flow from city 1 to city n one first determines a "complete flow," a flow with the property that each route from 1 to n contains a road section whose flow is equal to its capacity. To obtain a complete flow, start with the flow $f(i,j) = 0$ for each pair i,j and use the fact that, given an arbitrary flow that is not complete, a larger flow can be obtained as follows: Find a route from 1 to n in which no road section is used to capacity; now increase the flow in each road section of this route by 1. A complete flow is not always maximal. A maximal flow can be found, however, from a complete flow F by performing the following process:

Step 1. Define for each city i of N a "label" $l(i)$: Let $l(1) = 1$ and let $l(i) = 0$ for $i = 2, 3, \ldots, n$.

Step 2. If there exists a number j such that $l(j) = 0$ and for some i with $l(i) \neq 0$ either $f(i,j) < c(i,j)$ or $f(j,i) > 0$, then let $l(j) = i$ and go to Step 2.

Step 3. If $l(n) = 0$, then stop. (In this case F is maximal.)

Step 4. If $l(n) \neq 0$, then there exists a sequence S: $y_1, y_2, \ldots, y_k$ of cities such that $y_1 = 1, y_k = n$, and $l(y_{i+1}) = y_i$ for $i = 1, 2, \ldots, n - 1$. For each pair (y_i, y_{i+1}) in S change F as follows: If $c(y_i, y_{i+1}) > 0$, increase $f(y_i, y_{i+1})$ by 1; otherwise decrease $f(y_{i+1}, y_i)$ by 1.

Step 5. Go to Step 1.

EXAMPLE

Consider eight cities 1, 2, 3, 4, 5, 6, 7, and 8 where the capacities of existing road sections are as follows: $c(1,2) = c(1,3) = c(1,4) = c(5,8) = c(6,8) = c(7,8) = 2$, $c(4,5) = c(4,6) = c(4,7) = c(3,5) = c(3,6) = c(3,7) = c(2,5) = c(2,6) = c(2,7) = 1$ and $c(i,j) = 0$ otherwise. Further consider a flow F defined by $f(1,4) = f(1,3) = f(6,8) = f(5,8) = 2$, $f(1,2) = f(2,7) = f(7,8) = f(3,6) = f(3,5) = f(4,6) = f(4,5) = 1$, and $f(i,j) = 0$ otherwise. The flow F can easily be seen to be a complete flow and is shown graphically in Fig. 15-2: Solid lines indicate road sections used to capacity, dashed lines indicate road sections used but not to capacity, and dotted lines indicate unused road sections. Using the algorithm described above, the cities are first labeled in Step 1 as $l(1) = 1$, $l(2) = l(3) = l(4) = l(5) = l(6) = l(7) = l(8) = 0$. Now Step 2 is used repeatedly: Since $l(2) = 0$, $l(1) \neq 0$, and $f(1,2) < c(1,2)$, one obtains $l(2) = 1$; since $l(6) = 0$, $l(2) \neq 0$, and $l(2,6) < c(2,6)$, one obtains $l(6) = 2$; since $l(5) = 0$, $l(2) \neq 0$, and $f(2,5) < c(2,5)$, one gets $l(5) = 2$; since $l(3) = 0$, $l(6) \neq 0$, and $f(3,6) > 0$, $l(3) = 6$; since $l(4) = 0$, $l(6) \neq 0$, and $f(4,6) > 0$, one gets $l(4) = 6$; since $l(7) = 0$, $l(4) \neq 0$, and $f(4,7) < c(4,7)$, one obtains $l(7) = 4$; finally, $l(8) = 0$, $l(7) \neq 0$, and $f(7,8) < c(7,8)$ yields $l(8) = 7$.

The sequence of cities 1, 2, 6, 4, 7, 8 has the property described in Step 4 that the label of every city is the preceding city. Thus $f(1,2) = f(1,2) + 1 = 2$ since $c(1,2) > 0$; $f(2,6) = c(2,6) + 1 = 1$ since $c(2,6) > 0$; $f(4,6) =$

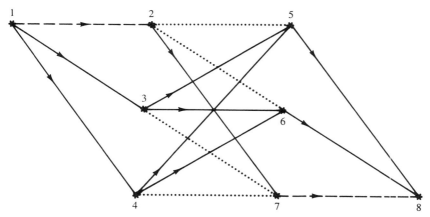

Figure 15-2

$f(4,6) - 1 = 0$ since $c(6,4) = 0$; $f(4,7) = f(4,7) + 1 = 1$ since $c(4,7)$ > 0; and $f(7,8) = f(7,8) + 1 = 2$ since $c(7,8) > 0$.

This new flow obtained is easily seen to be a maximal flow since all roads leaving city 1 are used to capacity. It is graphically shown in Fig. 15-3.

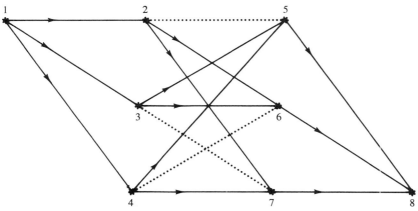

Figure 15-3

15.2 MISCELLANEOUS PROBLEMS

Using Backus Naur Form as explained in Section 10.1, Example 8, define a set $\langle E \rangle$ as follows:

$$\langle \text{digit} \rangle :: = 0 \mid 1 \mid 2 \mid 3 \mid 4 \mid 5 \mid 6 \mid 7 \mid 8 \mid 9$$
$$\langle \text{integer} \rangle :: = \langle \text{digit} \rangle \mid \langle \text{digit} \rangle \langle \text{integer} \rangle$$
$$\langle \text{operator} \rangle :: = + \mid - \mid \cdot \mid / \mid \uparrow$$
$$\langle E \rangle :: = \langle \text{integer} \rangle \mid [\langle E \rangle] \mid \langle E \rangle \langle \text{operator} \rangle \langle E \rangle$$

The set $\langle E \rangle$ is a set of expressions involving integers; the operators $+$ (addition), $-$ (subtraction), $\cdot$ (multiplication), $/$ (integer division), and $\uparrow$ (exponentiation); and the brackets $]$ and $[$.

Typical members of $\langle E \rangle$ are

$$[[3+14]/10+2] \cdot [5+3 \cdot 2]$$
$$5+6-2 \cdot 3$$
$$5 \cdot 6-2+3$$
$$5 \cdot 6-[[[2+3]]], \quad \text{etc.}$$

The value $v(x)$ of any character string x in $\langle E \rangle$ can be defined recursively as follows:

Definition of $v(x)$

Step 1. If x is in $\langle$integer$\rangle$, then let $v(x) = x$ and stop.

Step 2. If $x = [y]$ with y in $\langle E \rangle$, then let $v(x) = v(y)$ and stop.

Step 3. If $x = y + z$ with y and z in $\langle E \rangle$, then let $v(x) = v(y) + v(z)$ and stop.

Step 4. If $x = y - z$ with y and z in $\langle E \rangle$, then let $v(x) = v(y) - v(z)$ and stop.

Step 5. If $x = y \cdot z$ with y and z in $\langle E \rangle$, then let $v(x) = v(y) \cdot v(z)$ and stop.

Step 6. If $x = y/z$ with y and z in $\langle E \rangle$, then let $v(x) = \text{floor}(v(y)/v(z))$ and stop.

Step 7. If $x = y \uparrow z$ with y and z in $\langle E \rangle$, then let $v(x) = v(y)^{v(z)}$ and stop.

EXAMPLE

$$\begin{aligned}
v(5+6-2 \cdot 3) &= v(5) + v(6-2 \cdot 3) = 5 + v(6) - v(2 \cdot 3) \\
&= 5 + 6 - v(2) \cdot v(3) = 11 - 2 \cdot 3 = 5 \\
v(5 \cdot 6-2+3) &= v(5 \cdot 6-2) + v(3) = v(5 \cdot 6) - v(2) + 3 \\
&= v(5) \cdot v(6) - 2 + 3 = 5 \cdot 6 + 1 = 31 \\
v(5 \cdot 6-[[[2+3]]]) &= v(5 \cdot 6) - v([[[2+3]]]) = v(5)v(6) - v([[2+3]]) \\
&= 5 \cdot 6 - v([2+3]) = 30 - v(2+3) = 30 - (v(2) + v(3)) \\
&= 30 - (2+3) = 25
\end{aligned}$$

Note that in the definition of $v(x)$ the order of the steps is of critical importance: Exchanging, e.g., Step 3 with Step 5 would yield

$$\begin{aligned}
v(5+6-2 \cdot 3) &= v(5+6-2) \cdot v(3) = (v(5+6) - v(2)) \cdot 3 \\
&= (v(5) + v(6) - 2) \cdot 3 = 9 \cdot 3 = 27
\end{aligned}$$

Problem 15.2.1 (*Integer Expressions*)

An integer n followed by n character strings $x_1, x_2, \ldots, x_n$ is available on punched cards. Write a program that determines for each x_i ($i = 1, 2, \ldots, n$) whether x_i is in $\langle E \rangle$, and if so, then additionally $v(x_i)$.

Problem 15.2.2 (*Polish Notation for Integer Expressions*)

Consider once more the set $\langle E \rangle$ defined in Problem 15.2.1. Define the "priority" p of the operators $+, -, \cdot, /, \uparrow$ (see Problem 9.3.7) by $p(+) = p(-) = 1$, $p(\cdot) = p(/) = 2$, and $p(\uparrow) = 3$.

To compute $v(x)$ for any x in $\langle E \rangle$ one can first find a character string y in the set $\langle \text{polish} \rangle$ of Problem 10.2.22 with $\text{res}(y) = v(x)$ and use the algorithm of Problem 10.2.24 to calculate $\text{res}(y)$.

For any element x of $\langle E \rangle$, $x = a_1, a_2, \ldots, a_n$ (where a_i is either in $\langle \text{integer} \rangle$ or in $\{+, -, \cdot, /, \uparrow, [,]\}$ for $i = 1, 2, \ldots, n$), the following algorithm will produce a character string $y = b_1 b_2 \cdots b_m$ in $\langle \text{polish} \rangle$ with $v(x) = \text{res}(y)$.

Step 1. Let $i = 1$, let $j = 1$, let $k = 1$, and let $c_0 = [$.

Step 2. If $i > n$ and $k = 1$, then stop.

Step 3. If $i > n$ and $k > 1$, then let $b_j = c_{k-1}$, let $j = j + 1$, let $k = k - 1$, and go to Step 2.

Step 4. If $a_i = [$, then let $c_k = [$, let $k = k + 1$, let $i = i + 1$, and go to Step 2.

Step 5. If a_i is in $\langle \text{integer} \rangle$, then let $b_j = a_i$, let $j = j + 1$, let $i = i + 1$, and go to Step 2.

Step 6. If $a_i =]$ and c_{k-1} is in $\langle \text{operator} \rangle$, then let $b_j = c_{k-1}$, let $k = k - 1$, let $j = j + 1$, and go to Step 6.

Step 7. If $a_i = [$ and $c_{k-1} = [$, then let $k = k - 1$, let $i = i + 1$, and go to Step 2.

Step 8. If a_i is in $\langle \text{operator} \rangle$, c_{k-1} is in $\langle \text{operator} \rangle$, and $p(c_{k-1}) \geq p(a_i)$, then let $b_j = c_{k-1}$, let $k = k - 1$, let $j = j + 1$, and go to Step 8.

Step 9. Let $c_k = a_i$, let $k = k + 1$, let $i = i + 1$, let $b_j = \#$, let $j = j + 1$, and go to Step 2.

To be able to explain the above algorithm informally call $a_1, a_2, \ldots, a_n$ the "input symbols" and $c_0, c_1, \ldots$ the "push-down stack." The algorithm will print a number of "output symbols" $b_1, b_2, \ldots, b_m$.

At the start the stack is empty except for one left bracket $[$ at the "top" of the stack, the first input symbol is a_1, and no output symbol has been printed yet. Now output symbols will be produced as follows:

Step 1. If there is no further input symbol and there is a left bracket at the top of the stack, then stop.

Step 2. If there is no further input symbol but there is an operator at the top of the stack, then print all operators appearing on the stack, starting at the top, removing each operator as it is printed, until a left bracket [is encountered. Then stop.

Step 3. Call the next input symbol *d*.

Step 4. If *d* is a left bracket [, add it to the top of the stack and go to Step 1.

Step 5. If *d* is an integer, print it and go to Step 1.

Step 6. If *d* is a right bracket], print all operators appearing on the stack, starting at the top, removing each operator as it is printed, until a left bracket [is encountered. Now remove that left bracket [from the stack and go to Step 1.

Step 7. If *d* is an operator, print all operators appearing on the top of the stack one by one if their priority is not less than the priority of *d*, removing each operator from the stack as it is printed, until a left bracket [or an operator with priority less than *d* is encountered. Then print the output symbol $\#$, add the operator *d* to the top of the stack, and go to Step 1.

EXAMPLE

If $x = 5 \cdot 6 - [[[2+3]]]$ is given, the above algorithm works as follows: To start with, the *stack* = [and the *output* is nothing. By Step 3, $d = 5$; by Step 5, output = 5; by Step 3, $d = \cdot$; by Step 7, *output* = $5\#$, *stack* = [·; by Step 3, $d = 6$; by Step 5, *output* = $5\#6$; by Step 3, $d = -$; by Step 7, *output* = $5\#6 \cdot \#$, *stack* = [−; by Step 3, $d = [$; by Step 4, *stack* = [−[; by Step 3, $d = [$; by Step 4, *stack* = [−[[; by Step 3, $d = [$; by Step 4, *stack* = [−[[[; by Step 3, $d = 2$; by Step 5, *output* = $5\#6 \cdot \#2$; by Step 3, $d = +$; by Step 7, *output* = $5\#6 \cdot \#2\#$, *stack* = [−[[[+; by Step 3, $d = 3$; by Step 5, *output* = $5\#6 \cdot \#2\#3$; by Step 3, $d =]$; by Step 6, *output* = $5\#6 \cdot \#2\#3+$, *stack* = [−[[; by Step 3, $d =]$; by Step 6, *stack* = [−[; by Step 3, $d =]$; by Step 6, *stack* = [−; by Step 2, *output* = $5\#6 \cdot \#2\#3+-$; and the process terminates.

The reader unfamiliar with polish notation is urged to check carefully how both of the above algorithms transform $5+6-2 \cdot 3$ into $5\#6+\#2\#3 \cdot -$, $5 \cdot 6-2+3$ into $5\#6 \cdot \#2-\#3+$, $5 \cdot 6-[[[2+3]]]$ into $5\#6 \cdot \#2\#3+-$, and $[[3+14]/10+2] \cdot [5+3 \cdot 2]$ into $3\#14+\#10/\#2+\#5\#3\#2 \cdot +\cdot$.

An integer *n* followed by *n* character strings $x_1, x_2, \ldots, x_n$ is available on a punched card. Write a program that determines for each x_i ($i = 1, 2, \ldots, n$) whether x_i is in $\langle E \rangle$ or not; if x_i is in $\langle E \rangle$, the program should also determine a character string *y* with $v(x_i) = \text{res}(y)$ and the value res(*y*) using Problem 10.2.24.

Problem 15.2.3 (*A Simple Compiler*)

Using Backus Naur Form as explained in Section 10.1, Example 8, consider a set $\langle P \rangle$ as follows:

$\langle P \rangle :: = \langle \text{program} \rangle \langle \text{input} \rangle$

$\langle \text{digit} \rangle :: = 0 \mid 1 \mid 2 \mid 3 \mid 4 \mid 5 \mid 6 \mid 7 \mid 8 \mid 9$

$\langle \text{integer} \rangle :: = \langle \text{digit} \rangle \mid \langle \text{digit} \rangle \langle \text{integer} \rangle$

$\langle \text{letter} \rangle :: = A \mid B \mid C \mid D \mid E \mid F \mid G \mid H \mid I \mid J \mid K \mid L \mid M \mid N \mid O \mid P \mid Q \mid R \mid$
$\qquad S \mid T \mid U \mid V \mid W \mid X \mid Y \mid Z$

$\langle \text{identifier} \rangle :: = \langle \text{letter} \rangle \mid \langle \text{letter} \rangle \langle \text{identifier} \rangle$

$\langle \text{label} \rangle :: = \langle \text{identifier} \rangle$

$\langle \text{variable} \rangle :: = \langle \text{identifier} \rangle$

$\langle \text{program} \rangle :: = \langle \text{statement} \rangle ; \text{END}; \mid \langle \text{statement} \rangle ; \langle \text{program} \rangle$

$\langle \text{input} \rangle :: = \langle \text{integer} \rangle , \langle \text{input} \rangle \mid *$

$\langle \text{statement} \rangle :: = \langle \text{label} \rangle : \langle \text{st} \rangle \mid \langle \text{st} \rangle$

$\langle \text{st} \rangle :: = \langle \text{assignment-st} \rangle \mid \langle \text{read-st} \rangle \mid \langle \text{print-st} \rangle \mid \langle \text{goto-st} \rangle \mid$
$\qquad \langle \text{if-st} \rangle \mid \langle \text{stop-st} \rangle$

$\langle \text{assignment-st} \rangle :: = \text{LET}(\langle \text{variable} \rangle = \langle \text{expression} \rangle)$

$\langle \text{expression} \rangle :: = \langle \text{integer} \rangle \mid \langle \text{variable} \rangle \mid (\langle \text{expression} \rangle) \mid$
$\qquad \langle \text{expression} \rangle \langle \text{operator} \rangle \langle \text{expression} \rangle$

$\langle \text{operator} \rangle :: = + \mid - \mid \cdot \mid / \mid \uparrow$

$\langle \text{read-st} \rangle :: = \text{READ}(\langle \text{variable-list} \rangle)$

$\langle \text{print-st} \rangle :: = \text{PRINT}(\langle \text{variable-list} \rangle)$

$\langle \text{variable-list} \rangle :: = \langle \text{variable} \rangle \mid \langle \text{variable} \rangle , \langle \text{variable-list} \rangle$

$\langle \text{goto-st} \rangle :: = \text{GOTO}(\langle \text{label} \rangle)$

$\langle \text{if-st} \rangle :: = \text{IF}(\langle \text{expression} \rangle \langle \text{c-op.} \rangle \langle \text{expression} \rangle) \langle \text{goto-st} \rangle$

$\langle \text{c-op.} \rangle :: = < \mid > \mid =$

$\langle \text{stop-st} \rangle :: = \text{STOP}$

Each element of $\langle P \rangle$ represents a "program" followed by some "input": The program consists of optionally labeled statements that are separated by semicolons, the last being followed by the word END; the input is a sequence of integers separated by commas, the last being followed by an asterisk *.

The statements of a program are performed one after the other (starting with the first statement), unless a GOTO or IF statement designates a different next statement explicitly. The meaning of each individual statement should be obvious.

All variables represent integers. The value of an expression is defined analogous to Problem 15.2.1. The READ statement assigns the integers in the input one by one to the variables in the variable-list of the READ statement. The PRINT statement prints the values of the variables specified one by one, separated by commas.

Write a program C that will read a character string X and that will determine whether X is in $\langle P \rangle$, i.e., is a "program" p in $\langle program \rangle$ followed by some "input" i in $\langle input \rangle$. If this is the case, the program C should print whatever p and i specify.

The program C is called a "compiler" for the given programming language. For simplicity you may assume that p has not more than 100 "statements," that no "identifier" has more than 8 "letters," and that no "integer" has more than 8 "digits."

EXAMPLE

Given as input

$$\text{REPEAT:READ(X);IF(X=0)GOTO(FIN);LET(R=X}\cdot\text{X);}$$
$$\text{PRINT(X,R);GOTO(REPEAT);FIN:STOP;END;3,16,9,0*}$$

the output should be

$$3,9,16,256,9,81$$

Problem 15.2.4 (*A Simple Translator*)

Consider once more the set $\langle P \rangle$ defined in Problem 15.2.3. Write a program T that will read a character string X and that will determine whether X is in $\langle P \rangle$, i.e., is a "program" p in $\langle program \rangle$ followed by some "input" i in $\langle input \rangle$. If this is the case, the program T should print a character string Y that represents a "program" q and "input" j in some other programming language of your own choice (e.g., FORTRAN, Algol 60, PL/1, some assembly language, etc.) such that the effect of running the program q with input j is the same as running the program p with input i.

The program T is called a "translator" for the given programming language.

Problem 15.2.5 (*Symbolic Differentiation*)

Using Backus Naur Form as explained in Section 10.1, Example 8, define a set $\langle F \rangle$ as follows:

$\langle digit \rangle :: = 0 \mid 1 \mid 2 \mid 3 \mid 4 \mid 5 \mid 6 \mid 7 \mid 8 \mid 9$

$\langle integer \rangle :: = \langle digit \rangle \mid \langle digit \rangle\langle integer \rangle$

$\langle quantity \rangle :: = \langle integer \rangle \mid X$

$\langle operator \rangle :: = + \mid - \mid \cdot \mid / \mid \uparrow$

$\quad\quad \langle F \rangle :: = \langle quantity \rangle \mid [\langle F \rangle] \mid \langle F \rangle\langle operator \rangle\langle F \rangle \mid \langle function \rangle[\langle F \rangle]$

$\langle function \rangle :: = LN \mid COS \mid SIN$

The set $\langle F \rangle$ is a set of expressions similar to the set $\langle E \rangle$ of expressions in Problem 15.2.1 but also involves a "variable" X and three "functions" LN, COS, and SIN representing the natural logarithm, the trigonometric cosine, and the trigonometric sine, respectively.

Typical members of $\langle F \rangle$ are

$5 \cdot X \uparrow 3 - 6 \cdot X \uparrow 2 + 3$	(representing $5X^3 - 6X^2 + 3$)
$[X + 3 \cdot X \uparrow 2] \uparrow 3$	(representing $(X + 3X^2)^3$)
$LN[X \uparrow 2 - 3]$	(representing $\ln(X^2 - 3)$), etc.

Write a program that will read a character string f followed by a positive integer $n \leq 15$. If f is not in $\langle F \rangle$, a message to that extent should be printed. Otherwise the program should determine character strings $f^0, f^1, f^2, \ldots, f^n$, where f^i represents the "ith derivative of f with respect to X"; the character strings f^i ($i = 0, 1, \ldots, n$) can be obtained as follows: $f^0 = f$, $f^i = d(f^{i-1})$ for $i = 1, 2, \ldots, n$, where d is defined by the following recursive algorithm:

Definition of the function $d(f)$

Step 1. If $f = [g]$ and g is in $\langle F \rangle$, then let $d(f) = d(g)$ and stop.

Step 2. If $f = g + h$ with g and h in $\langle F \rangle$, then let $d(f) = d(g) + d(h)$ and stop.

Step 3. If $f = g - h$ with g and h in $\langle F \rangle$, then let $d(f) = d(g) - [d(h)]$ and stop.

Step 4. If $f = g \cdot h$ with g and h in $\langle F \rangle$, then let $d(f) = [d(g)] \cdot [h] + [g] \cdot [d(h)]$ and stop.

Step 5. If $f = g/h$ with g and h in $\langle F \rangle$, then let $d(f) = [[d(g)]] \cdot [h] - [g] \cdot [d(h)]/[h] \uparrow 2$.

Step 6. If $f = g \uparrow h$ with g and h in $\langle F \rangle$, then let $d(f) = [g \uparrow h] \cdot [[d(h)] \cdot LN[g] + [[h][d(g)]]/[g]]$ and stop.

Step 7. If f is in $\langle$integer$\rangle$, then $d(f) = 0$ and stop.

Step 8. If $f = X$, then $d(f) = 1$ and stop.

Step 9. If $f = LN[g]$ and g is in $\langle F \rangle$, then let $d(f) = [d(g)]/[g]$ and stop.

Step 10. If $f = COS[g]$ and g is in $\langle F \rangle$, then let $d(f) = 0 - [SIN[g]] \cdot [d(g)]$ and stop.

Step 11. If $f = SIN[g]$ and g is in $\langle F \rangle$, then let $d(f) = [COS[g]] \cdot [d(g)]$ and stop.

The program should not only find $f^0, f^1, \ldots, f^n$ but should also simplify the expressions obtained 'to some extent by removing redundant brackets, 0's, and 1's as factors; reducing $[g \uparrow n]/[g \uparrow m]$ to $g \uparrow k$ (if g is in $\langle F \rangle$, n,m are in $\langle$integer$\rangle$, $n \geq m$ and $k = n - m$); reducing $g \uparrow 0$, $g \uparrow 1$, $0 \uparrow g$, $1 \uparrow g$ to 1, g, 0, and 1, respectively (if g is in $\langle F \rangle$); etc.

EXAMPLE

Suppose that $f = 5 \cdot X \uparrow 3 - 6 \cdot X \uparrow 2 + 3$ is given. Then $f^0 = f$ and $f^1 = d(f)$ is obtained as follows:

$$d(5 \cdot X \uparrow 3 - 6 \cdot X \uparrow 2 + 3) = d(5 \cdot X \uparrow 3) - [d(6 \cdot X \uparrow 2 + 3)]$$

Since

$$d(5 \cdot X \uparrow 3) = [d(5)] \cdot [X \uparrow 3] + [5] \cdot [d(X \uparrow 3)]$$
$$= [0] \cdot [X \uparrow 3] + [5] \cdot [d(X \uparrow 3)]$$

and

$$d(X \uparrow 3) = [X \uparrow 3] \cdot [[d(3)] \cdot \mathrm{LN}[X] + [[3] \cdot [d(X)]]/[X]]$$
$$= [X \uparrow 3] \cdot [[0] \cdot \mathrm{LN}[X] + [[3] \cdot [1]]/[X]]$$
$$= [X \uparrow 3] \cdot [3]/[X] = [X \uparrow 2] \cdot 3$$

one obtains $d(5 \cdot X \uparrow 3) = 15 \cdot X \uparrow 2$. Similarly, $d(6 \cdot X \uparrow 2 + 3) = 12 \cdot X$ is obtained, giving the final result $f^1 = 15 \cdot X \uparrow 2 - 12 \cdot X$.

Problem 15.2.6 (*Series Expansion*)

Many functions $f(X)$ such as those defined by $\langle F \rangle$ in Problem 15.2.5 can be written as "infinite series"

$$f(X) = a_0 + a_1 X + a_2 X^2 + \cdots + a_n X^n + \cdots$$

If a function can be written in this form, it is known from calculus that

$$a_i = \frac{f^i(0)}{i!} \qquad \text{for } i = 0, 1, 2, \ldots$$

where f^i is the ith derivative of f with respect to X (see Problem 15.2.5) and $f^i(0)$ is the value obtained from f^i by replacing each occurrence of the variable X by 0.

Write a program that reads a character string f and determines whether f is in $\langle F \rangle$. If this is the case, the program should attempt to determine the numbers $a_0, a_1, \ldots, a_{10}$ in the infinite series $f(x) = a_0 + a_1 x + a_2 x^2 + \cdots$. In particular, apply the program to SIN[x], COS[x], and LN[$x+1$] using the fact that SIN[0] = LN[1] = 0 and COS[0] = 1.

Note: Infinite series representing functions $f(x)$ are often used to find approximate values for $f(x)$ (see Section 11.4), they can be used to determine $\int_a^b f(x) \, dx$ approximately, etc.

Problem 15.2.7 (*Family Tree*)

Write a program to produce a family tree given an unordered collection of "name cards," "birth cards," "marriage cards," "death cards," and "end cards" as follows.

There is a single name card per family tree indicating the name of the family. The tree will contain only members of this family born with that name and persons who have married a member of the family at issue.

A birth card indicates the birth of a new member of the family. It contains the date of birth, the sex and the first name of the child, and the first name of the father; if this does not determine the father uniquely, it also contains the first name of the father of the father, etc.

A marriage card indicates the marriage of a member of the family with a person not belonging to the family or a member of the family not closely related. It contains the date of the wedding and the names of bride and groom involved; for members of the family only the first name is given (with the first name of the father, of the father of the father, etc., added, if necessary to ensure uniqueness); for a person not belonging to the family, the full name is given.

A death card indicates the death of a member of the family. The information on it is analogous to the one on a birth card.

The occurrence of an end card indicates that the information concerning the family tree is now complete.

The program is to print the family tree as a tree using a number of pages both horizontally and vertically, if necessary. The input data should be checked carefully: Marriages of members of the same sex, of persons whose life-spans do not overlap, and of more than two people are quite unlikely. The life-span of the average person is neither negative nor does it exceed 180 years, etc.

Problem 15.2.8 (*Border Crossings*)

Information is available on punched cards indicating which of a number of countries $C_1, C_2, \ldots, C_n$ ($n \leq 200$) have common borders. Write a program to read this information together with the names of eight pairs of countries and determine for each pair of countries D,E which and how many borders have to be crossed to travel from country D to country E.

Problem 15.2.9 (*Four-Color Problem*)

Information is available similar to Problem 15.2.8 for $n \leq 25$ countries. Determine one way of coloring the map of the countries using only four different colors such that countries with a common borderline appear in different colours.

Note: This problem is known as the "four-color problem": It is not known to date whether for every arrangement of countries such a coloring is possible. However, for an arrangement of only 25 countries a coloring can always be found. To solve this problem use backtracking (see Problem 5.1.6).

Problem 15.2.10 (*Electrical Network*)

Information is available on punched cards representing an electrical network (see Problem 13.5.11) with $n \leq 25$ wires 1, 2, . . . , n and giving the current x_1 entering the network through wire 1 and leaving through wire n and the resistances $r_2, r_3, \ldots, r_{n-1}$ of all other wires.

Using Kirchhoff's first law and Ohm's law as explained in Problem 13.5.11, write a program to determine the currents $x_2, x_3, \ldots, x_{n-1}$ flowing through the wires 2, 3, . . . , $n - 1$.

Problem 15.2.11 (*RPG*)

A very large percentage of the time of the world's computers is spent in preparing and printing reports on sales figures, production figures, accounting figures, etc. Much of this report preparation follows the same basic system of steps:

Read in the raw data.

Perform a few calculations.

Print out the raw data with the relevant totals.

Because the production of reports is a standard procedure most computer manufacturers supply what is known as a report program generator (RPG for short). An RPG sys em is usually designed to accept a few "parameters" describing the raw data file, a few more giving the purpose of the report (what totals to take, etc.), and a few final parameters describing how the report is to appear on the printed page. After digesting these parameters the RPG system produces the desired report or generates a program that will produce the required report. In general there will be one line of output produced for each "record" of the input file. A record may consist of one or more data cards.

Consider now an RPG system in which the following parameters are available. The fields of the input record are called $F1, F2, F3, \ldots$ in that order and the parameters describing the input file are punched, one per card, in the form $Fi = S$ (for $i = 1, 2, 3, \ldots n$), where S is a specification that can be of three types:

> Iw this field consists of a w-digit integer
>
> Cw this field consists of a character string w characters long
>
> Xw this field consists of w blanks

For example, for the input file described in Problem 1.3.2 each record would be described as

> $F1 = C1$ column 1 of the first card
>
> $F2 = I5$ five-digit account number
>
> $F3 = C21$ customer's name
>
> $F4 = X2$ two empty columns, 28 and 29

$F5 = I1$ form of address

$F6 = X50$ blanks at the end of the first card

$F7 = C1$ character code at the start of the second card

$F8 = I5$ five-digit account number

$F9 = C2$ two-digit code in columns 7 and 8

$F10 = X2$ two blank columns, 9 and 10

$F11 = C20$ street address

$F12 = C20$ city

$F13 = C20$ province

$F14 = X10$ blank columns at the end of the second card

There are also parameters available to define constants. These parameters are of the form *letter* $= S$, *constant*, where S is one of the three specifications explained before. For example, to define a five-digit integer constant of value 1 called A one would use a parameter of the form $A = I5,00001$ or to define an 11 character string B having the contents RPG PROBLEM it would require a parameter $B = C11$,RPG PROBLEM. To be able to do simple arithmetic operations on the input data another parameter is available that essentially indicates that a new data item must be generated while the report is being produced. The general form of this parameter is $Gi = D \mathbin{\#} D$, where D is either the name of an input field or the name of a constant and $\#$ stands for any of the arithmetic operators $+$, $-$, $*$ (multiplication), or $/$ (division, only the integer quotient being kept as a result). For example, $G1 = F20 - F39$ would result in field $F39$ being subtracted from field $F20$ and the result being called $G1$. This computation would be done for each record of the report.

The output parameters specify (between them) one complete line of print in the report. The general form is $Pk,j = D$ (where D is either an Fi, a Gi, or the single letter identifying a constant), which specifies that item D should be printed in print positions k through j. A conditional output parameter also exists of the form IF $(X = Y)$UOP, where X and Y are any field (Fi or Gi) or constant names and UOP is any unconditional output parameter. For example, IF $(F1 = F7)P10,14 = F2$ would check to see if field 1 was identical to field 7, and if so, print out the contents of field 2 in print positions 10 to 14.

The fields that are to be totaled are specified by parameters of the form

TOTAL D,k,j (where D is any Fi, Gi, or constant name)

which causes a running total of the contents of field D to be kept and printed out at the end of the report in print positions k through j of a separate line. A final item, END, indicates the end of the parameter list. As a total example, consider the data file (punched on cards) as described below:

Cols. 1–5   five-digit account number

Cols. 6–35   30-character name

Cols. 40–46   seven-digit integer representing the amount of money this customer owes

Cols. 50–56   seven-digit integer representing the amount of money this customer has paid in the last month

A report is to be produced as follows: A customer has one line of print produced on the report giving his name, his account number, his old debt (the amount he owes), the amount of his payment, and his new debt (amount owed minus amount paid) as follows:

Print positions 1–30   customer's name

Print positions 35–39   his account number

Print positions 40–46   his old debt

Print positions 48–54   his payment

Print positions 56–62   his new debt

If a customer does not have an old debt (i.e., it is zero), then a row of asterisks is printed beside his line in print positions 70 to 79. The total of all the old debts, total receipts, and total new debts should be printed at the end of the report in positions 38 to 46, 48 to 56, and 58 to 66, respectively.

The final parameters to the RPG system would now be

$$F1 = I5$$
$$F2 = C30$$
$$F3 = X4$$
$$F4 = I7$$
$$F5 = X3$$
$$F6 = I7$$
$$A = I7,0000000$$
$$B = C10,**********$$
$$G1 = F4-F6$$
$$\text{TOTAL } G1,58,66$$
$$\text{TOTAL } F4,38,46$$
$$\text{TOTAL } F6,48,56$$
$$P1,30 = F2$$
$$P35,39 = F1$$
$$P40,46 = F4$$
$$P48,54 = F6$$
$$P56,62 = G1$$
$$\text{IF}(F4=A)P70,79 = B$$
$$\text{END}$$

Write a RPG system that will accept parameters similar to those described above and, based on these parameters, produce the required report or print out a program in some language of your own choice (e.g., FORTRAN, PL/I, Algol 60, some assembly language) that would produce the report.

Problem 15.2.12 (*Complete Graphs*)

The networks mentioned in Section 15.1 are often called "graphs." An "undirected" graph consists of a set of "vertices" and a set of "edges" joining pairs of these vertices. A "complete graph" on n vertices (generally called K_n) is a graph in which each pair of vertices is joined by an edge. Any graph will always contain some complete graphs. For example, it may contain a K_1 (a simple isolated vertex), or a K_2 (a pair of vertices joined by an edge), or a K_3 (three vertices joined to form a triangle), etc.

A number of cards are given containing a number P followed by a series of pairs of numbers (A,B) followed by the pair $(0,0)$. This input defines a graph on P vertices with each pair (A,B) being joined by an edge. Write a program to read these data and find the largest complete graph contained in the given graph.

Hint: Each K_n will consist of a number of K_{n-1}'s; thus one can eliminate from consideration for K_n any vertices that do not appear as part of a K_{n-1}. It is known that an edge e (with end vertices A,B) that is part of a K_n will have at least $n - 2$ other vertices joined, by edges, to both A and B. Care must be taken when using the last bit of information as there exist many graphs in which each edge has its end points joined to $n - 2$ other vertices but that are not K_n graphs.

Problem 15.2.13 (*Isomorphic Graphs*)

Two graphs, G_1 and G_2 (see Problem 15.2.12), are called "isomorphic" if a one-to-one correspondence can be established between the vertices of G_1 and those of G_2 in such a way that pairs of vertices of G_1 are connected by an edge if and only if the corresponding pairs of vertices of G_2 are connected by an edge. Write a program that will read in the details of two graphs in a form similar to that indicated in Problem 15.2.12 and determine if the two graphs are isomorphic or not. Note that the vertex numbering scheme of the first graph need not be the same as that of the second graph.

Problem 15.2.14 (*Plotting of a Three-Dimensional Object*)

All the problems in Chapter 14 deal with plotting a two-dimensional entity on a two-dimensional surface. It is much more interesting to attempt to plot a picture of how a three-dimensional object will look when viewed from some point P in space. A three-dimensional object (say a cube) can be specified by a sequence of eight triples (x,y,z) giving the coordinates of each corner. The coordinates (X, Y) of the two-dimensional picture of a point (x,y,z) may be obtained as follows:

(a) Choose the point P in three-dimensional space from which the object is being viewed.

(b) Determine the equation of the line A going from the point $(0,0,0)$ to P and A's projection, B, on the xy-plane and A's projection, C, on the xz-plane.

(c) The angle β is that angle made between the line C and the x-axis and the angle α is that angle made between the line B and the x-axis.

(d) $X = x(-\sin(\alpha)) + y(\cos(\alpha))$
$Y = x(-\cos(\alpha)\sin(\beta)) + y(-\sin(\alpha)\sin(\beta)) + z(\cos(\beta))$

Write a program that will read in a sequence of eight triples (x,y,z) giving the coordinates of the corners of a cube, followed by one triple that specifies the point in space from which this object is viewed. The program should then produce a picture of the cube when viewed from the indicated position.

Problem 15.2.15 *(Stereoplot)*

Write a program that will read in a series of triples (x,y,z) giving the coordinates of the corners of a solid figure, followed by one triple that gives the point P in space from which the figure is viewed. The program should make two plots of the figure—one when viewed from $1\frac{1}{2}$ inches to the "right" of P and one when viewed from $1\frac{1}{2}$ inches to the "left" of P. Note that the program will have produced these two plots so that they could be viewed under a stereoscope to produce a three-dimensional "plot" of the figure concerned.

Problem 15.2.16 *(Hidden Lines)*

One of the hardest problems to deal with when plotting a picture of a solid object is to eliminate all lines from the plot that would normally be hidden from view. For example, when viewing a cube from directly in front of one of its faces only four lines, forming the edges of that face, are visible; in general, nine lines are visible on a cube. One method of doing this is to compute the equation of the line from the point of vision to each point on the intended plot. If this line passes through a surface of the solid object, then the point in question is not visible.

Write a program to produce a plot of a solid cube (see Problem 15.2.14) such that only those lines visible from the indicated point of view are actually drawn.

Hint: For a cube it is necessary only to test one point on the line in question to determine if it is visible or not. Be sure to choose this point somewhere other than on a corner of the object because a corner may be visible, while all the lines joined to it may not be visible.

Problem 15.2.17 (*Hidden Lines Stereoplot*)

Write a program to produce a stereoscopic view of a cube (see Problem 15.2.15) such that only the lines normally visible appear in each of the plots (see Problem 15.2.16).

Problem 15.2.18 (*Send More Money*)

A man on a business trip requires an additional amount of money. He cables the three-word telegram SEND+MORE = MONEY to his business partner, who, after some thinking, sends an amount of $10652 since the addition SEND+MORE = MONEY only makes sense if one takes $S = 9$, $E = 5$, $N = 6$, $D = 7$, $M = 1$, $O = 0$, $R = 8$, and $Y = 2$, yielding 10652 for the word MONEY.

Write a program that reads three words x, y, and z of five characters each and that determines all valid additions that can be obtained from $x + y = z$ by replacing each character by one of the digits 0, 1, ... , 9 using different digits for different characters.

Problem 15.2.19 (*Compiler*)

One of the problems associated with the current proliferation of different computers and different languages is that a program written for an ABC computer will not, in general, run on an XYZ machine.

Choose a simple† assembly language L not available on the computer you are using. Write a program C that, given a character string X representing an arbitrary program p (written in the language L) with some input i, produces whatever output p would produce if supplied with input i. C is called a "compiler" for the language L.

Problem 15.2.20 (*Translator*)

Choose a simple† assembly language L not available on the computer you are using and another assembly language M available on the machine you are using. Write a program T that, given a character string X representing an arbitrary program p in the language L, produces a character string Y representing a program q in the language M such that the effect of p and q is the same. T is called a "translator" of L into M.

Problem 15.2.21 (*Simulator*)

Choose a simple‡ computer A different from the one you are using. Write a program S, that, given as input a character string X representing

† To keep this problem down to size use a language with a small instruction repertoire, where each individual instruction is reasonably simple and reasonably independent of special properties of a certain computer such as buffers, timing considerations, etc.

‡ To keep this problem down to size choose a "first-generation computer" with a simple instruction set.

a part P of the storage of the computer A containing some machine instructions I and data, will "simulate" the execution of the instructions I. The output is to consist of (a) whatever the instructions I would have printed when executed on computer A and (b) a character string Y representing the part P of the storage of A after the instructions I have been performed. S is called a "simulator" of the computer A.

APPENDIX

This section of the book gives enough information for most problems to determine if a program is running correctly. This is generally supplied by showing some of the lines of output that the program should have produced. If the output from a program can be easily checked, then no sample output is given. If the question requires the writing of a program to print out a table, then three or four lines of the table, taken at random, are displayed. Beside each problem is given an estimate of the number of elementary statements needed in the program. An elementary statement is assumed to be the equivalent of one statement of about 15 characters in FORTRAN, PL/1, or BASIC. This figure is only a guide and should not be considered in any way accurate. The size of the program is estimated as 10 statements or less—indicated by (10), between 10 and 20 statements—indicated by (20), between 20 and 50 statements—indicated by (50), between 50 and 100 statements—indicated by (100), and greater than 100 statements—indicated by (> 100).

Different computers will have different capabilities when it comes to storing and manipulating data. For this reason it is not impossible that the results produced by one computer will differ slightly from those produced by another. However, it is unlikely that correct results will differ from those presented here by more than one digit in the last decimal place.

CHAPTER 1

Section 1.2

Problem 1.2.1 (10)

Problem 1.2.2 (10)

205

Problem 1.2.3   (10)

Kilometers	Feet	Yards	Nautical Miles	Miles
34	111,554	37,182.4	18.3464	21.1276
112	367,472	122,483.2	60.4352	69.5968
187	613,547	204,503.2	100.9052	116.2018

Problem 1.2.4   (10)

Centigrade	Fahrenheit
−29	−20.2
0	32.0
32	89.6
95	203.0

Problem 1.2.5   (10)

Integer	Square
32	1024
52	2704
84	7056

Problem 1.2.6   (20)

For the data 1, 2, 34, 3, 4, 5, 6, 67, 5, and 6 the program should produce

THE LARGEST NUMBER IS 67 IT WAS PUNCHED ON CARD 8

Problem 1.2.7   (50)

Problem 1.2.8   (50)

Problem 1.2.9   (50)

Problem 1.2.10   (20)

For the example given in the problem,

Month	Principal ($)	Interest ($)	Tax ($)	Payment ($)	New Principal ($)
41	13,743.99	68.72	58.33	300.00	13,571.04
64	9,539.50	47.70	58.33	300.00	9,345.53
108	FINAL PAYMENT OF $78.00				

Problem 1.2.11   (50)

Ticket Price ($)	Total Profit ($)
2.35	245.85
1.95	265.05
1.30	9.60

Problem 1.2.12   (20)

The value of π (to three decimal places) is 3.141.

Problem 1.2.13   (20)

Problem 1.2.14   (20)

Problem 1.2.15   (10)

Mass	Spring Constant	Frequency
0.5	20	1.006
1.1	50	1.073
2.3	60	0.813

Problem 1.2.16   (20)

Mass	Mercury	Venus	Earth	Moon	Mars	Jupiter	Saturn	Uranus	Neptune
16	4.32	13.60	16.00	2.56	6.08	42.24	18.72	14.72	17.92
66	17.82	56.10	66.00	10.56	25.08	174.24	77.22	60.72	73.92
160	43.20	136.00	160.00	25.60	60.80	422.40	187.20	147.20	179.20

Problem 1.2.17   (10)

$F_{21} = 10{,}946$, $F_{30} = 832{,}040$.

Problem 1.2.18   (20)

Section 1.3

Problem 1.3.1   (20)

Problem 1.3.2   (20)

Problem 1.3.3   (20)

Problem 1.3.4   (20)

Problem 1.3.5   (50)

The program should have generated, among others, the strings

    ABBABBB
    ABABAABBAB
    ABABAAAABBBABBBABB

Altogether 276 strings should be generated.

Section 1.4

Problem 1.4.1   (20)

    7 11   8   IS SUNDAY NOVEMBER 8
    2 11 32   IS INVALID

Problem 1.4.2   (50)

Problem 1.4.3   (50)

Problem 1.4.4 (10)

$$5! = 120$$
$$7! = 5040$$

Problem 1.4.5 (10)

15	10	6	GENERAL
15	10	15	ISOSCELES
15	10	30	NONE

Problem 1.4.6 (20)

For the data

JOHN SMITH FTFTTTFTFFFFTTTFFFFTFTFTFFTFFTTTTFFFFTT
FTFFTFFTFFFTTTTFFFFFTTF

the program should produce

JOHN SMITH 31 OUT OF 60

Problem 1.4.7 (20)

The two solutions to $x^2 - 8x + 15 = 0$ are $x = 3$ and $x = 5$.

Problem 1.4.8 (20)

Some of the triples are

5	12	13
39	52	65

Altogether the program should generate 29 triples.

Problem 1.4.9 (10)

If anyone finds a solution to $abs(a^n + b^n - c^n) = 0$, the authors would very much like to hear about it. The program should have generated eight triples such that $abs(a^n + b^n - c^n) \le 15$.

CHAPTER 2

Section 2.2

Problem 2.2.1 (20)

The first five lines of the table should be

Miles	Kilometers
0.621	1.000
1.000	1.610
1.242	2.000
1.863	3.000
2.000	3.220

The last four lines of the table should be

Miles	Kilometers
62.112	100.000
63.000	101.430
64.000	103.040
65.000	104.650

Problem 2.2.2   (20)

The first four lines of the table are

Pounds	Kilograms
1.000	0.454
2.000	0.907
2.205	1.000
3.000	1.361

The last four lines are

Pounds	Kilograms
198.000	89.813
198.413	90.000
199.000	90.266
200.000	90.720

Problem 2.2.3   (20)

Choosing 1 German mark = 0.334 Canadian dollars, the first four lines of the table are

Canadian $	German Marks
0.334	1.000
0.668	2.000
1.000	2.994
1.002	3.000

Assuming that the table goes from 1 to 66 Canadian dollars and from 1 to 200 German marks, then the last four lines are

Canadian $	German Marks
66.000	197.605
66.132	198.000
66.466	199.000
66.800	200.000

Problem 2.2.4   (20)

The first four lines are

Fahrenheit	Centigrade
−40.000	−40.000
−39.000	−39.444
−38.200	−39.000
−38.000	−38.889

The last four lines are

Fahrenheit	Centigrade
210.000	98.889
210.200	99.000
211.000	99.444
212.000	100.000

Problem 2.2.5   (20)

Choosing the $n = 5$ pairs of numbers 6,19; 13,21; 15,22; 18,23; and 30,36, the program should produce 6, 13, 15, 18, 19, 21, 22, 23, 30, 36.

Problem 2.2.6   (20)

Choosing the $n = 3$ groups of surnames Adam, Conolly, Epp, Erhart, Aalborg; Brown, Eby, Harris, Turlock, Theed; and Rurka, Miller, Mauch, Wilde, Vender, the program should produce Aalborg, Adam, Brown, Conolly, Eby, Epp, Erhart, Harris, Miller, Mauch, Rurka, Theed, Turlock, Vender, Wilde.

Problem 2.2.7   (50)

The first four lines of the table are

Miles	Kilometers	Geog. Miles	Naut. Miles	It. Miles	Aust. Miles
0.621	1.000	0.135	0.541	0.549	0.138
1.000	1.610	0.217	0.870	0.885	0.222
1.130	1.820	0.245	0.984	1.000	0.251
1.149	1.850	0.249	1.000	1.016	0.276

The last four lines are

Miles	Kilometers	Geog. Miles	Naut. Miles	It. Miles	Aust. Miles
67.547	108.750	14.656	58.784	59.753	15.000
67.795	109.150	14.710	59.000	59.973	15.055
67.826	109.200	14.717	59.027	60.000	15.062
68.943	111.000	14.964	60.000	60.992	15.311

Problem 2.2.8   (50)

Choosing

1 German mark = 0.334 Canadian dollars

1 Canadian dollar = 0.97 U.S. dollars

1. U.S. dollar = 26 Austrian shillings

1 Austrian shilling = 23 Italian lire

1 U.S. dollar = 4 Swiss franks

and assuming that the table is to show 1, 2, 3, . . . , 50 German marks; 1, 2, 3, . . . , 14 Canadian dollars; 1, 2, 3, . . . , 13 U.S. dollars; 1, 2, 3, . . . , 60 Swiss franks; 10, 20, 30, . . . , 350 Austrian shillings; and 200, 400, 600, . . . , 8000 Italian lire, the first four lines of the table are

Canadian $	U.S. $	German Marks	Swiss Franks	Aust. Shillings	It. Lire
0.258	0.250	0.772	1.000	6.500	149.500
0.334	0.324	1.000	1.296	8.423	193.740
0.345	0.334	1.032	1.338	8.696	200.000
0.397	0.385	1.187	1.538	10.000	230.000

Problem 2.2.9   (50)

The first four lines of the table are

Centigrade	Fahrenheit	Reaumir	Kelvin
−273.000	−459.400	−218.400	0.000
−272.000	−457.600	−217.600	1.000
−271.000	−455.800	−216.800	2.000
−270.000	−454.000	−216.000	3.000

The last four lines of the table are

Centigrade	Fahrenheit	Reaumir	Kelvin
98.889	210.000	79.111	371.889
99.000	210.200	79.200	372.000
99.444	211.000	79.556	372.444
100.000	212.000	80.000	373.000

Problem 2.2.10   (20)

Problem 2.2.11   (50)

Choosing the list Drake, A; Hoirch, A; Demarco, B; Demers, B; Taylor, B; Cain, C; Mitchel, C; Mutsch, D; Frost, F; Hanarth, F; Kersch, F, the program should produce Cain, C; Demarco; B; Demers, B; Drake,

A; Frost, F; Hanarth, F; Hoirch, A; Kersch, F; Mitchel, C; Mutsch, D; Taylor, B.

Problem 2.2.12   (100)

CHAPTER 3

Section 3.2

Problem 3.2.1   (20)

In the integers $2, 3, \ldots, 200$ there are 47 abundant, 150 deficient, and 2 perfect numbers.

Problem 3.2.2   (20)

$P(10) = 42.$

Problem 3.2.3   (20)

$$15^3 = 3375 = 211 + 213 + 215 + 217 + 219 + 221 + 223$$
$$+ 225 + 227 + 229 + 231 + 233 + 235 + 237 + 239$$

$$20^3 = 8000 = 381 + 383 + 385 + 387 + 389 + 391$$
$$+ 393 + 395 + 397 + 399 + 401 + 403 + 405$$
$$+ 407 + 409 + 411 + 413 + 415 + 417 + 419$$

Problem 3.2.4   (20)

Problem 3.2.5   (20)

Problem 3.2.6   (20)

There are 303 prime numbers form 2 to 2000.

Problem 3.2.7   (50)

n	P_n	Q_n
203	1237	1196.2
267	1709	1646.3
303	1999	1906.6

Problem 3.2.8   (50)

There are 61 prime twins between 2 and 2000, the first pair being 3 and 5 and the last pair 1997 and 1999.

Problem 3.2.9   (20)

According to the formula there should be about 31 prime twins between 1 and 1500.

Problem 3.2.10   (50)

Problem 3.2.11   (50)

There are 87 complex prime numbers between 2 and 1000.

Problem 3.2.12   (50)

There are two values of n ($1 \leq n \leq 43$) such that x_n is not prime.

Problem 3.2.13 (20)

There are four values of n ($1 \leq n \leq 90$) for which y_n is not prime.

Problem 3.2.14 (50)

There are 22 permutable primes between 2 and 2000.

Problem 3.2.15 (20)

There are three prime numbers, less than 2000, of the form $n^n + 1$.

Problem 3.2.16 (20)

There are three prime numbers, less than 2000, of the form $n! + 1$.

Problem 3.2.17 (50)

There are 20 different arithmetic progressions of consecutive primes ≤ 2000 whose constant difference is less than 10. Of these, 18 consist of three consecutive primes and 2 consist of four consecutive primes.

Problem 3.2.18 (50)

Two arithmetic progressions of constant difference 6 are 11, 17, 23, 29 and 601, 607, 613, 619.

Problem 3.2.19 (20)

The number in question is 200.

Problem 3.2.20 (20)

There are four values of P ($2 \leq P \leq 12$) that result in the number $2^P - 1$ being prime.

Problem 3.2.21 (20)

Problem 3.2.22 (20)

The integer 123456 has the following factors: 1, 2, 3, 4, 6, 8, 12, 16, 24, 32, 48, 64, 96, 192, 643, 1286, 1929, 2572, 3858, 5144, 7716, 10288, 15432, 20576, 30864, 41152, 61728, 123456.

Problem 3.2.23 (50)

The first sequence of seven numbers, none of which is a prime, is 90, 91, 92, 93, 94, 95, 96.

Problem 3.2.24 (20)

$$\text{lcf}(306,68) = 34$$
$$\text{lcf}(10784619,27) = 9$$

Problem 3.2.25 (20)

$$\text{lcf}(21,12,9) = 3$$
$$\text{lcf}(64,32,24) = 8$$

Problem 3.2.26 (20)

$$\text{scm}(21,9) = 63$$
$$\text{scm}(306,68) = 612$$

Problem 3.2.27 (50)

$\text{mod}(2179^{76},33) = 1$.

Problem 3.2.28   (50)

There are 66 pseudoprimes from 1500 to 2000 of which 2 are not prime numbers.

Problem 3.2.29   (50)

The rightmost seven digits of 2^{5186} are 7739264 and of 3^{5186} are 3189129.

CHAPTER 4

Section 4.2

Problem 4.2.1   (20)

Height (miles)	Orbital Velocity (ft/sec)	Orbit Time (min)	Additional Velocity for Escape (ft/sec)
109	25,482	88	10,555
144	25,373	89	10,510
207	25,180	91	10,430
290	24,933	94	10,328

Problem 4.2.2   (10)

The square root of 16 = 4.000

The cube root of 16 = 2.5198

The fourth root of 16 = 2.0000

The fifth root of 16 = 1.7411

The eighth root of 16 = 1.4142

The tenth root of 16 = 1.3195

Problem 4.2.3   (20)

The value of π, correct to four decimal places, is 3.1415.

Problem 4.2.4   (20)

Given the pairs of numbers, $-2,1; 3,2; 4,6; 3, -2; 7,3; 5,2; 9, -3; -9, -3; 6, -14;$ and 4,3, the program should indicate that the following vectors are perpendicular: (4,6) and (3,−2), (7,3) and (6,−14).

Problem 4.2.5   (20)

If

$$M = \begin{pmatrix} 1 & 2 & 3 & 4 \\ 2 & 1 & 4 & 3 \\ 3 & 4 & 2 & 1 \\ 4 & 3 & 1 & 2 \end{pmatrix} \qquad N = \begin{pmatrix} 1 & 0 & 0 & 1 \\ 0 & 1 & 0 & 0 \\ 0 & 0 & 0 & 1 \\ 1 & 0 & 1 & 0 \end{pmatrix}$$

then

$$P = \begin{pmatrix} 5 & 2 & 4 & 4 \\ 5 & 1 & 3 & 6 \\ 4 & 4 & 1 & 5 \\ 6 & 3 & 2 & 5 \end{pmatrix} \qquad Q = \begin{pmatrix} 5 & 5 & 4 & 6 \\ 2 & 1 & 4 & 3 \\ 4 & 3 & 1 & 2 \\ 4 & 6 & 5 & 5 \end{pmatrix}$$

Problem 4.2.6 (50)

If there exists a road network joining cities 1 and 3, 2 and 6, 2 and 9, 3 and 4, 4 and 10, 5 and 6, 5 and 7, and 7 and 9, and an air route linking (in both directions) cities 1 and 10, 2 and 3, 2 and 4, 2 and 9, 3 and 7, 4 and 9, 5 and 7, 6 and 10, and 8 and 9, then the following table gives the number of ways of going from city i to city j, doing the first leg of the journey by road and the second by air:

					J					
	1	**2**	**3**	**4**	**5**	**6**	**7**	**8**	**9**	**10**
1	0	1	0	0	0	0	1	0	0	0
2	0	1	0	1	0	0	0	1	0	1
3	0	1	0	0	0	0	0	0	1	1
4	1	1	0	0	0	1	1	0	0	0
I **5**	0	0	1	0	1	0	0	0	0	1
6	0	0	1	1	0	0	1	0	1	0
7	0	1	0	1	0	0	1	1	0	0
8	0	0	0	0	0	0	0	0	0	0
9	0	0	2	1	1	0	0	0	1	0
10	0	1	0	0	0	0	0	0	1	0

Problem 4.2.7 (50)

Problem 4.2.8 (50)

Problem 4.2.9 (20)

If $A(x) = 1 + 2x + 3x^2 + 4x^3 + 5x^4 + 6x^5 + 7x^6 + 8x^7 + 9x^8 + 10x^9 + 11x^{10}$ and $B(x) = 5 + 6x + 7x^2 + 8x^3 + 9x^4 + 10x^5 + 11x^6 + 1x^7 + 2x^8 + 3x^9 + 4x^{10}$ then $C(x) = 5 + 16x + 34x^2 + 60x^3 + 95x^4 + 140x^5 + 196x^6 + 253x^7 + 312x^8 + 374x^9 + 440x^{10} + 446x^{11} + 435x^{12} + 406x^{13} + 358x^{14} + 290x^{15} + 201x^{16} + 90x^{17} + 88x^{18} + 73x^{19} + 44x^{20}$.

Problem 4.2.10 (50)

For $A(x) = x^5 - x^3 - x^2 + 1$ and $B(x) = x^4 - 2x^2 + 1$ one obtains $C(x) = x$ $\qquad R(x) = x^3 - x^2 - x + 1$.

Problem 4.2.11 (50)

If $A(x)$ and $B(x)$ are the polynomials given in the answer to Problem 4.2.10, then $F(x) = x^3 - x^2 - x + 1$.

Section 4.3

Problem 4.3.1 (10)

The decimal number 27 has a binary representation of 11011. The decimal number 205 has a binary representation of 11001101.

Problem 4.3.2 (10)

See the results given in the answer to Problem 4.3.1.

Problem 4.3.3 (10)

The binary number 0111111111111111111111111111111 has a decimal value of $2^{31} - 1 = 2147483647$.

Problem 4.3.4 (20)

Problem 4.3.5 (20)

The 182nd day of the year is a Tuesday. The 256th day of the year is a Saturday. The 323rd day of the year is a Wednesday.

Problem 4.3.6 (20)

Problem 4.3.7 (20)

Problem 4.3.8 (20)

Problem 4.3.9 (20)

Problem 4.3.10 (50)

Section 4.4

Problem 4.4.1 (50)

A magic square of order 9 is

71	64	69	8	1	6	53	46	51
66	68	70	3	5	7	48	50	52
67	72	65	4	9	2	49	54	47
26	19	24	44	37	42	62	55	60
21	23	25	39	41	43	57	59	61
22	27	20	40	45	38	58	63	56
35	28	33	80	73	78	17	10	15
30	32	34	75	77	79	12	14	16
31	36	29	76	81	74	13	18	11

The numbers forming the first row of the 81 by 81 magic square are 5741, 5734, 5739, 5678, 5671, 5676, 5723, 5716, 5721, 5174, 5167, 5172, 5111, 5104, 5109, 5156, 5149, 5154, 5579, 5572, 5577, 5516, 5509, 5514, 5561, 5554, 5559, 638, 631, 636, 575, 568, 573, 620, 613, 618, 71, 64, 69, 8, 1, 6, 53, 46, 51, 476, 469, 474, 413, 406, 411, 458, 451, 456, 4283, 4276, 4281, 4220, 4213, 4218, 4265, 4258, 4263, 3716, 3709, 3714, 3653, 3646, 3651, 3698, 3691, 3696, 4121, 4114, 4119, 4058, 4051, 4056, 4103, 4096, 4101.

Problem 4.4.2 (20)

A magic square of order 5 is

11	18	25	2	9
10	12	19	21	3
4	6	13	20	22
23	5	7	14	16
17	24	1	8	15

A magic square of order 7 is

```
22  31  40  49   2  11  20
21  23  32  41  43   3  12
13  15  24  33  42  44   4
 5  14  16  25  34  36  45
46   6   8  17  26  35  37
38  47   7   9  18  27  29
30  39  48   1  10  19  28
```

Problem 4.4.3   (50)

The first row of a magic square of order 25 is 261, 268, 275, 252, 259, 436, 443, 450, 427, 434, 611, 618, 625, 602, 609, 36, 43, 50, 27, 34, 211, 218, 225, 202, 209. The second row of this magic square is 260, 262, 269, 271, 253, 435, 437, 444, 446, 428, 610, 612, 619, 621, 603, 35, 37, 44, 46, 28, 210, 212, 219, 221, 203.

Problem 4.4.4   (20)

Given the integers 0, 1, 2, 3, 4, 5, 6, 7, and 8 a magic square is

```
7  0  5
2  4  6
3  8  1
```

For the integers 3, 6, 12, 18, 19, 24, 30, 34, and 36 no magic square exists.

Problem 4.4.5   (20)

A magic square of order 4 is

```
 1  12   7  14
 8  13   2  11
10   3  16   5
15   6   9   4
```

Problem 4.4.6   (50)

A border square of order 6 is

```
 1   6  10  29  30  35
 9  11  22  17  24  28
32  18  23  12  21   5
33  20  13  26  15   4
34  25  16  19  14   3
 2  31  27   8   7  36
```

Problem 4.4.7   (20)

Problem 4.4.8   (50)

There are two diagonal Latin squares of order 4 such that $L_{11} = 1, L_{14} = 2$, $L_{41} = 3$, and $L_{44} = 4$.

Problem 4.4.9   _ (50)

There are six diagonal Latin squares of order 5 such that $L_{11} = 1, L_{15} = 2$, $L_{51} = 4$, and $L_{55} = 5$.

Problem 4.4.10   (50)

There are four Greco–Latin squares of the type described in the problem.

Problem 4.4.11   (50)

If the two diagonal Latin squares are

$$
\begin{array}{cccc}
1 & 2 & 3 & 4 \\
4 & 3 & 2 & 1 \\
2 & 1 & 4 & 3 \\
3 & 4 & 1 & 2
\end{array}
\quad \text{and} \quad
\begin{array}{cccc}
1 & 2 & 3 & 4 \\
3 & 4 & 1 & 2 \\
4 & 3 & 2 & 1 \\
2 & 1 & 4 & 3
\end{array}
$$

then the magic square of order 4 is

$$
\begin{array}{cccc}
5 & 10 & 15 & 20 \\
16 & 19 & 6 & 9 \\
18 & 13 & 12 & 7 \\
11 & 8 & 17 & 14
\end{array}
$$

Section 4.5

Problem 4.5.1   (50)

For the alloys

ALUMINUM 30 IRON 50 NICKEL 20

ZINC 10 COPPER 70 NICKEL 20

IRON 60 NICKEL 20 COPPER 20

the specific weights are 6.23, 8.70, and 8.23, respectively.

Problem 4.5.2   (50)

Formula	Molecular Weight
ALCL(3)	133.33
NO(2)	46.01
C(5)H(12)	72.146

Problem 4.5.3   (20)

12 POUNDS 3 SHILLINGS 6 PENCE = $29.22

2 POUNDS 0 SHILLINGS 0 PENCE = $4.80

5 POUNDS 9 SHILLINGS 11 PENCE = $13.19

Problem 4.5.4   (20)

m_1 d_1	m_2 d_2	Days Between
1 2	1 7	4
8 12	8 3	8
13 2	8 12	INVALID

Problem 4.5.5   (50)

Year	Date of Easter
1800	APRIL 13
1810	APRIL 22
1991	MARCH 31
2000	APRIL 23

Problem 4.5.6   (20)

Date	Day of Week
1942,8,9	SUNDAY
1970,11,22	SUNDAY
2000,4,23	SUNDAY

CHAPTER 5

Section 5.1

Problem 5.1.1   (50)

Problem 5.1.2   (50)

If $M = 2$ and $P = 20$, then the knight can (in three moves or less) visit every square on the board except 2, 6, 34, 38, 56, 57, 59, 61, and 63.

Problem 5.1.3   (50)

Problem 5.1.4   (100)

Problem 5.1.5   (50)

If the black rook is on square 50 and the white queen on square 22 and there are other pieces on squares 13, 21, 25, 30, 37, 40, 42, 43, 47, and 54, then the rook must move from square 50 to 52, from 52 to 4, from 4 to 6, and finally from 6 to 22 and capture the queen.

Problem 5.1.6   (100)

One of the 92 possible solutions is to place a queen on squares 3, 14, 20, 26, 40, 45, 55, and 57.

Problem 5.1.7   (100)

One of the positions for five dominating queens is on squares 14, 19, 29, 39, and 44.

Problem 5.1.8   (100)

One of the positions for 12 dominating knights is to place them on squares 14, 18, 19, 21, 22, 27, 38, 43, 44, 46, 47, and 51.

Problem 5.1.9   (50)

One of the many possible knight's tours starts on square 42 and then moves in turn to squares 57, 51, 41, 58, 52, 62, 56, 39, 24, 7, 13, 3, 9, 26, 11, 1, 18, 33, 50, 60, 45, 35, 25, 10, 4, 19, 2, 17, 34, 49, 59, 44, 61, 55, 40, 23, 8, 14, 29, 46, 47, 64, 54, 48, 63, 32, 15, 30, 36, 53, 38, 28, 43, 37, 20, 5, 22, 12, 27, 21, 6, 16, and 31.

Problem 5.1.10   (50)

The longest journey a knight can make does not always start in a corner; however, for a board with five rows and columns (the squares being numbered from 1 to 25, 1 to 5 in the first row, 6 to 10 in the second, etc.) the longest journey does start on square 1 and proceeds to squares 12, 21, 18, 25, 14, 17, 8, 15, 4, and 7.

Problem 5.1.11 (>100)

Problem 5.1.12 (>100)

Section 5.2

Problem 5.2.1 (50)

Problem 5.2.2 (100)

Problem 5.2.3 (100)

Problem 5.2.4 (100)

There is no known winning strategy for this game.

Problem 5.2.5 (100)

The positions $(1,4,5)$, $(2,1,3)$, $(2,3,1)$, $(0,3,3)$, and $(0,1,1)$ are a few of the possible winning positions.

Problem 5.2.6 (100)

Problem 5.2.7 (>100)

Problem 5.2.8 (>100)

CHAPTER 6

Section 6.2

Problem 6.2.1 (20)

A solution is $s = 2.3112946$.

Problem 6.2.2 (20)

A solution is $s = 0.74828625$.

Problem 6.2.3 (20)

A solution for $e = 0.03$ is $s = -0.963$. A solution for $e = 0.00001$ is $s = -0.9625$.

Problem 6.2.4 (20)

A solution is $s = 1.27826$.

Problem 6.2.5 (20)

One solution is $s = 1.470989$. The other solution is between 7 and 8.

Problem 6.2.6 (20)

A solution is $s = 1.21246$.

Problem 6.2.7 (20)

For $a = 2$, $b = 3.73$, $c = 9.1$, and $e = 0.001$, a solution is $s = -2.1921$. For $a = -0.1$, $b = 2.6$, $c = -8$, and $e = 0.0001$, a solution is $s = 1.6$.

Problem 6.2.8 (50)

For $a = -1.9$, $b = -1.7$, $c = 3.4$, and $e = 0.0001$, a solution is $s = -1.3239$ and the remaining solutions are 1.7858 and 1.4381. For $a = -6.2$, $b = 8.3$, $c = -47$, and $e = 0.00001$, a solution is $s = 6.10205$ and there are no more real solutions.

Problem 6.2.9 (20)

A solution is $s = 1.6699449392$.

Problem 6.2.10   (20)

For $a = 1$, $b = 2$, $c = 1.5$, $d = -3$, $e = 5$, and $t = 0.0003$, a solution is $s = -1.65834$. For $a = -8$, $b = 0$, $c = 0$, $d = 0.8$, $e = 19.3$, and $t = 0.000001$, a solution is $s = -1.1887460$.

Problem 6.2.11   (50)

For $a = -8$, $b = 0$, $c = 0$, $d = 0.8$, $e = 19.3$, and $t = 0.000001$, a solution is $s = 7.9937070$. For $a = 1$, $b = 2$, $c = 1.5$, $d = -3$, $e = 5$, and $t = 0.0003$, a solution is $s = -1.65834$.

Problem 6.2.12   (50)

Four iterations are required with the Newton–Raphson method and 32 iterations with interval halving. The solution obtained is between 1.96 and 1.97.

Problem 6.2.13   (20)

For $p = 1.3$ and $q = -5$, a solution is $s = 1.45868176$. For $p = -1$ and $q = -6.9$, a solution is $s = 2.07842$.

Problem 6.2.14   (50)

For $a = 1$, $b = 3$, and $c = -7.787$, a solution is $s = 1.3$. For $a = -2.6$, $b = 4.1$, and $c = -0.7$, a solution is $s = 0.193$.

Problem 6.2.15   (50)

The solutions are 13, $-\frac{1}{3}$, $\frac{1}{3}$, $\frac{7}{3}$, $-\frac{7}{3}$, and $-\frac{1}{17}$.

Problem 6.2.16   (50)

The solutions are $\frac{13}{10}$, $-\frac{13}{10}$, and $-\frac{23}{10}$.

Problem 6.2.17   (50)

For $a = 4$, $b = -28$, $c = -1$, and $d = 7$, one obtains the solutions $\frac{1}{2}$, $-\frac{1}{2}$, and 7. For $a = 338$, $b = -169$, $c = -8$, and $d = 4$, one obtains the solutions $\frac{2}{13}$, $-\frac{2}{13}$, and $\frac{1}{2}$.

Problem 6.2.18   (50)

For $a = -7$, $b = 0$, $c = 0$, $d = -4$, and $e = 28$, there is only one solution $s = 7$ of the desired form. For $a = 5$, $b = -5$, $c = -25$, $d = 4$, and $e = 20$, the solutions obtained are 1, -1, 2, -2, and -5.

Problem 6.2.19   (100)

The equation can be reduced to $x^5 - 3x^3 - 2x^2 + 6 = 0$, which has three real solutions: $+\sqrt{3}$, $-\sqrt{3}$, and $\sqrt[3]{2}$.

Problem 6.2.20   (50)

Problem 6.2.21   (50)

CHAPTER 7

Section 7.2

Problem 7.2.1   (20)

Problem 7.2.2   (20)

Problem 7.2.3   (50)

Problem 7.2.4   (50)

Problem 7.2.5   (20)

Problem 7.2.6   (50)

Problem 7.2.7   (100)

For sorting 200 random numbers between 1 and 99999 using the method of Problem 7.2.6, between 2 and 12 rearrangements are necessary.

Problem 7.2.8   (50)

Using 80 random numbers $x_1, x_2, \ldots, x_{80}$ between -100 and 900 generated by the algorithm in Section 8.1 with starting value $Y = 568731$ a total of 1626 exchanges is necessary.

Problem 7.2.9   (20)

Problem 7.2.10   (100)

Considering the following customer file, payment cards, and charge cards,

631502	Legg T.	2839 Lionel Ave.	+16.30
180003	Hofstra M.	225 Smith Str.	−6.00
000963	Malioney P.J.	4344 Nero Rd.	+366.92
517724	Morier G.E.	19 Cumberland Ave.	+60.40
432649	Hauser M.	2940 Toronto Rd.	0.00
817387	Currie W.D.	281 Harvard Str.	+55.00
180003		PAYMENT	4.00
000963		CHARGE	23.88
817387		PAYMENT	55.00
000963		CHARGE	10.00
000963		PAYMENT	60.00
517724		CHARGE	3.43
631502		CHARGE	118.60

one obtains

Account No.	Prev. Bal.	Handling Fee	Charges	Payments	New Balance
631502	16.30	0.24	118.60	—	135.14
180003	−6.00	—	—	4.00	−10.00
000963	366.92	5.50	33.88	60.00	346.30
517724	60.40	0.91	3.43	—	64.74
432649	—	—	—	—	—
817387	55.00	0.83	—	55.00	0.83

Problem 7.2.11   (50)

Problem 7.2.12   (50)

Problem 7.2.13   (50)

Given the $k = 7$ integers 200, 37, 603, 1025, 3, 8, 17 one obtains 3, 8, 17, 37, 200, 603, 1025 in decimal and 11, 1000, 10001, 100101, 11001000, 1001011011, 1000000001 in binary.

Problem 7.2.14   (20)

Problem 7.2.15   (100)

Problem 7.2.16   (100)

Problem 7.2.17   (20)

Problem 7.2.18   (50)

Problem 7.2.19   (50)

Considering the following membership lists,

Vegetarian Club:	Woods, Vander, Pertl, Mautner, Turner, Feed, Moore, Chimino, Bowden, Birchull, McBee, Lust
Hunting Assoc.:	Harris, Hauser, Meyers, Melin, Pertl, Pearson, Woodman, Vandenberg, Witter, Foorts, Smith, Moore
Fly-to-the-Moon Club:	Moore, Turner, Witter, Woodman, Burrit, Bur, Britton, Brock, Zander, Anglin
Stay-on-Earth Assoc.:	Vander, Mautner, Moore, Turner, Harris, Smitte, Harman

one obtains

People belonging to all four associations:	Moore
People belonging to at least two associations:	Vander, Pertl, Mautner, Turner, Moore, Harris, Woodman, Witter
Hypocrites:	Pertl, Moore, Turner

Problem 7.2.20   (50)

There are 27 such quadruples.

Problem 7.2.21   (50)

Some of the quadruples obtained are (1,2,1,0), (2,3,4,1), (6,9,29,2), (15,20,14,22), and (8,21,49,19).

Problem 7.2.22   (50)

There are 23 quadruples (a,b,c,d) satisfying $a < 59$, $b < 158$, $c < 133$, $d < 134$, $0 < a < b$, $a < c < d$, and abs$(a^4 + b^4 - c^4 - d^4) \leq 5$.

Problem 7.2.23   (50)

There are 222 such sextuples.

Problem 7.2.24   (50)

There are 32 such sextuples.

Problem 7.2.25   (50)

There are 51 such sextuples.

Problem 7.2.26   (50)

The desired pair is $(x,y) = (0.60, -0.47)$.

Problem 7.2.27   (50)

There are nine such pairs; two of them are $(0.70, -0.48)$ and $(0.80, 0.85)$.

CHAPTER 8

Note: Throughout this chapter *RG* is the random number generator given in Section 8.1 with initial value $Y = 568731$.

Section 8.1

Problem 8.1.1 (20)

Using *RG*, 1 occurs 28 times, 2 occurs 35 times, . . . , 31 occurs 38 times and 32 occurs 33 times.

Problem 8.1.2 (20)

Using *RG*, there are 103 numbers between zero and 0.099, 100 numbers between 0.1 and 0.199, . . . , 114 numbers between 0.9 and 0.999.

Problem 8.1.3 (20)

Using *RG*, 1 occurs 300 times, . . . , 4 occurs 347 times.

Section 8.2

Problem 8.2.1 (50)

Using *RG* for one simulation of 600 throws, the number 1 occurs 109 times, the longest run of 1's is 5, two consecutive 1's occur 17 times, the number 2 occurs 91 times, the longest run of 2's is 3, and two consecutive 2's occur 12 times. A run 1,2,3,4,5,6 does not occur.

Problem 8.2.2 (20)

Using *RG*, a run 1,1,1 occurs 2 times, a run 1,1,3 occurs 8 times, and a run 1,5,2 occurs 9 times.

Problem 8.2.3 (50)

Using *RG* for generating 2400 random numbers $X_1, X_2, \ldots, X_{2400}$ between 1 and 6 where each triple X_n, X_{n+1}, X_{n+2} for $n = 1, 4, 7, \ldots$, 2398 represents a throw of three six-sided dice, one obtains: a throw of 3 points occurs 3 times, a throw of 4 points occurs 12 times, a throw of 6 points occurs 37 times; the successive totals 3,3 do not occur; the successive totals 5,5 occur twice.

Problem 8.2.4 (50)

The best choice for *n* in strategy (a) is between 6 and 14; the best choice for *n* in strategy (b) is between 20 and 54.

Problem 8.2.5 (100)

In 500 hands more than 7 cards in any suit will occur between 10 and 28 times and a slam bid between 7 and 13 times.

Problem 8.2.6 (50)

The average score will be between 21 and 27.

Section 8.3

Problem 8.3.1 (50)

A typical simulation yields

	Average	*Maximum*
Time of ship in harbor	75.54	283
Waiting time of ship	10.89	230
Number of ships in waiting line	0.668	6

Problem 8.3.2   (100)

The best switching period for green in direction 1 is between 20 and 40 seconds. A switching period for green of 30 seconds is encountered in most simulations.

Problem 8.3.3   (50)

The average number of customers in the waiting line is between 2 and 4.

Problem 8.3.4   (100)

Problem 8.3.5   (100)

Problem 8.3.6   (50)

Using *RG* for one simulation of 500 steps one obtains that the person does not leave the city, the junction Centre Street–Centre Avenue is encountered 4 times, and a closed road is encountered 42 times.

Problem 8.3.7   (50)

Using *RG* to generate 500 random numbers $X_1, X_2, \ldots, X_{500}$ between zero and 3 (zero indicating north, 1 indicating east, 2 indicating south, and 3 indicating west), one obtains

	5	4	3	2	1	C	1	2	3	4	5
5							E	E	E	S	
4							N			S	
3						E	N		E	S	
2						N	W			S	
1						E	N		S	W	
C						N			E	S	
1								E	T	S	
2								N	W	S	
3									N	W	
4											
5											

Problem 8.3.8   (100)

Problem 8.3.9   (50)

Using $A = B = C = D = 25\%$, the results agree with those of Problem 8.3.6.

Problem 8.3.10   (100)

In simulating 100 times the situation for 800 steps, the persons meet in 37 simulations.

Problem 8.3.11   (50)

Problem 8.3.12   (50)

Between 150 and 500 bags of paint are required.

Problem 8.3.13   (100)

The largest catch is obtained by throwing the bait between every 30 and 50 seconds.

Problem 8.3.14   (20)

Between 61 and 79 matches can be removed.

Problem 8.3.15   (50)

Section 8.4

Problem 8.4.1   (20)

Using 2000 random points, one obtains $m = 3.3 \cdot 10^{10}$.

Problem 8.4.2   (20)

Using 2000 random points, the number of lattice points in the region is found to be $m = 9 \cdot 10^7$.

Problem 8.4.3   (20)

Using RG to generate 2000 random numbers between 2 and 3, one obtains $\sqrt{5} = 2.2. \ldots$

Problem 8.4.4   (20)

Using 2000 random numbers, $\sqrt[3]{7} = 1.9 \cdots$ and $\sqrt[7]{3} = 1.17 \cdots$ are obtained.

Problem 8.4.5   (20)

Using 2000 random numbers for $n = 7$, one obtains $\sqrt{7} = 2.6 \cdots$ and $\sqrt[3]{7} = 1.9 \cdots$.

Problem 8.4.6   (20)

Problem 8.4.7   (20)

Using 4000 random points, $\pi = 3.1$ is obtained.

Problem 8.4.8   (20)

Using 4000 random numbers (i.e., 2000 random points), the area obtained is 185.

Problem 8.4.9   (20)

Using 6000 random numbers (i.e., 2000 random points), the area obtained is 2600.

Problem 8.4.10   (20)

There are roughly 8500 prime numbers among the 100,000 integers floor$(1.93x + 0.82)$, $x = 1, 2, \ldots, 1000000$.

Problem 8.4.11 (20)

The value obtained for 6000 random numbers is 3333; i.e., there are roughly 3300 perfect squares among the 20,000,000 numbers floor (2.1111*x*), *x* = 1, 2, . . . , 20000000.

Problem 8.4.12 (20)

The area of the region obtained is 1.27.

CHAPTER 9

Section 9.1

Problem 9.1.1 (20)

Problem 9.1.2 (50)

A data card of

-,· · · ·,·,·,-· ·,---,-- ·,·,· ·,· · ·,·,-· · ·,-· ·,·-,-· ·,-· ·

would translate as THE DOG IS BLACK.

Problem 9.1.3 (20)

Problem 9.1.4 (100)

A card containing the characters

ZX213E-2B-4.9E-2YWP2R425B,9/8;B

would cause the program to print

2.13   −0.049   2   425   9   8

Problem 9.1.5 (50)

The telephone number 2442536 results in a printout containing the word CHICKEN as well as 2186 other words (mostly unpronounceable).

Problem 9.1.6 (100)

The data 015021030032030021009401002402003 should be interpreted as the expression 2+(3*(2+9)+2)*3.

Problem 9.1.7 (50)

The character string THISCODEISHARDTOBREAK would encode to 20,28,37,16,19,34,38,3,12,31,39,0,18,22,2,17,19,37,2,3,14.

Problem 9.1.8 (50)

Problem 9.1.9 (20)

The first two things said on earth are both able to be read forward or backward. Adam, upon first seeing Eve, is supposed to have said *MADAM IM ADAM*, to which Eve replied *EVE*.

Problem 9.1.10 (50)

Section 9.2

Problem 9.2.1 (50)

Problem 9.2.2 (50)

Problem 9.2.3   (50)

See Problem 14.2.3 if any problem develops in scaling the values to be plotted.

Problem 9.2.4   (20)

Problem 9.2.5   (20)

Problem 9.2.6   (50)

Problem 9.2.7   (>100)

Problem 9.2.8   (20)

Problem 9.2.9   (50)

03245698 should be printed as $3,245,698 and 213 should be printed as $213.

Problem 9.2.10   (50)

Problem 9.2.11   (100)

Problem 9.2.12   (>100)

Problem 9.2.13   (>100)

Section 9.3

Problem 9.3.1   (100)

See the problem for a sample output.

Problem 9.3.2   (100)

See the problem for a sample output.

Problem 9.3.3   (>100)

See the problem for how a pawn may be represented.

Problem 9.3.4   (100)

$$IIII + VIIII = XIII$$
$$LXXXXI + XXII = CXIII$$

Problem 9.3.5   (>100)

$$IV \cdot XI = XLIV$$
$$XIX - XV = IV$$

Problem 9.3.6   (100)

See the problem for a sample output.

Problem 9.3.7   (100)

The character string

    24*(2+3**(3+9)+4−2*(2**(2−6+9)−4))**2−3+6

should be printed as

$$24(2 + 3^{3+9} + 4 - 2(2^{2-6+9} - 4))^2 - 3 + 6$$

Problem 9.3.8 (>100)

The character string $2*R(I)+S(K-L+2**P)**R(I)$ would be printed as

```
                    R
                      I
      2 R   + S
        I                     P
              K - L + 2
```

Problem 9.3.9   (100)

CHAPTER 10

Section 10.2

Problem 10.2.1   (10)

$fact(6) = 720$; $fact(9) = 362880$.

Problem 10.2.2   (10)

$$lcf(7219645,1234567) = 1$$
$$lcf(4000000,1000000) = 1000000$$
$$lcf(6172835,1234567) = 1234567$$

Problem 10.2.3   (20)

$$A(1,2,3) = 5 \qquad d = 7$$
$$A(2,3,4) = 12 \qquad d = 33$$
$$A(3,4,6) = 4096 \qquad d > 2000$$

Problem 10.2.4   (50)

See answers from Problem 10.2.3.

Problem 10.2.5   (20)

$P(9) = 30$; $P(11) = 56$.

Problem 10.2.6   (20)

See the answers to problem 10.2.5.

Problem 10.2.7   (20)

$Q(9,10) = 41$; $Q(18,20) = 625$.

Problem 10.2.8   (20)

$rem(738512^{118},7) = 2$; $rem\ (21797^{6},33) = 1$.

Problem 10.2.9   (20)

$b_{15,15} = 1$; $b_{12,10} = 66$; $b_{20,15} = 15504$.

Problem 10.2.10   (20)

$F_5 = 5$; $F_{10} = 55$; $F_{15} = 610$.

Problem 10.2.11   (20)

$r(5,1,0.0001) = 2.2360$; $r(256,1,0.0001) = 16.000$; $r(300,1,0.0001) = 17.3205$.

Problem 10.2.12   (20)

For $n = 5$ the moves are

P_1	P_2	P_3
5,4,3,2,1		
5,4,3,2	1	
5,4,3	1	2
5,4,3		2,1
5,4	3	2,1
5,4,1	3	2
5,4,1	3,2	
5,4	3,2,1	
5	3,2,1	4
5	3,2	4,1
5,2	3	4,1
5,2,1	3	4
5,2,1		4,3
5,2	1	4,3
5	1	4,3,2
5		4,3,2,1
	5	4,3,2,1
1	5	4,3,2
1	5,2	4,3
	5,2,1	4,3
3	5,2,1	4
3	5,2	4,1
3,2	5	4,1
3,2,1	5	4
3,2,1	5,4	
3,2	5,4,1	
3	5,4,1	2
3	5,4	2,1
	5,4,3	2,1
1	5,4,3	2
1	5,4,3,2	
	5,4,3,2,1	

Problem 10.2.13   (20)

The general formula for n discs is $f(n) = 1 + 2f(n - 1)$, and $f(50) = 1,125,899,906,842,623$ which comes to slightly less than half a million centuries.

Problem 12.2.14   (50)

Problem 12.2.15   (50)

The positions $(1,4,5)$, $(2,1,3)$, $(2,3,1)$, and $(0,1,1)$ are a few of the possible winning positions.

Problem 10.2.16   (50)

Problem 10.2.17   (50)

Problem 10.2.18 (100)

Problem 10.2.19 (20)

There are 372 integers not exceeding 2000 that are members of the set *Prop*.

Problem 10.2.20 (100)

$2+37/49\cdot276159$ and $571964326-4132\cdot36+92/42/3/6$ are both elements of ⟨expression⟩, while $213+729\cdot-3241$ is not.

Problem 10.2.21 (100)

See the problem for an example.

Problem 10.2.22 (100)

See the problem for an example.

Problem 10.2.23 (>100)

The character string [[[[3+14]/10]+2]·[[3·2]+5]] is in ⟨ex⟩ and has an equivalent expression in ⟨polish⟩ of 3#14+#10/#2+#3#2·#5+·.

Problem 10.2.24 (100)

See the problem for an example.

Problem 10.2.25 (20)

$f(5) = 22$; $f(10) = 92$; $f(15) = 212$.

CHAPTER 11

Section 11.1

Problem 11.1.1 (20)

For $a = 98765432120191817185$ and $b = 12345678910111213145$,
$a + b = 111111111030303030330$.

Problem 11.1.2 (20)

For a and b as in Problem 11.1.1, $a - b = 86419753210080604040$.

Problem 11.1.4 (20)

$F_{80} = 23416728348467685$ and $F_{95} = 31940434634990099905$, where $F_1 = 1$, $F_2 = 1$, and $F_i = F_{i-1} + F_{i-2}$ for $i \geq 3$.

Problem 11.1.5 (20)

$2^{105} = 40564819207303340847894502572032$.

Problem 11.1.6 (20)

$25! = 15511210043330985984000000$.

Problem 11.1.7 (50)

For a and b as in Problem 11.1.1, $ab =$
$1219326312374272716898800618342408896825$.

Problem 11.1.8 (50)

For a and b as in Problem 11.1.1, floor $(a/b) = 8$.

Problem 11.1.9   (50)

For a and b as in Problem 11.1.1, mod$(a,b) = 839302112025$.

Problem 11.1.10   (50)

For a and b as in Problem 11.1.1, lcf$(a,b) = 5$.

Problem 11.1.11   (20)

For $a = 638927$ and $b = 259431$ one obtains

$$\frac{a}{b} = 2.4628012843492103873476955336871846463992352494497573535930$$
$$5557161634500117564978741939089777242327470502754104174134$$
$$9337588800104844833501007975145607117113991774306077531212$$
$$5382086180911302041776040 64$$

Problem 11.1.12   (50)

For $a = 597$ and $b = 109$ one obtains

$$\frac{a}{b} = 5.47706422018348623853211009174311926605504587155963302752 2$$
$$935779816513761467889908256880733944954128440366972\cdots$$

and all 109 digits behind the decimal point repeat.

Section 11.2

Problem 11.2.1   (20)

$(37,601) + (29,13) = (17910,7813)$.

Problem 11.2.2   (20)

For $n = 3$ and $a_1/b_1 = \frac{13}{6}$, $a_2/b_2 = \frac{19}{15}$, $a_3/b_3 = \frac{8}{7}$ one obtains $s = \frac{961}{210}$ and $m = \frac{961}{630}$.

Problem 11.2.4   (20)

For $a = 2$, $x_4 = \frac{577}{408}$; for $a = 5$, $x_5 = \frac{2207}{987}$.

Problem 11.2.5   (50)

For $a = 4$, $x_7 = 17168419101462562423289245446 41/8584209550731281$ 21164462272320; for $a = 2$, $x_6 = 886731088897/627013566048$.

Problem 11.2.6   (20)

For $a_{11} = \frac{1}{7}$, $a_{12} = -\frac{13}{51}$, $b_1 = \frac{8}{3}$, $a_{21} = \frac{7}{1}$, $a_{22} = \frac{9}{19}$, and $b_2 = \frac{17}{3}$, the solution is $(s_1,s_2) = (55097/37686, -121125/12562)$.

Problem 11.2.7   (50)

The system

$$\frac{1}{5}x_1 - \frac{6}{7}x_2 + \frac{13}{17}x_3 = \frac{18}{1}$$
$$\frac{2}{3}x_1 + \frac{1}{5}x_2 - \frac{2}{9}x_3 = -\frac{17}{3}$$
$$\frac{15}{2}x_1 - \frac{7}{12}x_2 + \frac{2}{1}x_3 = 0$$

has the solution $(s_1,s_2,s_3) = (7907/1530, 668529/1785, 387443/4590)$.

Problem 11.2.8   (20)

$1 + \frac{1}{2} + \frac{1}{3} + \cdots + \frac{1}{18} = 14274301/4084080$.

Problem 11.2.9   (50)

$1 + \frac{1}{2} + \frac{1}{3} + \cdots + \frac{1}{45} = 5914085889685464427/1345655451257488800.$

Problem 11.2.10   (50)

The first four lines of the table are

Fahrenheit	Centigrade
-40	-40
-39	$-\frac{355}{9}$
$-\frac{191}{50}$	-39
-38	$-\frac{350}{9}$

Section 11.3

Problem 11.3.1   (20)

For $n = 5$ and $[a_1,a_2,a_3,a_4,a_5] = [1,2,6,3,2]$, one obtains $[a_1,a_2,a_3] = \frac{19}{13}$ $= 1.461538461538\ldots$.

Problem 11.3.2   (20)

$p_6/q_6 = \frac{99}{70} = 1.4142\ldots$.

Problem 11.3.3   (20)

$\frac{98}{67} = [1,2,6,5]$.

Problem 11.3.4   (50)

For $a = 698335$, $b = 201924$, and $c = 0.00001$, such a fraction c/d is $c/d = \frac{1954}{565}$.

Problem 11.3.5   (20)

For $(2 + 3\sqrt{5})/7$, one obtains $[a_1,a_2,a_3,a_4,a_5,a_6] = [1,4,10,4,1,1]$.

Problem 11.3.6   (50)

For $b = 13$ and $e = 0.000001$, one obtains $c/d = \frac{4287}{1189}$.

Problem 11.3.7   (50)

There are two such pairs; the first is $(x,y) = (649,180)$.

Problem 11.3.8   (50)

One solution of $19x_1 + 15x_2 = 87$ is $(s_1, s_2) = (3,2)$. One solution of $19x_1 - 15x_2 = 8$ is $(s_1,s_2) = (3,3)$. The equation $20x_1 + 16x_2 = 33$ has no integer solutions.

Problem 11.3.9   (50)

For $A = 31$, $B = 13$, $C = 50$, and $D = 28$, use 3 trucks and 5 boats.
For $A = 52$, $B = 28$, $C = 200$, and $D = 20$, use 9 trucks and 16 boats.

Section 11.4

Problem 11.4.1   (20)

$\cos(0.03) = 0.99550$; $\cos(6.00) = 0.960170$.

Problem 11.4.2   (20)

$\sin(0.09) = 0.08987855$; $\sin(1.3) = 0.96355819$.

Problem 11.4.3   (20)

$\sin(50°) = 0.766044$; $\cos(50°) = 0.642788$.

Problem 11.4.4   (20)

$e = 2.71828183$.

Problem 11.4.5   (20)

$e^{0.05} = 1.0513$; $e^{1.8} = 6.0496$.

Problem 11.4.6   (20)

$(p_9, q_9) = (1457,536)$.

Problem 11.4.7   (20)

The last four digits are 5235.

Problem 11.4.8   (20)

The last four digits are 3238.

Problem 11.4.9   (100)

The last ten digits are 8327950288.

Problem 11.4.10   (100)

The last 20 digits are 21529734355312037422.

Problem 11.4.11   (50)

$\sqrt[3]{1.5} = 1.164993$; $\sqrt[4]{3} = 1.316074$.

Section 11.5

Problem 11.5.1   (10)

$a = 31$, $b = 27$, and $c = 36$ is a triangle; $a = 31$, $b = 27$, and $c = 59$ is no triangle.

Problem 11.5.2   (10)

For $a = 31$, $b = 27$, and $c = 36$, one obtains $V = 406.74292$.

Problem 11.5.3   (20)

There are 31 such triangles.

Problem 11.5.4   (10)

For $A = (3,9)$ and $B = (28,31)$, the length of the segment is 33. For $A = (12,20)$ and $B = (-1,19)$, the length of the segment is 13.0384.

Problem 11.5.5   (10)

For $A = (3,9,-5)$ and $B = (28,31,6)$, the length of the segment is 34.

Problem 11.5.6   (20)

The area of the triangle determined by $A = (3,9)$, $B = (28,31)$, and $C = (-5,11)$ is 110.14279.

Problem 11.5.7   (20)

The area of the triangle determined by $A = (3,9,-5)$, $B = (28,31,5)$, and $C = (-5,11,83)$ is 1458.52417.

Problem 11.5.8   (10)

See Problem 11.5.6.

Problem 11.5.9   (20)

See Problem 11.5.7.

Problem 11.5.10   (10)

For $a = 6$, $b = 31$, and $\gamma = 0.83$, one obtains $c = 29.422386$.

Problem 11.5.11   (20)

For $a = 25.5$, $\beta = 0.6$, and $\gamma = 0.83$, one obtains $\alpha = 1.712857$, $b = 14.544904$, and $c = 19.008738$.

Problem 11.5.12   (20)

For $a = 31$, $b = 27$,and $c = 36$, the distance of A from a is 26.2415.

Section 11.6

Problem 11.6.1   (20)

Problem 11.6.2   (20)

Problem 11.6.3   (20)

$\sqrt{5} = 2.235$; $\sqrt{800} = 28.284$.

Problem 11.6.4   (20)

$\ln(2.3) = 0.8329$; $\ln(2) = 0.6931$.

Problem 11.6.5   (20)

$\arcsin(0.06) = 0.06004$; $\arcsin(0.55) = 0.56102$.

Problem 11.6.6   (50)

For $a = 66$, $b = 102$, and $\beta = 0.96$, one obtains $\alpha = 0.558$, $\gamma = 1.624$, and $c = 124.412$.

Problem 11.6.7   (50)

For $a = 31$, $b = 27$, and $c = 36$, one obtains $\alpha = 0.416$, $\beta = 1.393$, and $\gamma = 1.333$.

Section 11.7

Problem 11.7.1   (20)

$\int_4^7 ((\sqrt{x + 1} + x^3)/\sqrt{x^3 - 1})\, dx = 35.071$.

Problem 11.7.2   (20 for each part)

The exact value of the integral is $0.9166\ldots$; for $n = 10$, the rectangle formula gives 1.0725; for $n = 20$, the trapezoidal formula gives 0.918123; for $n = 2$, the tangent formula yields 0.84375 and Simpson's formula yields 0.916667.

Problem 11.7.3   (20 for each part)

$\int_0^{0.2} e^{(x^2)}\, dx = 0.20269888\ldots$.

Problem 11.7.4   (20)

$\int_2^8 x(4 + x^2)^{-1/3}\, dx = 15.49493\ldots$.

Problem 11.7.5   (20)

arctan(0.2) = 0.197395. . . .

Problem 11.7.6   (20)

ln(2) = 0.693147. . . .

Problem 11.7.7   (20)

π = 3.14159265358979323846. . . .

Problem 11.7.8   (20)

See Problem 11.7.7.

CHAPTER 12

Section 12.1

Problem 12.1.1   (20)

For the data on the heights of students given in the introduction to the chapter, the median is 70 inches and the mean is 69.43 inches.

Problem 12.1.2   (20)

For the data on heights of students, the average deviation is 2.099 inches and the standard deviation is 2.6207.

Problem 12.1.3   (50)

Problem 12.1.4   (50)

For the data on the heights of students, the skewness is -0.6525.

Problem 12.1.5   (100)

Problem 12.1.6   (50)

For the random number generator given in Chapter 8, with a starting value of 568731, the average (mean) is 25, the standard deviation is 14, and the skewness is 0.

Section 12.2

Problem 12.2.1   (50)

For the random number generator given in Chapter 8, with a starting value of 568731, the χ^2 value is 12.63, which indicates that the random number generator is not very good. This value shows that the sequence of numbers produced has only 20% chance of being truly random.

Problem 12.2.2   (50)

With the same initial conditions as in the answer to Problem 12.2.1, the χ^2 value is 8.89, which indicates that the serial correlation has a better than 99% chance of being random.

Problem 12.2.3   (50)

With initial conditions as in the answer to Problem 12.2.1, the χ^2 value is 20.19, which indicates that the triples are generated with about 80% chance of being truly random.

Problem 12.2.4   (50)

Starting Value of Random Number Generator	χ^2
568731	12.63
999999	26.21
100000	33.93
100005	42.25
457862	49.09

So a starting value of 568731 is the best of these five.

Problem 12.2.5   (20)

The coins are biased.

Problem 12.2.6   (20)

Intelligence Score	Sales
30	21.7
52	36.7
81	56.5
100	69.5

Problem 12.2.7   (20)

The χ^2 value is 31, which would indicate that our assumption of a direct relation is unlikely.

Problem 12.2.8   (20)

The correlation coefficient is 0.82, which indicates a reasonable correlation between intelligence and sales ability.

CHAPTER 13

Section 13.5

Problem 13.5.1   (50) for (a) and (b); (100) for (c)

The system

$$x_1 + 2x_2 - x_3 = 1$$
$$-x_1 + 3x_2 + 2x_3 = -1$$
$$x_1 + 11x_2 + x_3 = 3$$

has the solutions $s_1 = 15$, $s_2 = -2$, and $s_3 = 10$; the system

$$3x_1 + 7x_2 - x_3 = 7$$
$$x_1 + 3x_2 + 3x_3 = 1$$
$$2x_1 + 5x_2 + x_3 = 4$$

has no unique solution; the system

$$5x_1 + x_2 \qquad\qquad\quad = 9$$
$$x_2 + x_3 + x_4 = 16$$
$$-x_1 + x_2 + 8x_3 - x_4 = 0$$
$$10x_1 - x_2 - x_3 + 2x_4 = 1$$

has the solutions $s_1 = -0.21875$, $s_2 = 10.09375$, $s_3 = -0.48958$, and $s_4 = 6.3958$; the system

$$x_1 + x_2 - x_3 + x_4 = 6$$
$$- x_2 + 9x_3 - x_4 = 1$$
$$2x_1 + x_2 - 5x_3 + x_4 = 3$$
$$3x_1 + x_2 + 3x_3 + x_4 = 11$$

has no unique solution; the system

$$x_1 + x_2 + x_3 + x_4 + x_5 + x_6 + x_7 + x_8 = 8$$
$$x_2 + x_3 \qquad + x_5 + x_6 \qquad\qquad = 6$$
$$x_1 + x_2 \qquad\qquad + x_5 - x_6 - x_7 - x_8 = 0$$
$$3x_1 + x_2 - 3x_3 - 6x_4 + x_5 \qquad\qquad + 9x_8 = 51$$
$$x_1 - 2x_2 + 2x_3 + 5x_4 - 7x_5 + x_6 - x_7 + 2x_8 = 10$$
$$x_1 + x_2 + x_3 + x_4 + x_5 - x_6 - 3x_7 - 4x_8 = -1$$
$$10x_1 - x_2 + 19x_3 - 7x_4 \qquad\qquad + x_7 + 19x_8 = 100$$
$$-x_1 + x_2 - 11x_3 + x_4 - 2x_5 + 6x_6 + x_7 - x_8 = 6$$

has the solutions $s_1 = 0.455112$, $s_2 = -3.667763$, $s_3 = -0.7207262$, $s_4 = 3.359$, $s_5 = 5.893$, $s_6 = 4.495$, $s_7 = -9.081$, and $s_8 = 7.267$.

Problem 13.5.2   (100)

The system

$$101.3x_1 + 2.8x_2 - 6.8x_3 + x_4 - x_5 + x_6 - x_7 + 8.2x_8 - 9x_9 + x_{10} = 3$$
$$x_1 - 44x_2 + 16x_3 - 2.3x_4 \qquad\qquad\qquad\qquad\qquad = -11$$
$$2x_2 + 50x_3 - x_4 \qquad + x_6 - 1.1x_7 + 23x_8 \qquad\qquad = 4$$
$$x_1 \qquad\qquad - 49x_4 \qquad + x_6 + x_7 + x_8 - 10x_9 \qquad = 0$$
$$3.3x_2 - x_3 + x_4 - 42.6x_5 + 1.6x_6 \qquad\qquad\qquad + 7.3x_{10} = 16$$
$$23x_1 \qquad\qquad - 7x_4 + 18x_5 + 60x_6 + 2x_7 \qquad\qquad - 2.9x_{10} = 2$$
$$x_1 + 2x_2 + 3x_3 + 4x_4 + 5x_5 + 36x_6 + 149x_7 - 15x_8 - 13x_9 - 7x_{10} = 11$$
$$-3x_1 - 2x_2 - 6x_3 - 4x_4 - 6x_5 + 30x_6 \qquad + 88x_8 - 9x_9 - 10x_{10} = 2$$
$$2x_1 + 7x_2 + 8.1x_3 + 8x_4 + 6x_5 \qquad - 7x_7 \qquad - 93x_9 \qquad = 1.3$$
$$x_1 + 5x_2 - 6x_3 + 6.3x_4 - 3x_5 \qquad + 7x_7 \qquad - 7x_9 + 45x_{10} = 200$$

has the solutions $s_1 = -0.0644$, $s_2 = 0.1931$, $s_3 = -0.1493$, $s_4 = 0.0191$, $s_5 = 0.3889$, $s_6 = 0.1461$, $s_7 = 0.2803$, $s_8 = 0.4895$, $s_9 = -0.0082$, and $s_{10} = 4.3829$. The system

$$\begin{aligned}
x_1 + x_2 &= 1 \\
x_2 + x_3 &= 2 \\
x_3 + x_4 &= 3 \\
x_4 + x_5 &= 4 \\
x_5 + x_6 &= 5 \\
x_6 + x_7 &= 6 \\
x_1 + 2x_2 + 2x_3 + 2x_4 + 2x_5 + 2x_6 + 2x_7 - 2x_8 - 2x_9 - x_{10} &= 100 \\
x_1 - x_2 + x_3 \qquad\qquad\qquad\qquad + x_8 + x_9 + x_{10} &= 31 \\
- 2x_7 + 4x_8 + 4x_9 + 2x_{10} &= 60 \\
x_{10} &= 3
\end{aligned}$$

has no unique solution.

Problem 13.5.3   (50) for (a) and (b); (100) for (c)

$$\mathrm{val}\left(\begin{vmatrix} 1 & 2 & -1 \\ -1 & 3 & 2 \\ 3 & 11 & 1 \end{vmatrix}\right) = 15$$

$$\mathrm{val}\left(\begin{vmatrix} 2 & 1 & 0 & -1 \\ 0 & 1 & 3 & 2 \\ 0 & 0 & 2 & 1 \\ 0 & -5 & 0 & 0 \end{vmatrix}\right) = 10$$

$$\mathrm{val}\left(\begin{vmatrix} 1 & 2 & 3 & 4 & 5 & 6 & 7 & 8 \\ 2 & 3 & 4 & 5 & 6 & 7 & 8 & 1 \\ 3 & 4 & 5 & 6 & 7 & 8 & 1 & 2 \\ 4 & 5 & 6 & 7 & 8 & 1 & 2 & 3 \\ 5 & 6 & 7 & 8 & 1 & 2 & 3 & 4 \\ 6 & 7 & 8 & 1 & 2 & 3 & 4 & 5 \\ 7 & 8 & 1 & 2 & 3 & 4 & 5 & 6 \\ 8 & 1 & 2 & 3 & 4 & 5 & 6 & 7 \end{vmatrix}\right) = 9437184$$

Problem 13.5.4   (100)

$$\mathrm{val}\begin{vmatrix} 1 & -1 & -4 & 6 & 3 & 2 & 0 & 2 & -1 & -9 \\ -2 & 2 & 0 & 8 & 5 & 2 & 6 & 5 & 7 & 8 \\ -3 & -5 & 3 & 0 & 5 & 1 & 11 & 0 & 3 & -2 \\ 2 & 1 & 17 & 4 & 5 & -2 & 7 & -1 & 13 & 7 \\ 0 & 1 & 1 & 3 & 5 & -6 & 9 & 0 & 12 & 0 \\ -3 & 2 & 2 & 0 & 3 & 6 & -7 & 6 & 0 & 6 \\ -5 & -7 & 8 & 9 & 3 & -2 & 7 & 1 & 5 & 5 \\ 2 & 2 & 2 & 2 & 2 & 2 & -8 & 8 & 0 & 3 \\ 11 & 17 & 8 & 2 & 1 & -6 & 7 & -9 & 9 & 3 \\ 1 & 6 & 5 & 3 & 0 & 8 & 8 & 13 & -10 & 10 \end{vmatrix} = 574978851$$

Problem 13.5.5   (50)

The person should travel 100 miles by car and 800 miles by plane.

Problem 13.5.6   (20)

For the system

$$3x_1 + x_2 + x_3 = 9$$
$$x_1 + 2x_2 \quad\quad = 3$$
$$-x_1 - x_2 + 4x_3 = 16$$

the first six approximations obtained when starting with $(0,0,0)$ are

$$(3,0,4.75),$$
$$(1.417,0.792,4.552), \quad (1.219,0.891,4.527),$$
$$(1.194,0.903,4.524), \quad (1.191,0.904,4.524),$$
$$(1.191,0.905,4.524)$$

Problem 13.5.7   (20)

Problem 13.5.8   (50)

For the system

$$9x_1 + x_2 + x_3 + 2x_4 - 3x_5 = 1$$
$$x_1 - 16x_2 + 3x_3 \quad\quad + x_5 = 8$$
$$x_1 + 3x_2 - 6x_3 \quad\quad + x_5 = 7$$
$$7x_2 + 3x_3 - 20x_4 + 2x_5 = 1$$
$$x_1 + x_2 + x_3 - 2x_4 - 10x_5 = 10$$

$e = 0.0001$ and starting with $s_1 = s_2 = s_3 = s_4 = s_5 = 0$ one obtains $s_1 = 0.2021172$, $s_2 = -0.885729$, $s_3 = -1.758765$, $s_4 = -0.7335718$, and $s_5 = -1.097523$ after seven iterations.

Problem 13.5.9   (50) if no reordering is attempted; (>100) for the general case

For the first system given in Problem 13.5.2, $e = 0.01$ and starting with $s_1 = s_2 = \cdots = s_{10} = 0$, one obtains $s_1 = -0.06439675$, $s_2 = 0.1932406$, $s_3 = -0.1492963$, $s_4 = 0.01904954$, $s_5 = 0.3889043$, $s_6 = 0.1460654$, $s_7 = 0.2802927$, $s_8 = 0.4895478$, $s_9 = -0.008189645$, and $s_{10} = 4.382883$ after eight iterations. For the system

$$2x_1 - x_2 \quad\quad = 4$$
$$x_2 + x_3 = 2$$
$$2x_1 \quad\quad - 4x_3 = 1$$

one obtains the solutions $s_1 = 2.5$, $s_2 = 1$, and $s_3 = 1$ after about 25 iterations despite the fact that the convergence condition (12) of Section 13.4 is not satisfied.

Problem 13.5.10   (50)

The amount of spinach is 14.9397, grams; the amount of milk is 583.865 grams.

Problem 13.5.11   (100)

For $r_2 = r_3 = r_4 = \cdots r_{12} = 1$ and $x_1 = 8$, one obtains $x_2 = 1.5$, $x_3 = 1.5$, $x_4 = 0$, $x_5 = 1.5$, $x_6 = 1.5$, $x_7 = 2$, $x_8 = 3$, $x_9 = 1$, $x_{10} = 1$, $x_{11} = 4$, and $x_{12} = 4$.

CHAPTER 14

Section 14.2

Problem 14.2.1   (50)

Problem 14.2.2   (50)

The plot should cross the x-axis between the values $x = -8$, and $x = -9$ and again between the values $x = 6$ and $x = 7$.

Problem 14.2.3   (50)

If there are 100 units on the $f(x)$-axis, then for the function $f(x) = 3x^2 + 9x - 120$ plotted from $x = -30$ to $x = +30$, a suitable scaling formula would be $g(x) = 100((f(x) + 130)/(3130))$.

Problem 14.2.4   (50)

For an input of (3,6,3), the circle generated should just touch the y-axis at the point $y = 6$.

Problem 14.2.5   (50)

The plot will consist of two lines that meet as they cross the x-axis at the two points $x = 0$ and $x = 10$.

Problem 14.2.6   (50)

Problem 14.2.7   (100)

Problem 14.2.10   (100)

The two plots should intersect at the two points (3,2) and (6,-1).

Problem 14.2.11   (50)

For the parabola $y = 2x^2 + 3x + 4$ (evaluated between $x = -10$ and $x = +10$) with the tangent and normal lines constructed at the point $x = 1$, the tangent line should pass through the points (0,2) and (2,16), while the normal line should pass through the points $(-6,10)$ and (8,8).

Problem 14.2.12   (50)

There is one zero of the function between $x = 1.6$ and $x = 3.6$.

Problem 14.2.13   (20)

The plot should be a circle, centered on the origin, with a radius of 25 units.

Problem 14.2.14   (50)

The lemniscate should look like a figure 8 on its side.

Problem 14.2.15   (50)

The folium should have a loop in the first quadrant and a line going out to infinity in the second and fourth quadrants.

Section 14.3

Problem 14.3.1   (50)

For the input data (0,0,1,3), the first three moves of the pen would be to the points (0,0.01), (0.01,0.02), and then to (0.01,0.03).

Problem 14.3.2   (100)

Both of the functions are always positive and thus have no zeroes.

Problem 14.3.3   (20)

Problem 14.3.4   (50)

CHAPTER 15

Section 15.1

Problem 15.1.1   (100)

Given the road network $(A,B,21.3)$, $(A,C,30)$, $(A,D,40)$, $(B,C,21.3)$, $(B,F,23.8)$, $(C,D,28.8)$, $(C,E,18.7)$, $(C,F,31.9)$, $(C,G,35)$, $(D,E,21.3)$, $(E,G,26.5)$, $(E,K,21.3)$, $(F,G,46)$, $(F,H,34)$, $(F,L,15)$, $(G,H,21)$, $(G,I,20)$, $(G,K,29.5)$, $(H,I,30)$, $(H,L,30)$, and $(I,K,40)$, the shortest road connection from city A to city I is 85; the shortest road connection from city D to city H is 68.8.

Problem 15.1.2   (>100)

Note that for certain road networks it is sometimes impossible to find a road map if cities are connected by a straight line. For example, the distance between cities E and G in the network of Problem 15.1.1 is already determined by other information and must be 26.5. In solving the problems, first construct a road map using only part of the information supplied, and then check whether the rest agrees roughly (say $\pm 2\%$) with the map obtained.

The network of Problem 15.1.1 determines a unique road map once the locations of A, B, and C have been fixed according to the mileage information. The air distance between cities A and I is 85, and between cities D and H it is 61.5.

Problem 15.1.3   (>100)

The network of Problem 15.1.1 determines a unique road map once the locations of A, B, and C have been fixed according to the mileage information. It is shown in Fig. A-1.

Problem 15.1.4   (>100)

Given the road network (A,B), (A,D), (A,E), (A,J), (A,M), (A,N), (B,N), (C,E), (C,F), (C,G), (C,H), (C,I), (C,J), (D,E), (D,G), (D,N), (E,G), (F,G), (F,H), (F,O), (G,O), (G,P), (H,O), (H,P), (I,J), (I,L), (I,P), (J,K), (J,L), (J,M), (K,M), (M,N), and (O,P), a Euler line is H-F-C-J-M-A-B-N-A-D-E-A-J-K-M-N-D-G-E-C-I-J-L-I-P-O-F-G-O-H-P-G-C-H.

Problem 15.1.5   (>100)

For the network of Problem 15.1.4, a Hamiltonian circuit is A-B-N-D-E-G-P-O-H-F-C-I-L-J-K-M-A.

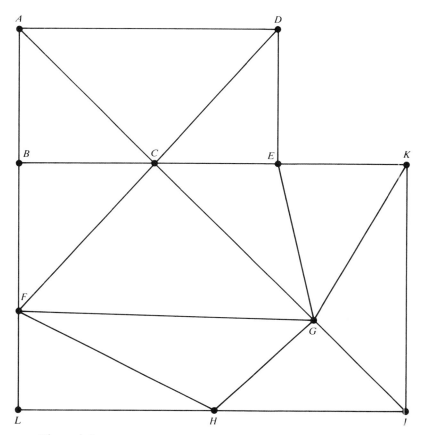

Figure A-1

Problem 15.1.6   (>100)
For the network of Problem 15.1.1, a shortest Hamiltonian circuit is
H-L-F-B-A-C-D-E-K-G-I-H.

Problem 15.1.7   (>100)

Section 15.2

Problem 15.2.1   (100)

Problem 15.2.2   (100)

Problem 15.2.3   (>100)

Problem 15.2.4   (100)

Problem 15.2.5   (>100)

Problem 15.2.6   (>100)
For SIN[x] one obtains $a_0 = 0, a_1 = 1, a_2 = 0, a_3 = -0.1666667, a_4 = 0,$
$a_5 = 0.0083333, a_6 = 0, a_7 = -0.0001984, a_8 = 0, a_9 = 0.0000028,$ and
$a_{10} = 0.$

Problem 15.2.7   (>100)

Given the following input information,

name card:	Smith
birth card:	James (father: unknown) 3/2/1843
death card:	James (father: unknown) 12/4/1899
marriage card:	Joyce (Winderhill) to James (father: unknown) 6/8/1869
birth card:	James (father: James) 15/11/1870
death card:	James (father: James) 3/7/1946
marriage card:	Petra (Doe) to James (father: James) 24/12/1899
birth card:	Diana (father: James (father: unknown)) 3/9/1872
death card:	Diana 4/6/1938
marriage card:	Diana to John (Brust) 6/6/1892
birth card:	Peter (father: James (father: unknown)) 1/10/1875
death card:	Peter (father: James (father: unknown)) 3/2/1916
birth card:	Richard (father: James (father: unknown)) 8/9/1876
death card:	Richard 5/4/1941
marriage card:	Gay (Higst) to Richard 9/2/1902
birth card:	Ronald (father: James (father: James)) 5/6/1903
death card:	Ronald 9/4/1907
birth card:	Regina (father: James (father: James)) 1/7/1907
marriage card:	Regina to Walt (Burrit) 10/3/1930
birth card:	Peter (father: Richard) 3/5/1904
death card:	Peter (father: Richard) 9/9/1970
marriage card:	Sylvia (Tinn) to Peter (father: Richard) 5/3/1930
birth card:	Susan (father: Richard) 15/11/1908
birth card:	James (father: Peter) 22/2/1931
marriage card:	Audrey (Newster) to James (father: Peter) 3/8/1952
birth card:	John (father: James (father: Peter)) 6/7/1954
birth card:	Walt (father: James (father: Peter)) 26/7/1956

the program should produce a family tree similar to the one shown in Fig. A-2.

Problem 15.2.8   (50)

The following pairs indicate the mutual position of ten countries: A pair (i,j) is listed if and only if countries i and j have a common border. (1,2), (1,4), (2,3) ,(2,4), (2,5), (3,5), (3,6), (4,5), (4,7), (4,8), (4,10), (5,6), (5,7), (6,7), (6,8), (6,9), (7,8), (8,9), (8,10). To go from country 1 to country 9 one has to go through at least the two additional countries 4 and 8. To go from country 3 to country 10 one has to go through at least two additional countries, choosing either 5 and 4 or 6 and 8.

Problem 15.2.9   (100)

One possible coloring of the countries in Problem 15.2.8 is the following: blue: countries 4 and 6; black: countries 5 and 8; green: country 2; red: countries 1, 3, 7, 9, and 10.

Problem 15.2.10   (>100)

Problem 15.2.11   (>100)

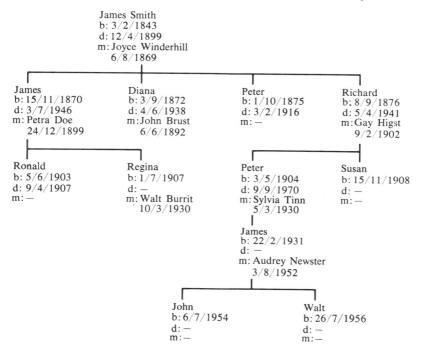

James Smith
b: 3/2/1843
d: 12/4/1899
m: Joyce Winderhill
6/8/1869

James	Diana	Peter	Richard
b: 15/11/1870	b: 3/9/1872	b: 1/10/1875	b: 8/9/1876
d: 3/7/1946	d: 4/6/1938	d: 3/2/1916	d: 5/4/1941
m: Petra Doe	m: John Brust	m: —	m: Gay Higst
24/12/1899	6/6/1892		9/2/1902

Ronald	Regina	Peter	Susan
b: 5/6/1903	b: 1/7/1907	b: 3/5/1904	b: 15/11/1908
d: 9/4/1907	d: —	d: 9/9/1970	d: —
m: —	m: Walt Burrit	m: Sylvia Tinn	m: —
	10/3/1930	5/3/1930	

James
b: 22/2/1931
d: —
m: Audrey Newster
3/8/1952

John	Walt
b: 6/7/1954	b: 26/7/1956
d: —	d: —
m: —	m: —

Figure A-2

Problem 15.2.12   (>100)

The following pairs define a graph with eight vertices: A pair (i,j) is listed if and only if there is an edge joining vertex i with vertex j. (1,2), (1,3), (1,4), (1,5), (1,7), (2,3), (2,4), (2,5), (2,6), (3,4), (3,5), (3,6), (3,7), (3,8), (4,5), (4,6), (4,7), (4,8), (5,6), (5,7), (5,8), (6,8), (7,8). The largest complete graph contained is a K_5.

Problem 15.2.13   (>100)

The two graphs G and H below, defined by sets of pairs as in Problem 12.2.12, are isomorphic. The graph G is not isomorphic to the graph given in Problem 15.2.12.

$G:$ (1,2), (1,5), (1,6), (1,7), (2,3), (2,4), (2,5), (2,6), (2,7), (2,8), (3,4), (3,6), (3,8), (4,5), (4,6), (5,6), (5,7), (6,7), (6,8)

$H:$ (1,2), (1,4), (1,6), (1,7), (2,3), (2,6), (2,7), (3,6), (3,7), (4,5), (4,6), (4,7), (4,8), (5,6), (5,7), (5,8), (6,7), (6,8), (7,8)

The correspondence of points of G and H is as follows: 1-8, 2-6, 3-2, 4-1, 5-4, 6-7, 7-5, 8-3.

Problem 15.2.14   (100)

Problem 15.2.15   (100)

Problem 15.2.16   (>100)

Problem 15.2.17   (>100)

Problem 15.2.18   (100)

One of the solutions of $ABEND + AMACE = MANEF$ is $A = 0, B = 9,$ $C = 8,\ D = 7,\ E = 5,\ F = 2,\ M = 1,\ N = 6$. The addition $ABCDE + FGHII = JKMLA$ has no solution (too many letters). The addition $AAAAB + AAAAA = AAAAC$ has no solution. The addition $AAAXB + AAAAX = AADAC$ has six different solutions.

Problem 15.2.19   (>100)

Problem 15.2.20   (>100)

Problem 15.2.21   (>100)

INDEX